Experimental Theatre

from Stanislavsky to Peter Brook

Other titles by James Roose-Evans

Directing a Play (Studio Vista, 1968)
Experimental Theatre (Studio Vista and Universe, 1970,
    revised edition, 1974; major new edition Routledge and
    Kegan Paul, 1984)
London Theatre: From the Globe to the National (Phaidon,
    1977)
84 Charing Cross Road (a play, French's, 1983; Fireside, New
    York, 1983)
Inner Journey, Outer Journey (Rider, 1987)
The Adventures of Odd and Elsewhere (André Deutsch, 1971,
    1988)
The Secret of the Seven Bright Shiners (André Deutsch, 1972,
    1988)
Odd and the Great Bear (André Deutsch, 1973)
Elsewhere and the Gathering of the Clowns (André Deutsch,
    1974)
The Return of the Great Bear (André Deutsch, 1975)
The Secret of Tippity-Witchit (André Deutsch, 1975)
The Lost Treasure of Wales (André Deutsch, 1977)
Darling Ma (edited letters of Joyce Grenfell to her mother)
    (Hodder & Stoughton, 1988)

James Roose-Evans in rehearsal with Sir John Gielgud in Hugh
Whitemore's *The Best of Friends,* Apollo Theatre, London 1988
(courtesy of John Haynes)

Experimental Theatre

from Stanislavsky to Peter Brook

James Roose-Evans

London and New York

This new edition is dedicated
to Anna Halprin and all those
who continue the search

First published 1970
by Studio Vista
Second edition 1973
Third edition 1984
by Routledge & Kegan Paul
Fourth edition, revised and updated, 1989
by Routledge
11 New Fetter Lane, London EC4P 4EE
29 West 35th Street, New York, NY 10001

Reprinted 1990, 1991, 1994, 1996, 1999, 2000, 2001, 2002

Routledge is an imprint of the Taylor & Francis Group

© *1970, 1973, 1984, 1989 James Roose-Evans*

Phototypeset by Input Typesetting Ltd, London
and Printed in Great Britain by
T. J. International Ltd, Padstow, Cornwall

British Library Cataloguing in Publication Data
Roose-Evans, James
  Experimental theatre. — 4th ed
  1. Experimental theatre, 1896–1989
  I. Title
  792'.022

Library Congress Cataloguing in Publication Data
A catalogue record for this book is available from
the Library of Congress

ISBN 0–415–00963–4

CONTENTS

Illustrations   vii
Acknowledgments   x

1 Introduction   1
2 Stanislavsky's Life in Art   6
3 The School of Realism   14
4 Meyerhold and the Russian Avant-garde   21
5 Taïrov and the Synthetic Theatre   31
6 Vakhtangov's Achievement   35
7 Craig and Appia – Visionaries   40
8 Copeau – Father of the Modern Theatre   53
9 Reinhardt, Piscator and Brecht   62
10 The Theatre of Ecstasy – Artaud, Okhlopkov, Savary   74
11 The Contribution of the Modern Dance –
   Martha Graham and Alwin Nikolais   91
12 Further Experiments Today – in America   101
13 Richard Foreman, Robert Wilson and the Bread
   and Puppet Theatre   114
14 Anna Halprin and the Dancers' Workshop   131
15 Grotowski and the Poor Theatre   145
16 Grotowski and the Journey to the East   152
17 Eugenio Barba and the Third Theatre   163
18 The Mountain with Many Caves: Peter Brook,
   Alfred Wolfsohn and Roy Hart   174
19 Towards AD 2,000   187

   Epilogue   201
   Bibliography   203
   Recommended Further Reading   215
   Index   220

ILLUSTRATIONS

Between pages 30 and 31
  1 Vsevelod Meyerhold (Theatre Museum)
  2 The 1928 revival of Meyerhold's constructivist production
    of *The Magnanimous Cuckold* (Theatre Museum)
  3 Eugene Vakhtangov (Theatre Museum)
  4 Adolphe Appia, 1882 (courtesy of the Appia Foundation)

Between pages 64 and 65
  5 Jacques Copeau
  6 Olympia transformed into a medieval cathedral for Max
    Reinhardt's production of *The Miracle*, 1911 (drawing by
    J. Duncan and Theatre Museum)
  7 Bertolt Brecht, 1959 (photo by Ernestine Costa)

Between pages 84 and 85
  8 Designs by Jacob Schtoffer showing playing areas (white)
    and audience areas (grey) for various productions of the
    Realistic Theatre under the direction of Okhlopkov
  9 Moment from the Grand Théâtre Panique (later the Grand
    Magic Circus) production of Arrabal's *Labyrinth* (photo by
    Frazer Wood)

Between pages 100 and 101
  10 Martha Graham (courtesy of Anthony Crickmay)
  11 Martha Graham as Jocasta and Erick Hawkins as Oedipus
     in Martha Graham's *Night Journey*, music by William
     Schuman
  12 Martha Graham and Robert Cohan in Martha Graham's
     Dark Meadow
  13 Alwin Nikolais (*Hampstead and Highgate Express*)

14 *Sanctum*, a Dance Theatrepiece by Alwin Nikolais (photo by Ken Kay, courtesy of Alwin Nikolais)
15 *Galaxy*, a Dance Theatrepiece by Alwin Nikolais (photo by Susan Schiff-Faludi)
16 *Triptych*, a Dance Theatrepiece by Alwin Nikolais (photo by Basil Langton)
17 Julian Beck of the Living Theatre (photo by Jean Marquis)
18 The Living Theatre's production of *Frankenstein* (photo by Jean Marquis)

Between pages 112 and 113
19 Scene from *Motel*, from *America, Hurrah!*, a play by Jean-Claude van Itallie, produced by the Open Theatre.
20 Founded in 1978, in San Francisco, *A Travelling Jewish Theatre* 'combine the spontaneity of improvisation with the dazzling language of the mystics' (Susan Griffin). Like Peter Schumann they recognise that the roots of theatre lie in the realm of the mythic, the sacred and the communal; and like Grotowski and Brook, they believe that theatre can be an instrument of healing (courtesy of a Travelling Jewish Theatre, San Francisco)
21 Peter Schumann, founder of the Bread and Puppet Theatre (photo by Richard Bellak)

Between pages 130 and 131
22 Bread and Puppet Theatre, Peace Parade, New York, April 1969 (photo by Marc Kaczmarek)
23 Bread and Puppet Theatre, *Fire* (photo by Marc Kaczmarek)
24 The Bread and Puppet Theatre in Glover, Vermont, USA (courtesy of Chris Braithwaite and the *Chronicle*)
25 A play at dusk, Bread and Puppet Circus, Glover, Vermont (courtesy of Chris Brathwaite and the *Chronicle*)

Between pages 144 and 145
26 Anna Halprin (courtesy of Anna Halprin and the Dancers' Workshop)
27 The San Francisco Dancers' Workshop in a ritual created in 1970 for the Beth Sinai Temple in Oakland, USA (Dancers' Workshop)
28 Aerial view of the Polish Laboratory Theatre's setting for

The Constant Prince with the audience placed like voyeurs peeping down on a forbidden act (courtesy of the Polish Laboratory Theatre)

29 Cieslak, Grotowski's leading actor as the Constant Prince (courtesy of the Polish Laboratory Theatre)

Between pages 162 and 163

30 Sketches for Grotowski's *mises-en-scène, for* (a) *Dr Faustus*, Marlowe's text, (b) *Kordian*, Slowacki's text, and (c) *The Constant Prince*, Calderón-Slowacki (courtesy of H. Martin Berg, Odin Teatret Vorlag and J. Grotowski)

31 The final procession from the Polish Laboratory Theatre's production of *Acropolis* (courtesy of the Polish Laboratory Theatre)

32 Peter Brook and Jerzy Grotowski (photo by Ryszard Wolinski, courtesy of Ossia Trilling)

33 *Min Fars Hus* (My Father's House), created by Eugenio Barba and the Odin Teatret (courtesy of Tony d'Urso)

34 *Min Fars Hus* (courtesy of Tony d'Urso)

Between pages 178 and 179

35 Peter Brook and his actors in Africa, one of many versions of *The Conference of Birds* (photo by Mary Ellen Mark, and Centre International de Recherche Théâtrale)

36 Hywel Jones in *Deaths and Entrances* (courtesy of Zoë Dominic, London)

37 Judgment scene from *Deaths and Entrances* (courtesy of North of England newspapers)

38 Alfred Wolfsohn and Roy Hart (courtesy of the Roy Hart Theatre)

39 Roy Hart and the Roy Hart Theatre on Paxos, Greece, July 1973 (courtesy of the Roy Hart Theatre)

Between pages 194 and 195

40 Eugene O'Neill's *The Hairy Ape*, part of INTERNATIONAL THEATRE '87 presented by the Schaubühne Company from West Berlin, in the Lyttelton Theatre from 11–16 May 1987. Photo by Ruth Walz (courtesy of the National Theatre)

41 and 42 Scenes from Peter Brook's production of *The Mahabharata*

ACKNOWLEDGMENTS

I should like to thank the many who have opened doors for me, and assisted me in my research, especially the following: Anna Halprin, Elka Schumann, Peter Schumann, Eric Shorter, Karl-Heinz Westarp of the University of Aarhus who was my host in Denmark, and Eugenio Barba and the actors of Odin Teatret, Ron Vawter of the Performance Group, Richard Armstrong and the Roy Hart Theatre, Frank Marcus, John and Wendy Trewin, Emma Dickinson, Horace Judson of *Time Magazine*, Lady Diana Cooper, Chris Bazely who translated some of the Copeau material, Tom Leabhart, editor of the *Mime Journal*, and also of Mask Mime and Marionette; Rosemary Cole, Ethel Issler, Jane Nicholas of the British Council, and the ever-welcoming support of Mrs Foster and Miss Tracey of the British Theatre Associations Library, Alexander Schouvaloff of the Theatre Museum, and Barbara Wilkes who gave me for my library a precious collection of *Theatre Arts Monthly*; Maria Guther and Craig Barton from whose letters I have quoted; the Garrick Club, and McKenzie and Sutherland whose catalogue is always a feast of discoveries. I am extremely grateful to John Lahr for reading the revised manuscript, and for his invaluable suggestions. I also thank Marina Cantacuzino, who so cheerfully helped me over the last stages of this book.

1 Introduction

To experiment is to make a foray into the unknown – it is something that can be charted only after the event. To be avant-garde is truly to be way out in front. Each of the key figures in this book has opened up the possibilities of theatre as an art and for each of them experiment has implied something very different. For Stanislavsky it meant the importance of the actor, whereas for Craig the actor was practically dispensable, the emphasis being upon the scenic possibilities of theatre. Meyerhold and Reinhardt stressed the importance of the director; Appia the use of light. Brecht, like his master, Piscator, was concerned to explore the didactic nature of the theatre. Artaud, like Stanislavsky, came to believe that theatre should reflect not the everyday reality of naturalism, but rather those intimations that are beyond the reach of words. Much that was foreseen by the early pioneers has come to be realized in the American modern dance, while the theatre of Alwin Nikolais represents in many ways a synthesis of Artaud's concept of a non-verbal theatre and Craig's idea of moving abstract masses. Finally, like Copeau, Jerzy Grotowski, Peter Brook and Eugenio Barba have gone back to the essence of theatre, to the live relationship of actor and audience.

Of necessity, much has had to be omitted. If the role of the dramatist is not examined in this book it is not to depreciate the role of the author, far from it, but because there tend to be many more books written about the contribution of the writer, from the realistic plays of Chekhov to the socially and politically orientated dramas of Shaw and Brecht, and the work of such modern dramatists as Ionesco and the whole

1

school of the Theatre of the Absurd with its major contribution to the development of the drama, Samuel Beckett and Harold Pinter, each of whom has, in the words of Virginia Woolf, attempted to write 'about silence, about the things which people do not say'. It is precisely with this area that the avant-garde theatre of the 1970s and 1980s has come to be concerned.

Increasingly in this century, psychologists, painters, sculptors, writers, poets, dancers, have been concerned with the attempt to build a bridge between the known and the unknown, between the conscious world of the ego and the unconscious world that lies within. Yet the theatre has always lagged behind.

Although our knowledge of the psyche is still extremely limited, our own experience, at least, should convince us how all too easily we are possessed by moods, troubled by strange dreams and nightmares, become unreasonable and unpredictable in our behaviour. We have the impression that at bottom we know ourselves scarcely at all. Increasingly we are aware of other selves within the self. 'My selves the grievers', says Dylan Thomas in a poem, and Emily Dickinson,

> One need not be a chamber to be haunted,
> One need not be a house;
> The brain has corridors surpassing
> Material place . . .
> Ourself, behind ourself, concealed,
> Should startle most;
> Assassin, hid in our apartment,
> Be horror's least.

But how to express this reality that is within? How, for example, to express the reality of a dream? Julien Green, the American writer, in his journal, remarks of one dream,

> It was intensely real, far more so than everyday life . . . .
> This confirms my belief that a man who dreams is
> sometimes a far more gifted artist than the man who
> is awake. Words cannot express the length of time
> passed in a vision that lasted seconds.

And of a recurring dream he says that it brought 'a feeling of happiness such that human speech cannot give the faintest idea of it'.

Throughout the first half of this century painters in particular understood this need to create a language that would, in the words of Franz Marc, 'break the mirror of life so that we may look being in the face.' Marc, like Chagall, Kandinsky, Klee, sought to give expression to the mystical content of art. 'Therefore', wrote Kandinsky, 'the artist's eye should always be alert for the voice of inward necessity.' In this way, and this way alone, as Paul Klee observed, could 'the secretly perceived be made visible'.

In the 1930s Antonin Artaud declared that

> the theatre will never find itself again except by furnishing
> the spectator with the truthful precipitates of
> dreams . . . . I say that there is a poetry of the senses as
> there is a poetry of language and that this concrete
> physical language is truly theatrical only to the degree
> that the thoughts it expresses are beyond the reach of the
> spoken language.

Artaud's concept of a non-verbal theatre was to be developed first by such pioneers of the modern dance as Martha Graham who created a whole new form of theatre. Her works, which she described as graphs of the human heart, often bewildered audiences. As Robert Horan observed, in *Chronicles of the American Dance*, if her audiences were sometimes distraught at the imagery she used, it was because they were so ill-prepared to face the psychological reality which is the basis of her art. They were confronted with a form of theatre that sought not merely to entertain but to make demands.

At the climax of Virginia Woolf's novel, *Between the Acts*, the actors appear with bits of mirror and glass in order to portray the twentieth century. 'And the audience saw themselves . . . the hands of the clock had stopped at the present moment. It was now. Ourselves.' For several centuries the theatre in the West has held the mirror up to nature, but now the mirror seeks to reflect something else. The empty space, of which Peter Brook has spoken, is, in fact, the space within. As the manager of the Magic Theatre in Herman Hesse's *Steppenwolf* explains to the hero,

It is the world of your own soul that you seek. Only within yourself exists that other reality for which you long. I can give you nothing that has not already its own being within yourself. I can throw open to you no picture gallery but your own soul. All I can give you is the opportunity, the impulse, the key. I help you to make your own world visible. That is all.

In writing about contemporary figures I have tried to avoid making any critical judgments, being more concerned to catch something of the essence of an artist's work. I would agree with Henry Moore that 'what really counts is the vision a work of art expresses, that is, the quality of the mind revealed behind it, rather than the way it is done.'

In his journal, Isamu Noguchi, the American-Japanese sculptor, writes,

I wanted other means of communication – to find a way of sculpture that was humanly meaningful without being realistic, at once abstract and socially relevant. I wanted to find out what sculpture was fundamentally about. Sculpture, I felt, had become a captive, like the other arts, to coterie points of view.

If one substitutes for the word 'sculpture' the word 'theatre', this sums up exactly my own feelings and reflections during the latter half of the 1960s. Increasingly I came to see the importance of taking time out to search and *re*-search. It seemed to me, at that time, that the drama in England was merely repeating itself in varying styles of naturalism, and that it was being saturated with words.

I had first begun to experiment with non-verbal forms of theatre in 1955-6 when I was invited to join the faculty of the Julliard School of Music in New York 'in order to explore the possibilities of integrating music, dance and drama'. As a result of the work I did there, I was invited by Alwin Nikolais to found a school of drama at the Henry Street Playhouse in New York where he was based. Instead, I returned to England and, in 1959, started the Hampstead Theatre. The stresses and strains of mounting ten, sometimes more, productions a year, under-staffed, over-worked, and for seven years without subsidy, left little time for experimentation outside the narrow confines of particular productions. By 1968, however, the theatre was established; I was able to hand over to a successor and concentrate my energies upon establishing at Hampstead an experimental workshop with a permanent company. The company was called Stage Two, because I regarded it as the second stage in the development of the theatre. I managed to raise enough money to subsidize the experiment for just over a year. For a year the actors trained and then gave a ten-week season in London of two works: *Dreams*, and *Deaths and Entrances*, followed by a short tour. In spite of generous praise from critics, it proved impossible to raise further finance, and the venture folded. Since then my own explorations have continued in workshops here and abroad, especially in America. Some of this work I have touched on in *Inner Journey, Outer Journey* (Rider, 1987) and will be examined in more depth in my next book, *Journeys of the Heart*. The first edition of this book was published in 1970. A new edition appeared in 1974, followed by several reprints. In 1984 the book appeared in a major new edition, twice as long as the original, and rewritten from start to finish, incorporating much new research that had accumulated as I continued to study, read about, experience, talk with and, above all, listen to others. I am convinced that if one is a practitioner of the theatre it is an essential part of one's task to see and know what is going on in all the arts. We have much to learn from one another as well as from the lessons of history.

For this latest edition I have added a final chapter, bringing the book within sight of the end of the twentieth century.

2 Stanislavsky's Life in Art

At the turn of this century Russia was a land of giants. From the 1890s onwards was a time of volcanic eruption in the arts, bringing in its wake an entire social, religious and ideological upheaval – the emergence of a new society. A roll-call of that period catches some of the excitement – Tolstoy, Dostoevsky, Chekhov, Gogol, Tchaikovsky, Rimsky-Korsakov, Chaliapin, Diaghilev, Pavlova, Karsavina, Nijinsky, Bakst, Benois, Fokine and, of course, Stanislavsky.

Constantin Stanislavsky is the great patriarchal figure not only of the Russian theatre, but of theatre throughout the Western world. Of all the pioneers he casts the longest shadow. Great as were his achievements as director and actor, however, his most important contribution lay in the light he threw upon the technique of acting. His 'system', based upon the observation of good acting practice, has been developed and adjusted according to the needs of different temperaments and nationalities. It was never intended to be a rigid system: 'Create your own method,' he would say. The Method, as we know it, is merely the result of his system first taught in America by two of his protégés, Michael Chekhov and Richard Boleslavsky, and subsequently adapted to the needs of the American actor by Lee Strasberg and other members of the Group Theatre. The greatness of Stanislavsky lies as much in his own flexibility as in his adherence to the cardinal principle of inner truth on the stage. His legacy was, and remains, the Moscow Art Theatre. Kenneth Tynan, describing the giants at the Maly Theatre playing with a selfless economy and precision reminiscent of a group of chess champions at a tournament, records:

At the Moscow Art Theatre, ripe in years, robust as oaks, beaming in their beards and their supreme authority, the masters play together as Stanislavsky taught and as they can still teach the world. The joy of seeing master craftsmen working in unison, with the humane poetry and not just the neurotic trimmings of naturalism, is something I had never known until I saw these perdurable players. This is Stanislavsky without Freud, physiological acting without the psychiatric glosses beloved of so many American 'Method' actors; it has subtlety and absolute inevitability . . . The power and the glory of Soviet theatre resides in its older actors, who are by far the finest I have ever seen.

Whatever thread one takes up in the history of twentieth-century drama leads back to Stanislavsky. The most austere figure of contemporary theatre, Jerzy Grotowski, acknowledges his debt to him: 'His persistent study, his systematic renewal of the methods of observation, and his dialectical relationship to his own earlier work make him my personal ideal.' In his thinking, Stanislavsky anticipated many of the major developments in theatre. Through all the vicissitudes of fashion, however, he retained his belief in the essential creative power of the actor as the only source of vitality for the theatre.

Stanislavsky felt that the director of a theatre which was to fulfil a 'cultural mission' should have a first-hand and expert knowledge of all the elements of theatre: he should be familiar with it from the actor's, director's, producer's and administrator's points of view. One rarely comes across all these qualities in one person – but they were combined in Vladimir Nemirovich-Danchenko. 'He was that director of whom one could dream. It seems that he had also dreamed of such a theatre as I had imagined and sought a man such as he imagined me to be.'

His meeting with Danchenko in 1896 was to have a profound influence not only on the theatre in Russia but throughout the world. From it sprang one of the most important events in theatrical history. By founding the Moscow Art Theatre, both Stanislavsky and Nemirovich-Danchenko were rebelling against the conventional, declamatory style of acting; against a star system which prevented the development of an ensemble style of acting. 'Like all revolutionaries', wrote Stanislavsky, 'we broke the old and exaggerated the new.'

At the time, Nemirovich-Danchenko was one of the best of the younger Russian dramatists, and was considered to have inherited the mantle of Ostrovsky. He had shared the Griboyedov Prize with Chekhov who had submitted *The Seagull*. Because it seemed to him that Chekhov's play was immeasurably superior to his own, he declined his half of the prize in favour of his rival. With the founding of the Moscow Art Theatre it was his idea to include *The Seagull* in the first season, and it was he who suggested that Stanislavsky should direct it. In Anton Chekhov the Moscow Art Theatre found a dramatist whom they were uniquely gifted to interpret. As Stanislavsky said, 'Chekhov gave that inner truth to the stage which served as the foundation for what was later called the Stanislavsky System, which must be approached through Chekhov, or which serves as a bridge to the playing of Chekhov.'

By 1904 the plays of Chekhov, Gorki, Ibsen, Knut Hamsun, Tolstoy, Shakespeare and Maeterlinck, as well as the exceptionally high standard of design, acting and directing, had made the theatre a success. Diaghilev, writing on 'The Originality of the Moscow Art Theatre' in his publication *The World of Art*, observed that because of its proven success and popularity this company could risk innovations in the theatre which with any less well-established group would have been condemned to ridicule.

In spite of their success, however, Stanislavsky was filled with doubts. He felt that they had become trapped by the very realism they had set out to achieve. Compared with what was happening in the other arts, in the new painting, music and sculpture, the theatre seemed antiquated. It was during this period that he came into contact once again with Vsevolod Meyerhold, a former member of the company, who had created the part of Konstantin in *The Seagull* and had left in order to start up his own group in the provinces. Like Stanislavsky, he was seeking something new in art, something more contemporary and modern in spirit.

The difference between the two men lay in the fact that while Stanislavsky strained towards the new without knowing how to realize it, Meyerhold believed that he had already found it but was unable to realize it through lack of means and opportunity. Since the daily rehearsal and performance schedule of a repertory theatre provided no room for experimental laboratory work, Stanislavsky decided to help him. He opened the Theatrical Studio where, with a group of young actors, Meyerhold was to be free to carry out his ideas. The principle of the new studio was that realism and local colour had outlived their usefulness and no longer interested the public. 'The time for the unreal on the stage had arrived. It was necessary to picture not life itself as it takes place in reality', wrote Stanislavsky, 'but as we vaguely feel it in our dreams, our visions, our moments of spiritual uplift.'

After a summer in which Meyerhold and his young actors were left to work without interruption, Stanislavsky saw a dress rehearsal of Maeterlinck's *The Death of Tintagels*, and Hauptmann's *Schluck und Jan*. Although there was a great deal that was new, unexpected and often beautiful, Stanislavsky felt that the actors were too young and inexperienced. He was acutely conscious of the gulf between the director's dreams and their realization – since only the actor could fulfil this dream: *For the new art new actors were necessary, actors of a new sort with an altogether new technique.* But there were no such actors in the Studio and Stanislavsky felt that to open it in such an incomplete state would be harmful to its very *raison d'être*: 'A good idea, badly shown, dies for a long time.' It was at this moment that the First Revolution broke and so the opening of the Studio was delayed indefinitely. Stanislavsky had to pay off the actors, close the Studio and spend the next several years paying off its debts. Meyerhold returned to the Moscow Art Theatre to play Konstantin in *The Seagull*.

Meanwhile, Stanislavsky and Nemirovich-Danchenko saw clearly that they had reached a crossroads; that it was necessary to refresh themselves and the company. There seemed no point in remaining in Moscow, not simply because of the revolutionary climate, but because they had no concrete idea of what they might achieve there. The death of their beloved playwright Anton Chekhov, the death of their patron Morozov, the failure of the Maeterlinck plays, the catastrophic demise of the Studio project, as well as Stanislavsky's own dissatisfaction with himself as an actor, 'and the complete darkness that lay before me, gave me no rest, took away all faith in myself.' In this state of mind he went to spend the summer of 1906 in Finland.

It is at those moments of extreme despair and seeming disintegration in an artist's life that new life is often stirring; when an impasse seems to have been reached, a new path is discovered. So with Stanislavsky in the summer of 1906. 'Sitting on a bench in Finland and examining my artistic past' – was to prove the beginning of what is now known as the Stanislavsky System. In 1906 he enjoyed a world-wide reputation as an actor, director and co-founder of the Moscow Art Theatre. With more than thirty years' experience behind him, he had acquired a vast amount of knowledge about acting technique. But everything was thrown together indiscriminately and in such a form that, in order to make further progress, he had first to analyse his accumulated experience.

The results of his analysis were set out in his two books, *My Life in Art* and *An Actor Prepares*.

> The basis of my system [he wrote] is formed by the laws of the organic nature of the actor which I have studied thoroughly in practice. Its chief merit is that there is nothing in it I myself invented or have not checked in practice. It is the natural result of experience of the stage over many years .... Directors explain very cleverly what sort of result they want to get. They tell the actor what he should *not* do, but they do not tell him *how* to achieve the required result.

It is always interesting to trace the first influence upon any great artist, and none more so than Stanislavsky. One of a large and wealthy family, he was educated at home. As a boy he was taught ballet by Yekaterina Sankovskaya, one of the most outstanding ballerinas in Russia. Noted particularly for her strong dramatic talent and her interest in the psychological motivation of the characters she portrayed, she perhaps planted the first seed of inner truth in the young Constantin. He next came under the influence of Mikhail Shchepkin, the great Russian actor of the first half of the nineteenth century. He was the first in that country to introduce simplicity and life-likeness into a performance, and he taught his pupils to observe the manner in which emotions are expressed in real life. Stanislavsky records how, as a youth, he tried to acquaint himself with everything Shchepkin wrote about dramatic art in his letters to Gogol and other friends. 'Always have nature before your eyes,' he wrote to a fellow actor: 'enter, so to speak, into the skin of the role you are playing; study well the social background of the character . . . therefore study all classes of society.' He would repeat over and over to his students, 'It is not important that you play well or ill; it is important that you play truthfully.'

For the Stanislavskys, theatricals were a family pursuit. As the children grew older, and became more experienced, so they would stage whole plays, even operas. One year they decided to do *The Mikado*. All that winter their home resembled a corner of Japan, and they even had a troupe of Japanese acrobats, who were appearing in a circus, to stay with them. Returning from the office or factory, the young actors would put on their Japanese costumes, wearing them all evening and, during the holidays, all day as well. Stanislavsky records how they spent one whole day behaving not as themselves but as the characters in the play. The girls also practised walking about with their legs tied together as far as the knee, and learned how to use the fan. 'I do not doubt', he comments, 'that the work we then accomplished, although it was temporary and soon forgotten, nevertheless planted certain seeds of the future in our souls.'

The young Constantin was always studying, observing and absorbing. When the famous Meiningen Players came to Moscow he went to every one of their performances, 'not only to look but to study as well'. Similarly, years later, when he was famous, he attended every single one of Isadora Duncan's recitals. All his life he was relentless in his search for knowledge and in his quest for inner truth on the stage, the truth of feeling and experience.

In his experiments on himself as an actor, Stanislavsky displayed a determination and an objectivity that one can only parallel with the work of some of the modern dancers such as

Martha Graham, or a teacher like F. Mathias Alexander. The actor, the dancer, the singer, has to work through his own muscles, his own body, his own emotions; often there is no one to teach or guide him. He is his own instrument and laboratory. For years, like Graham or Alexander, Stanislavsky preached his artistic credo with enthusiasm but without any success. 'A wall rose between me and the company. For years our relationship was cold.'

As with Copeau when he founded the School of the Vieux-Colombier, the actors of the Moscow Art Theatre were jealous of Stanislavsky's work with the young actors. It was only after several years that his system began to be accepted by the older actors – at least in part. The danger, however, was that they learned the terminology but neglected the continuous exercises. Stanislavsky did not shut his eyes to the fact that his system required so much devotion to the art of the stage that only a few actors were equal to it. In later life he confessed to the many disappointments he had had; although he had worked with hundreds of actors, only a few of them had the will-power and perseverance necessary for 'real art'.

In order to help the young people who came to him he founded the first Studio under the leadership of Sulerjitsky, and entrusted their training to Evgeny Vakhtangov. He bought and presented to the Studio a large plot of land on the shores of the Black Sea, where the young actors built communal buildings, a small hotel, stables, cowsheds, barns. Each actor built his own house which then became his own property, while everyone took part in the communal tasks. It was a Tolstoyan existence. It was to prove an ideal, a way of life and a way of work that would haunt the imaginations of other artists at various times. Vera Komisarjevskaya, the sister of the director, Theodore Komisarjevsky, dreamed of such a community of artists; Copeau formed a group of actors and, twice in the career of the Vieux-Colombier, took them away to live and work in the country. His successor, Michel Saint-Denis, did likewise with the Compagnie des Quinze. So did Charles Dullin. So, too, the Group Theatre in America in the 1930s, the Living Theatre, and Peter Schumann's Bread and Puppet Theatre in the 1960s, and Peter Brook and Eugenio Barba. Vera Komisarjevskaya dreamed of a company of actors united by the same understanding of the art of acting. She came to the conclusion that a theatre of ideas needs interpreters who have been brought up on the ideas and methods of that particular theatre.

Every such theatre must be like a community, following a 'master', something like what in painting is called a 'school', in which all the disciples carry out freely and enthusiastically the ideas of their leader and are able to work together on the same picture.

3 The School of Realism

The movement towards greater truth on the stage, 'to hold, as't were, the mirror up to nature', stemmed, however, not from Russia but from Europe, and its first clear definition was provided by Victor Hugo. In 1827 Hugo, then twenty-five, published his famous manifesto in which he declared that life, and life alone in all its variety, was the only model for the stage. The stage should feel free to present any subject and to use any form or style.

> Let us take the hammer to theories and poetic systems [he pronounced]. Let us throw down the old plastering that conceals the façade of art. There are neither rules nor models; or, rather, there are no other rules than the general rules of nature which soar above the whole field of art and the special rules which result from the conditions appropriate to the subject of each composition.

He rejected as unnatural the division of comedy and tragedy, and the classical unities of time, place and action. Although the German playwrights of the *Sturm und Drang* school, fifty years previously, had fought for greater freedom to experiment, Victor Hugo's introduction to *Cromwell* became the most important manifesto of the new realism. His *Hernani*, presented at the Théâtre Français in 1830, created an uproar. It was soon followed by the plays of Zola, Ibsen, Strindberg – as well as a play by the Goncourt brothers who were ardent supporters of the new movement. As the nineteenth century became increasingly industrialized, its outlook more materialistic and scientific, so the movement towards realism in the theatre gathered momentum. And with the new plays there came the demand for an equal realism in their staging. Although there had been a vogue for illusionist sets in the Italian court theatres of the Renaissance, these had not been used naturalistically as part of the environment to which the characters in the play belonged, but merely as stunning backgrounds before which the actors strutted and exhibited themselves.

The new drama not only paved the way for a new approach to décor, but also led to the creation of the director-producer whose task it was to create an overall unity of design and style for the production. One of the first companies to demonstrate the importance of the director was that of the Meiningen Players, founded in 1874 by George II, Duke of Saxe-Meiningen, who designed and directed all the productions, assisted by the actor Ludwig Kronek. Of the various innovations for which the company became famous, that of historical accuracy of costumes and settings was derived from earlier experiments in the English theatre, the work of William Charles Macready, Madame Vestris, and Charles Kean. The latter used to engage antiquarians and scholars to help create 'authentic', historically correct sets. It is also probable that the Duke, who was related to Queen Victoria and often used to visit London, may have seen the production of Tom Robertson's *Caste*, with its very naturalistic set. The Duke was the first in Europe to set his actors within the environment of the décor, thereby breaking up that formality of grouping which was so characteristic of the period, especially on the French stage. He employed steps and rostra to keep the actors moving on different levels. He insisted that all gestures be within the period of the play's setting. Above all, he brought to the crowd scenes such detail of characterization as to astound the rest of the world and to have a profound effect on such directors as Stanislavsky in Russia and Antoine in France.

Many have attributed to the Duke the privilege of being the first to visualize a production in its entirety, thereby giving it a unity of style and characterization and interpretation. As an orchestra needs a conductor so, it is said, the Duke revealed the need for a theatre ensemble to have a director. It was, however, an English actor and director, Samuel Phelps who, from 1844 until 1862, at Sadler's Wells theatre, demonstrated for the first time that the classic repertory of the English stage could attract and hold a popular audience. From Macready, with whom he acted, he had learned how to handle crowds but, more than anything, he was the first to demonstrate the advantages of an ensemble style of acting. The German novelist, Theodor Fontane, from 1851-7, reviewed six of Phelps's productions and in 1860 he published his reviews in a long essay entitled *Die Londoner Theater*. The three things that most impressed him about Phelps's productions were the remarkable use of settings, the direction of the plays by a single intelligence, and the appeal of Shakespeare to many levels of society. He liked the immediacy, the sense of being within the scene, that he found at Sadler's Wells, in contrast to the German court theatres which tended to remove the scene from the audience. He also realized that a director could exercise much more power than was generally believed. The unity and coherence of performances at Sadler's Wells were unknown in the Berlin theatre.

The achievements of Phelps tend to be overshadowed by the greater fame of the Meiningen Players. The truth is that in theatre many die without seeing their work bear fruit. The more one knows of history, the more one learns to acquire a long perspective, learning not to think in terms of one life-time, but of many generations. In 1848 one man conceived the idea of a national theatre for England but it was to be more than a century before it was realized. As King Arthur says in *The Quest for the Holy Grail*: 'for this is the purpose for which God sent you to us: to consummate what others have had to renounce, and to bring to conclusion all those things that no other was ever able to resolve.' In the course of this book it will be salutory to remember those words.

What the Duke of Saxe-Meiningen did was to bring to a peak a new way of working. Thus, although Macready insisted on detailed and long rehearsals of his productions, it was the Duke who insisted on much longer periods of rehearsal, and that his actors should work with the sets, costumes and proper-ties from the very beginning. 'It is always an advantage', he wrote, 'for an actor to touch a piece of furniture or some object naturally; that enhances the impression of reality.'

Antoine, who founded the Théâtre Libre in Paris in 1887, was to develop this argument.

> We must not be afraid of an abundance of little objects, of a wide variety of props [he wrote]. These are the imponderables which create a sense of intimacy and lend authenticity to the environment which the director seeks to re-create . . . . Among so many objects . . . the performer's acting becomes more human, more intense, and more alive in attitude and gestures.

Antoine believed that a set should be designed with its four walls in mind 'without worrying about the fourth wall which will later disappear so as to enable the audience to see what is going on.' It was first necessary to create the environment; it was this that would determine the movements and 'business' of the actors within the given circumstances and physical environment of the play.

Just as Antoine, in his enthusiasm for realism, hung up chunks of real meat in a scene set in a butcher's shop; just as David Belasco in America had real buildings transferred in their entirety onto the stage; so, too, the Moscow Art Theatre was at first obsessed by a passion for historical and realistic detail. But such extremes were a natural phase in the process of experimentation, and gradually Stanislavsky moved away from his early emphasis on external or photographic realism, and began to search for an inner realism. He realized that the actor had to select those aspects of reality which would serve to create an *impression* of reality. Similarly, although Zola wanted drama to be 'unarranged', presented unequivocally as *une tranche de vie*, authors such as Ibsen, Shaw, Chekhov and Strindberg were aware of the need to select and arrange material.

There seems to be no trace in the available records of what happened to the Meiningen Players. One suspects that in the company's very success lay the seeds of its decline. It was an ensemble achieved at the price of autocracy: neither the Duke nor Kronek were concerned, as was Samuel Phelps, with the contribution of the individual actor. Stanislavsky himself was at first a despotic director. Faced with amateur, second-rate, or inexperienced actors, he admitted a need for the director to dictate the whole production. The amazing detail and inventiveness of his production of *The Seagull* were conceived and written down while on holiday and then dictated to the company. In the early days of the Moscow Art Theatre, in order to achieve a new style, Stanislavsky was obliged to impose his ideas. Gradually, as he came to realize the need to train new actors, his system was evolved. Where the Meiningen Players, having created a standard of external excellence in production and a brilliance of detail, did not continue to explore and develop, the Moscow Art Theatre was able to grow with the artistic growth of its director.

Although at first the Moscow Art Theatre was to perfect the naturalistic style and to become renowned for its realistic productions of Chekhov, it also experimented with other forms of theatre. Joshua Logan, in his foreword to Sonia Moore's book on Stanislavsky, records his surprise at Stanislavsky's interpretation of *The Marriage of Figaro* by Beaumarchais.

> It was done with a racy, intense, farcical spirit which we had not associated with Stanislavsky. It was as broad comedy playing and directing as anything we had ever seen. The high-styled members of the cast in flashing coloured costumes would run, pose, prance, caress, faint, stutter in confusion, and play out all the intricate patterns of the French farce with a kind of controlled frenzy.

Another outstanding memory of Logan's visit to Moscow was Tolstoy's *Resurrection*, directed by Nemirovich-Danchenko. In this the director took full advantage of the revolving stage of the Moscow Art Theatre and a great deal of the effect of the production was visual; André van Gyseghem, in *The Theatre in Soviet Russia, 1943*, described it as 'the most revolutionary production in the repertoire'. For it a new character was written into the play, that of Tolstoy, to fill in the gaps, speak the thoughts of the characters, comment on and add a counter-point to the action. Also in this production the Moscow Art Theatre broke the convention of the picture-frame stage. Katchalov, as Tolstoy, played in the orchestra pit, by the proscenium arch, at the side of the stage, in the auditorium, by the side of the characters whose thoughts he spoke, and for one whole scene he spoke alone while the actors on stage said nothing.

Unfortunately the success of the Moscow Art Theatre with its realistic productions was to dog its reputation for many years.

> There was an opinion extant at that time [wrote Stanislavsky], an opinion which it is impossible to overthrow, that our theatre was a realistic theatre only . . . and yet . . . who was it who was really interested in the quest for and creation of the abstract? But once an idea gets lodged in the mind of the public it is hard to dislodge it.

It is therefore worth recalling some of Stanislavsky's stylistic experiments. In an early production of Hauptmann's *The Sunken Bell* he broke up the surface of the stage as a challenge to the actors.

> Let them creep, I thought, or sit on stones. Let them leap on the cliffs or climb the trees. Let them descend into the trap and climb back again. This will force them, and myself too, to get used to a new mise-en-scène, and to play in a way that is new to the stage.

In *The Drama of Life* by Knut Hamsun, Stanislavsky achieved a special effect by the use of shadow play. The tents of the circus booths were made of oiled linen. By the use of back lighting the silhouettes of the crowds were obtained. The tents were placed on platforms, rising one above the other, so that the entire stage seemed filled with the whirling shadows of people rising and falling on roundabouts. The success of this particular production, so totally unlike the realism of Stanislavsky's Chekhov productions, caused the progressive element in the audience to shout out, 'Death to realism! Down with crickets and mosquitoes!' while the more conservative members retorted, 'Shame on the Art Theatre! Down with Decadence!'

For Andreyev's *The Life of Man* the stage was covered entirely with black velvet – when Isadora Duncan saw it she said, 'Mon Dieu, c'est une maladie!' – against which was a set made of rope, suggesting the outlines of doors, windows, etc. All the furniture and the costumes of the actors were in black and outlined in rope, the colour of which varied with each act. With this particular production it was said that the theatre had discovered new paths in art, but, as Stanislavsky remarked, 'these paths, as is always the way with scenic revolutions in the theatre, did not go any further than the scenery.' It was this production that was to prove an historical turning point in his life, for in spite of its success he did not feel that the actors had moved forward. From that moment on, his work and his attention were devoted almost completely to the study and teaching of inner creativeness. The more disappointed Stanislavsky became in the means of theatrical production, the more he entered into the inner creative work of the actor. In a production of *A Month in the Country* he even attempted to do away with all *mise-en-scène* and had the actors seated on a bench speaking their inmost thoughts. Ironically, as he observes,

> as the outward side of our productions retreated more and more to the background, so in the other theatres of Moscow and Petrograd more and more interest was displayed in the outer appearances in contra-distinction to the inner contents of the play.

4 Meyerhold and the Russian Avant-garde

Stanislavsky was referring, of course, to the productions of such avant-garde directors as Meyerhold and Taïrov who often cared more about the form than the content of the play. Norris Houghton vividly describes Meyerhold's general approach to a play in an account of a talk given by Meyerhold to his actors at the first rehearsal for a production of three one-act plays by Chekhov, *The Proposal*, *The Bear*, and *The Jubilee*.

> Two things are essential for a play's production, as I have often told you. First, we must find the thought of the author; then we must reveal that thought in a theatrical form. This form I call a *jeu de théâtre* and around it I shall build the performance . . . . In this production I am going to use the technique of the traditional vaudeville as the *jeu*. Let me explain what it is to be. In these three plays of Chekhov I have found that there are thirty-eight times when characters either faint, say they are going to faint, turn pale, clutch their hearts, or call for a glass of water – so I am going to take this idea of fainting and use it as a sort of leitmotif for the performance. Everything will contribute to this *jeu*.

In 1932 both Stanislavsky and Nemirovich-Danchenko were to come out with sharp criticism of formalistic innovators and to defend realism on the stage as the only sound tradition. This accorded with previous announcements condemning 'excessive experiment'. Already, in 1926, they had staged Ostrovsky's *The Burning Heart* as an answer to Meyerhold, affirming the theatre of the actor and of the psychological treatment of characters as opposed to the avant-garde treatment of the actor as a puppet.

After the ill-fated Experimental Theatre Studio, Vsevolod Meyerhold was invited to be the director of Vera Komisarjevskaya's theatre. Here he was given the opportunity to put into practice all his ideas. For *Hedda Gabler* he removed the proscenium arch and presented an entirely non-realistic production based on the French symbolists' principle of correspondence between moods and colours – each character having its own colour and fixed set of gestures. For Maeterlinck's *Sister Beatrice*, in order to bring audience and actors closer, he had the scenery (decorative flats) brought down stage, leaving only a shallow platform so that the actors resembled figures carved in a bas-relief. Instead of individualizing the crowd, as would have been done at the Moscow Art Theatre, he had groups moving in unison like a medieval frieze. His aim was to convey not the feelings of individual characters but purified 'extracts' of emotion. The actors were trained to speak in a form of recitative limited to three notes and to move in a slow, hieratic style. Often it seemed as though Meyerhold were trying to turn his actors into puppets, reminding one, as Marc Slonim observes, of the French nursery rhyme – '*Les petites marionettes font, font, font leurs trois petites tours et puis s'en vont.*'

Maeterlinck's *Pelléas et Mélisande* was interpreted by Meyerhold as a fairy tale with settings from a children's book. In *The Little Showbox* by Blok he mixed live actors and marionettes. Each and every production was daring and provocative, moving theatre away from realism: yet they never caught on with the general public. Also, Meyerhold increasingly neglected Vera Komisarjevskaya. Not only the owner of the theatre but also a great actress, she was not content to be treated as a marionette, however gifted the puppet-master. He barred her from several of his important productions and, although he went with her to Berlin in 1907 to study the work of Reinhardt, further collaboration between them became impossible. In 1908 he was asked to leave and another innovator, Nikolai Evreinov, replaced him. However, nothing could now save the situation and the theatre closed in 1909. Komisarjevskaya went on tour to America hoping to be able to make enough money to re-open her theatre. She caught pernicious smallpox and died in Russia on 10 February 1910.

For a while Meyerhold went to Minsk to stage plays, using screens instead of sets. He experimented with having the auditorium as well as the stage lit in order to heighten the mood of the spectator and, at the same time, permitting the actor to see exactly what effect he was having. Moving away from sculptural groupings and linear friezes, he became increasingly attracted to the techniques of the circus and the music hall. He came to see mime as superior to words, which were 'but a design on the fabric of movement'.

In 1912 Meyerhold declared in his seminal essay *The Fairground Booth* that pantomime and *cabotinage* were the only antidote to an excessive misuse of words in theatre.

> The cabotin is a strolling player [he wrote]; the cabotin is a kinsman to the mime, the historian, and the juggler; the cabotin can work miracles with his technical mastery; the cabotin keeps alive the tradition of the true art of acting.

By reviving the primordial elements of the theatre – such as the mask, gesture, movement and plot – theatre at last was able to free itself from the shackles of literature. Actors belonging to the school of 'realism' had become slaves to real life imitations, and the mask had been replaced by make-up. *Cabotinage*, Meyerhold claimed, would help the actor rediscover those basic laws of theatricality and would bring about a renaissance in the theatre of improvisation. The art of the actor consisted of shedding all traces of his environment and choosing a mask and costume with which to show off his tricks, quickly shifting character and situation with great technical mastery. Meyerhold compared the theatre of mask to a fairground show, noticing something of the 'eternal' in both forms of entertainment – 'Its heroes do not die; they simply change their aspects and assume new forms.'

Meyerhold's notion of *cabotinage* was closely associated with the *commedia dell'arte* as were his ideas on the grotesque. Realism concentrated on the typical and in so doing impoverished life by reducing the richness of the empirical world. The grotesque, on the other hand, sharpened the senses by mixing opposites and creating harsh incongruities. It was a means of making situations and events startling and dynamic whereas the verisimilitude of realism depended upon the audience's familiarity with what was being portrayed and was therefore ultimately banal. Theatre should not mirror reality but should transcend the commonplace of everyday life by deliberately exaggerating and distorting reality through stylized theatrical techniques. Only by concentrating on the design in its broadest sense – the setting, the architecture, mime, movements, gestures and poses – could theatre become expressive once more.

> When in the art of the grotesque [Meyerhold wrote], form triumphs over content, then the soul of the grotesque and the soul of the theatre will be one. The fantastic will exist in its own right on the stage; 'joie de vivre' will be rediscovered in the tragic as well as the comic.

More and more he aimed at breaking down the barrier between the stage and audience, building gangways and steps from the stage into the auditorium and having the actors moving in the aisles. In the House of Interludes, a theatre where he was able to try out many of his ideas, he had the hall arranged like a tavern with the audience seated at tables drinking while the action took place in their midst, as in a night club.

As a result of the revolution there were entirely new audiences coming in to the theatre, many of them for the first time, for whom theatre was a new experience. Audience participation was a subject much debated, with those like Meyerhold who were for it, and others who felt that the spectator should remain an observer. Vyachleslav Ivanov, a symbolist poet and playwright, agitated for the return of medieval mysteries in which actor and spectator would be united in a common religious experience. Platon Mikhailovich Kerzhentzev, a social theorist, suggested that the audience should not only take an active part in the performance but work in the various other departments of a theatre. Scriabin even advocated what he termed 'preparatory action': in order to be admitted the spectator would have to be initiated, wear special robes, and rehearse his part in a production. There were many, however, who considered that this kind of participation belonged to religious ceremonials, folk festivals, carnivals, political and sports meetings.

In 1911, at the Alexandrinsky Theatre in St Petersburg, Meyerhold was to develop these ideas on a larger and much grander scale. In his production of Molière's *Don Juan*, for instance, he removed the front curtains and the footlights and built a semi-circular proscenium. The stage was lit by huge candelabra and chandeliers, and all the lights in the auditorium were on so that it resembled a vast ballroom. Prompters sat behind Louis Quatorze screens, liveried servants brought on chairs, while little blackamoors ran to and fro arranging accessories, all to a background of music by Lully. The whole production was regarded as a triumph of theatricality, as well as a challenge to the Moscow Art Theatre.

At this period Meyerhold was deeply influenced by the conventions of the Chinese and Japanese theatre. He maintained that attempts to create reality on stage were doomed. He believed that the essence of theatre, as in the Kabuki or in the Kathakali dance theatre of India, lay in the appeal to the audience to use its imagination. This was the principle also of the Elizabethan stage and Shakespeare's 'On your imaginary forces work!' Meyerhold's ideas were influenced by Pavlov's theory of association which was currently fashionable. He considered that it was the task of the director to work consciously on the known associations of his audience, who know they are being asked to participate. 'The audience is made to see what we want them to see.'

In 1915, in *The Unknown* by Blok, in which he employed jugglers and Chinese boys throwing oranges into the audience, there was one scene, typical of his work at this period, in which an astronomer observes a falling star. This was represented by a stage-hand with a lighted torch on the end of a bamboo pole making a circle of flame in the air, and another stage-hand on the opposite side of the stage extinguishing it in a bucket of water.

When the House of Interludes was closed, he continued his experiments under the name of Dr Dappertutto in several of the many workshops that were springing up all over the country. By 1927 there were 24,000 theatre groups in Russia.

These were the years of experiment, of studios, workshops and theatre schools. It was almost entirely due to the influence of Meyerhold that the theatre of the revolution became the theatre of the avant-garde. As Marc Slonim points out, in no other country and at no other time were experimentalists given such financial and material opportunities as they were under Lenin, even though he was a conservative in art.

One of the most colourful and idiosyncratic experimenters was Nikolai Evreinov who succeeded Meyerhold as director of Vera Komisarjevskaya's theatre. In 1908 he published his ideas on theatre in a sensational article in which he claimed that theatre is an organic urge as basic as hunger or sex, an idea that Peter Brook was to pursue in the 1970s. From children's games of cops and robbers to military parades, public receptions, religious ceremonies and even the wearing of clothes, consciously or unconsciously, we all play a part, whether we are conforming to certain rules of etiquette or to what is expected of us in our particular profession or social status. Of course, granted such a premise, the theatre of naturalism is meaningless. The true aim of theatre, he argued, was 'theatricalization of life'. According to Evreinov the whole evolution of the European theatre towards realism was a ghastly mistake. Like Meyerhold, Taïrov and Vakhtangov, he believed the theatre should not attempt to make audiences forget they are watching a performance.

He set out, therefore, to revive the great theatrical spectacles of the past. At the Ancient Theatre in St Petersburg he revived medieval miracle plays and sixteenth-century farces. Typical of his productions was Adam de la Halle's *Robin and Marion*, a thirteenth-century pastorale in which he had the stage transformed to resemble a castle hall filled with knights, ladies, servants, minstrels – the audience of the play's period. The players were seen arriving, setting up their stage, unpacking their props, disclosing all the tricks of their trade.

The second season of the Ancient Theatre, 1911–12, was devoted to seventeenth-century playwrights: Calderón, Lope de Vega, Tirso de Molina. The stage usually represented the square of a Spanish town with a background of mountains. Evreinov laid great stress on the visual side of a production. His belief that 'words play but a subordinate role on the stage and we hear more with the eyes than with the ears' was in sympathy with Meyerhold's conviction of the superiority of mime.

In 1920 he staged in Petrograd *The Storming of the Winter Palace*, reproducing the highlights of the Bolshevik uprising. Eight thousand people took part in the show, an orchestra of five hundred played revolutionary songs, while a real blast from the warship *Aurora*, anchored on the Neva River, added to the theatricality of the occasion. More than one hundred thousand people watched the event which began at ten in the evening, and was staged in three main areas, the central area being the Winter Palace itself. Evreinov even went so far as to look for actual participants in the event to take part in the dramatic reconstruction. The performance was directed from a raised platform in the middle of the square. Using field phones, light signals and motorcycle couriers, the performance was orchestrated by Evreinov, with the aid of various assistants at strategic points. At the end he had a Tree of Freedom around which all the nations were united in brotherly celebration while the soldiers of the Red Army exchanged their rifles for sickles and hammers. From the darkened windows of the Winter Palace red stars with five points were lit. On the top of the building a huge red banner was raised. The performance ended with a mass singing of the International, fireworks, and a parade of the armed forces.

The idea of open air collective spectacles as the theatre form of the future had been discussed in Russia from the time of the 1905 revolution, and became popular after the October 1917 revolution. These mass spectacles were characterized by collective authorship, military-like organization, and the participation of different segments of society. They were not only conscious attempts to create a new, distinctly proletarian theatre but also an attempt to establish a new social ritual, re-enacting and celebrating the events of the revolution.

The idea of a theatre of the proletariat had been developed by Platon Kerzhentzev in an influential book, *The Creative Theatre*, published in 1918; he advocated a complete break with the professional theatre so that a people's theatre could originate from the people themselves. He was influenced by Romain Rolland's *The People's Theatre*, first published in

France in 1903, and translated into Russian in 1910. Kerzh-entzev was also influenced by the revival in England and America at this time of open air pageants, created collectively by members of the community.

It was in 1920 that Meyerhold began to develop his theory of bio-mechanics, a form of training that aimed at developing actors who would be part athletes, part acrobats, part anim-ated machines. Bio-mechanics was a gymnastic based upon:

Preparation for an action – pause –
the action itself – pause –
and its corresponding re-action.

Its aim was to discipline both the emotional and muscular response of the actor. As with a dancer, so every movement or gesture made on stage would be calculated, controlled and never spontaneous. The actor was taught to use the space around him as well as to relate in spatial terms to his fellow actors and the objects around him. Just as Alwin Nikolais demands from his dancers motion rather than emotion, so Meyerhold demanded from his actors the vigorous elimination of all human feeling and the creation of an order based upon mechanical laws; the actor was to function as a machine – a somersault, *salto-mortale*, or head-spring would suffice to convey different states of emotion.

In 1921 he began to train a company of actors according to this system of bio-mechanics. The company gave its first performance in April 1922 in *The Magnificent Cuckold* by Crommelynck, a comedy about a miller who, in an attempt to discover his wife's lover, gets all the men in the village to pass through her bedroom. For this production Meyerhold stripped the stage bare, removing the front curtains, borders, tormen-tors and backdrops. In the centre of this space stood a vertical construction suggestive of a mill, divided into various hori-zontal levels linked by staircases and gangways. This made it possible for a large number of scenes to be played without a break. There were also wheels, rolling discs, windmill sails, a trapeze, a bridge and ramps. On this constructivist set the actors, without make-up and in full light, dressed only in the light blue overalls of mechanics, ran, jumped and swung like acrobats in a gymnasium. Instead of 'true emotion' they presented a variety of athletic exercises and movements, performed to the accompaniment of a jazz orchestra. Meyerhold's theory was that the truth of human relationships and behaviour is best expressed not by words, but by gestures, steps, attitudes and poses.

In subsequent productions, like a ring-master, he put his actors through their paces; like a puppet-master he manipulated his marionettes in space. He used mobile constructions, moving walls, pivoting screens, as well as a revolving stage divided into concentric rings each of which could move independently. He aimed at creating a continuity on stage comparable to the cinema. Also, as Piscator and Jean-Louis Barrault were to do later, he used film in his productions. For the next seventeen years Meyerhold continued experimenting and each of his productions was a subject for debate and controversy. In *Terelkin's Death* by Sukhovo-Kobylin, against an abstract décor of geometric forms, his actors swung across the stage on ropes, juggled and struggled with objects that exploded or leaped into the air. In *Earth on its Hindlegs* by Marcel Martinet, the actors roared across the stage on motorbikes, pedalled on bicycles, or dragged on heavy cannons; and at one point a regiment of soldiers marched across the stage. In 1931, Charles Dullin, a contemporary of Jacques Copeau, referred to Meyerhold as 'a creator of forms, a poet of the theatre, who writes with gestures, rhythms, and a theatrical language invented for his needs'. People flocked from all over Russia and from every part of the world to see his productions and to learn his theory of bio-mechanics.

His most controversial and last great production was Gogol's *The Government Inspector*, staged in 1926. He transposed the text and altered the plot, moving the action from a small town to Moscow, turning the Mayor into a General, and so on. There was a semi-circular shaped dais, like the inside of a drum, in which were set fifteen doors. The main action took place on a sloping platform which emerged out of the darkness for each scene. In the scene where the officials arrive to bribe Kheslakov secretly, Meyerhold achieved one of his most startling effects. Suddenly, all the doors in the circular wall opened and in each appeared an official offering money. At the end, as the General was carried off in a strait-jacket on a stretcher, a white curtain was lowered, announcing in gold letters the arrival of the real Inspector-General. When it was raised, instead of the live actors, there were painted dummies arranged like a tableau of the final scene.

From 1928–53, however, the era of Stalin, experiment in art was banned; Meyerhold's powerful friends in the Party grew fewer, and between 1932–4 he was constantly reproached for his 'inimical attitude towards social realism'. Although he continued to do some outstanding productions, his theatre began to decline as the actors, rebelling against his autocratic methods, left his company. He tried hard to resist the Party's demand for ideological plays. In January 1932, *Pravda* led an all-out attack on experiment in the arts as a form of decadence. The political trials which had eliminated all Stalin's enemies were now extended to the arts: Meyerhold was denounced as an enemy of socialist realism and politically dangerous. In January 1938 his theatre was closed and he found himself unemployed, branded as an enemy of the State. Only Stanislavsky had the courage to offer him a job as his assistant at the Opera Theatre. He told Bakrushin, his deputy during some months of illness; 'Take care of Meyerhold; he is my sole heir in the theatre – here or anywhere else.' Stanislavsky died in August 1938 and Meyerhold took over direction of the Opera Theatre from Stanislavsky. In June 1939 there was an All-Union Conference of Stage Directors, intended by the Party as a public display of submission. It is said that Meyerhold was present – although the evidence is somewhat contradictory – and delivered an impassioned speech, declaring that what was happening in the theatre had nothing whatsoever to do with art. With great courage he defended the right of the creative artist to experiment, and denounced the uniformity that was being imposed upon the arts.

Three days later he was arrested and deported to a concentration camp in the Arctic. Shortly after his arrest, his wife – the actress Zinaida Raikh – was found assassinated, with her throat cut, her face disfigured and knife wounds all over her body. Whether Meyerhold died in exile or committed suicide is not known.

1 Vsevelod Meyerhold

2 The 1928 revival of
Meyerhold's constructivist
production of *The
Magnanimous Cuckold*

3 Eugene Vakhtangov

4 Adolphe Appia, 1882

5 Taïrov and the Synthetic Theatre

To Alexander Taïrov, as to many of his contemporaries, the actors of the Meyerhold Theatre were mere puppets in the hands of their director. At the same time, however, he considered that the actors of the Moscow Art Theatre were too dominated by the author. Of the school of naturalism he wrote scathingly, 'Little by little the theatre has turned into an experimental laboratory for psychopathological research . . . the naturalistic theatre suffers from a dysentery of formlessness'.

Taïrov believed that theatre was an art in itself and so he sought to train a company of master actors who would be capable of improvising upon an idea in the tradition of the *commedia dell'arte* and developing it before an audience. He believed in what he called 'the synthetic theatre', incorporating in one company all the talents of ballet, opera, circus, music hall and drama.

Like Meyerhold he insisted upon the spectator's being aware that he was in a theatre. Similarly he stressed the importance of gesture and movement, although he considered that Meyerhold imposed these arbitrarily from outside. Believing that the actor should be trained to create them from within himself, Taïrov always insisted that the main creator in the theatre is the master-actor.

For him the future of the theatre lay not only in a synthesis of all the arts but in complex stage machinery which would serve as an extension to the actor's craft. Influenced by Craig and Appia, he used space on the stage to create dynamics and spatial relationships, assisted by an imaginative use of lighting (based upon the theories of Appia), and the choreographed movement of actors. He consistently broke up the flat surface of the stage – 'the stage is the keyboard of the actor' – and used a variety of levels, ramps, stairways and abstract shapes. He would discuss the distance between levels in musical terms – according to the kind of movement required – speaking of intervals of a quarter or an eighth time etc. His critics accused him of being more concerned with beauty than with intellectual content. Marc Slonim records that in the 1920s the public went to his theatre as one goes to the ballet. Critics would write of certain productions, 'Alisa Koonen danced beautifully through her role', or 'Tseretelli's designs had delightful variations in a minor key.'

Like Appia he believed in music as the underlying principle, and often compared his actors to musical instruments and himself to a conductor: when staging Oscar Wilde's *Salome*, he would refer to the contra-bass of the soldiers, the flute of the young Syrian, the oboe of Salome, and so forth. He was often accused of paying more attention to the appearance of his actors than to their talent. When asked what kind of actor he hoped to produce he would reply by quoting the require-ments of the classical Hindu theatre: 'Freshness, beauty, plea-sant face, red mouth, good teeth, a neck round as a bracelet, arms of handsome form, gracious stature, powerful hips, charm, dignity, nobility, pride – without speaking of genius!' Like Grotowski he considered that actors should begin their training at the age of seven as in the ballet. In his own school the pupils (known as 'The Jumping Jacks') had to learn fencing, acrobatics, juggling, clowning, as well as various forms of movement and dance. He insisted that the actor's movement is more important than his diction, although both had to conform to strict rules of rhythm and dynamics.

In 1899 Adolphe Appia had published his most important work, *Die Musik und die Inszenierung*, in which, among many suggested reforms, he demanded for the singers a 'musical gymnastic' which would enable them to co-ordinate musical and bodily rhythm. Appia related everything to the concepts of Time and Space and, from 1906 onwards, worked with Jacques Dalcroze, the originator of eurhythmics, in his academy at Hellerau. What later became known as music-visualization was also developed in America by such modern dancers as

Ruth St Denis, Ted Shawn and Doris Humphrey. Under Taïrov rhythm became a distinctive feature at the Kamerny Theatre; for him music was the purest of the arts and he endeavoured to make his productions as musical as possible. Dialogue would be intoned, chanted, and, in addition, a musical score was composed for each production. Where Meyerhold's theatre was often as raucous as a circus ring, that of Taïrov resembled a mixture of opera and ballet. He foresaw a time when the actor would so master rhythm that he would be able to execute a performance not merely rhythmically but a-rhythmically. He foresaw the use of off-beat movement and a-tonal sound creating new possibilities in theatre. In many of his ideas he was to anticipate the discoveries of modern dance.

Taïrov, like Meyerhold, was a cosmopolitan. His theatre, the Kamerny, was a chamber theatre for connoisseurs. With greater patience than Meyerhold, he proved the better teacher, while his diplomacy steered him through many political intrigues. But even he was not able to escape the machinations of the Party entirely. In 1929 Stalin described the Kamerny as 'deeply bourgeois and alien to our culture', saying that recent plays there were trash. Taïrov's desire to continue his experiments with style and form was constantly in conflict with the growing demand to present ideological and propaganda plays. Because of his flexibility and tact, as well as a use of fashionable terminology which enabled him to put the label of 'socialist realism' on completely different, and often conflicting, plays and productions, he succeeded in surviving through the 1930s. Of all the theatres of the 1920s, the Kamerny had the longest life, but it was purchased at the price of sacrifice and compromise.

In 1946 he staged his last production – Chekhov's *The Seagull*. It was said in Moscow that Chekhov's seagull had become Taïrov's swansong. The play was given a concert performance against black drapes and all the actors wore black. Taïrov inserted discussions about naturalism and other trends in the theatre, while Konstantin's search for new forms sounded very much like an attack on the drabness of socialist realism. It was the same year in which Zhdanov and the Party Central Committee condemned all formalism and experimentation in literature and the arts. In 1949 the Kamerny was closed and in the following year Taïrov died.

For two decades the Communist Party under Stalin forced the Soviet theatre into a conforming line of socialist realism, producing hundreds of doctrinaire plays about collective farming, hydro-electric plants, dam building, and the heroes of the revolution and of the civil war. For almost twenty years the Soviet stage, which had been the greatest in the world, suffered an eclipse.

6 Vakhtangov's Achievement

If Taïrov rejected the theories of both Meyerhold and Stanislavsky, it was Evgeny Vakhtangov's unique achievement to fuse the contributions of these two great directors and thereby point the way to a richer and more varied form of theatre.

For Meyerhold [wrote Vakhtangov, who called Meyerhold 'dear, beloved master'] a performance is theatrical when the spectator does not forget for a second that he is in a theatre, and is conscious all the time of the actor as a craftsman. Stanislavsky (to whom Vakhtangov once wrote, 'I thank life for the opportunity of knowing you . . . . I do not know anyone superior to you') demands the opposite: that the spectator become oblivious to the fact that he is in a theatre and that he be immersed in the atmosphere in which the protagonists of the play exist.

What made the productions of Vakhtangov unique was precisely the fusion of psychological truth with a greater awareness of theatricality.

Realism does not take everything from life [he wrote], but only what it needs for the reproduction of a given scene . . . the form must be created by one's fantasy. That is why I call it fantastic realism. The means must be theatrical.

As a young man Vakhtangov became extremely interested in the work of Meyerhold. 'Each of his productions', he wrote in his diary, 'is a new theatre. Every one of them would have a whole new direction.' However, he also thought that Meyerhold acted merely from a desire to destroy the old, and this led him to impose upon a play a form that was often alien to its content.

Evgeny Vakhtangov, who was Stanislavsky's greatest pupil, studied first under Nemirovich-Danchenko and then, in 1911, was accepted into the Moscow Art Theatre company where he played over fifty roles. He believed completely in the teachings of Stanislavsky and soon became his assistant. When Stanislavsky formed the First Studio he entrusted to him the training of the young actors. He criticized Vakhtangov's first production in which he allowed the actors to perform for themselves, what he called 'trance acting', rather than for the audience. Indeed, in these first years, Vakhtangov was inclined to take his master's theories too far. For instance, in 1918, when directing *Rosmersholm*, he insisted that the actors should not only think *about* the character they were playing but *as* the character. 'An actor must live and think as the character,' he declared. Whereas Stanislavsky, who was continually revising his system, considered that the actor should not lose himself in the part.

Vakhtangov's was essentially a poetic approach to theatre without the preciousness or over-romanticism of Taïrov, and he remained, although of the younger generation, alien to the technological devices exploited by other avant-garde directors. In his production of Strindberg's *Eric IV* which, with Michael Chekhov in the lead, created a furore in Berlin in 1922, he interpreted the whole play through the diseased mind of the mad king. In the throne room the gold ornaments were rusted and columns bent. There were labyrinths of stairs and passageways, together with a use of wrong perspective, suggestive of the twisted demented turnings of the king's mind. The courtiers were portrayed as 'the dead souls' of the aristocracy and dressed as puppets or ghosts, while the common people were treated realistically.

One of his most famous productions was *The Dybbuk* for the Habima Theatre Studio in Moscow. Without forgetting Stanislavsky's principle of inner truth, he managed to forge a grotesque style that laid bare the atmosphere of fear and superstition in the ghetto which succeeds in destroying the young lovers. Sonia Moore describes how, wrapped in a great coat with a hot-water bottle at his side, he would rehearse through the long, cold nights, stopping only to swallow some bicarbonate of soda which helped to ease the pain of the cancer in his side. During this period, although he was gravely ill, he was also directing at his own studio as well as performing in the evenings. Sonia Moore describes how he would seek a different theatrical rhythm for each character, not imposed from without but discovered from within by each actor.

Forget the superfluous imitation of life [he would say]. Theatre has its own realism, its own truth. This truth is in the truth of experience and emotions which are expressed on the stage with the help of imagination and theatrical means.

When *The Dybbuk* opened on 31 January 1922, the critics were full of praise: 'Every gesture, every intonation, every step, every pose and acting detail is brought to such technical perfection that one can hardly imagine anything superior.' Tyrone Guthrie, the English director, in his autobiography, *A Life in the Theatre*, described the production as the most exciting he had ever seen.

It is still, after more than forty years, in its rejection of naturalism, its use of symbolism and ritual, its choreography, its musical approach, more 'advanced', more assured and more economical than the work of any director which I have since encountered .... Vakhtangov, who set the impress of his style on all Habima's earlier work, was a genius.

It was this same production that Lee Strasberg saw on a visit to Russia in 1934 with Stella Adler, Harold Clurman, and other members of the American Group Theatre. He wrote in his diary,

Vakhtangov's value lay in dissociating the Stanislavsky System as a technique for the actor from the Stanislavsky method of production; thus, of course, the System was enriched and improved. His own way certainly proved that the 'Method' in the proper hands did not produce only realistic acting, but that the process of 'inner justification' was a necessary technique in a creative process regardless

of the style desired. His second achievement was his sense
of perfection – his ability to penetrate every gesture,
intonation, etc. into the spirit of the play . . . . Meyerhold
uncovers the social content of the play. Vakhtangov
displays the play in all its manifestations. Thus
Vakhtangov's production of *The Dybbuk*, which I have
seen, was complete. Meyerhold's productions all appear like
fragments, episodes (his technique is episodic, too). Thus,
Meyerhold's production seems to be against the original
text, while Vakhtangov's somehow simply lays bare the
undiscovered content of the text and seems to remain true
to the author.

Vakhtangov's last production – he died in May 1922 – was
Carlo Gozzi's *Turandot*. At the first rehearsal he announced,
'Our work is senseless if there is no holiday mood. If there is
nothing to carry the spectators away. Let us carry them away
with our youth, laughter and improvisation.' The actors
worked on every word, gesture and intonation until it seemed
absolutely spontaneous, *as if* improvised. Actors would
compete with one another in invention. A scarf would become
a beard; a lampshade, an emperor's hat; a towel, a turban; a
shawl would become a dress, and so on. The rehearsals would
commence just after 11 p.m. when Vakhtangov's own performance had ended, and continue until eight the next morning.
His demands for discipline were so severe that actors were
actually afraid of him. They knew when he had arrived by the
sudden silence in the Studio. He could bring actors to elation
by his praise, and reduce them to tears with his keen criticism.
  Mortally ill, he demanded joy, infectious gaiety, from his
cast. 'Actors must have joy in their hearts from the feeling of
the stage. Without this, theatre is a layman's pastime.' He
knew that he had not long to live and yet he would sometimes
cancel in a moment what had been achieved during long
nights. 'Never stop searching', he would say, 'and cherish the
form which discloses the inner content.' Continually searching
for truth and force, he made each rehearsal new. 'Art is search,
not final form. If what an actor finds is good, it will be easy
to find something better. Even after the opening of the play
the role should grow.'

On 27 February a dress rehearsal was held especially for Stanislavsky, Nemirovich-Danchenko, and the actors and students of the Moscow Art Theatre. Vakhtangov himself was at home, dying. At the first break Stanislavsky telephoned to Vakhtangov, and at the second break he hired a sleigh and went to his home. He gave instructions that the performance was not to continue until his return.

'I wanted the actors to live truthfully, really cry and laugh,' said Vakhtangov. 'Do you believe in them?'

'Your success is brilliant,' replied Stanislavsky. He then returned to the theatre and the performance continued. At the end, Stanislavsky said to the actors, 'In the twenty-three years of the Moscow Art Theatre's existence there have been few triumphs such as this one. You have found what many theatres have sought in vain for a long time.'

At the beginning of *Turandot* the actors appear before the front curtain, wearing their ordinary clothes, to tell the audience what they are going to see. The curtain rises and, to a waltz tune, they all dress up in the bits and pieces they find lying about the stage, converting rags to riches by their imaginative use of them. Stage hands come on, dressed in dark blue kimonos and caps and, to the accompaniment of the lilting waltz, set the stage. Scenery descends from the flies, counterweighted with gaily-coloured sandbags; as these soar into the air, doors and windows, pillars and arches glide smoothly on. So the play begins.

The production exploded on that dark night in the Moscow of 1922 like a brilliant display of fireworks. Those were the days of poverty, hardship, and extreme cold in Moscow when everything was scarce – food, materials, warmth. Yet out of this very lack, Vakhtangov, with a Franciscan gaiety and lightness of heart, had created an experience of joy.

7 Craig and Appia – Visionaries

As I write, it is not easy to refrain from singing – the moment is the most lovely, the most hallowed in all my life – for in a few minutes I shall have given birth to that which has for a long while been preparing far back before I was born, and all during my life, and now I am the one selected to this honour and am amongst the creators.

Such words might the Virgin Mary have written to her cousin Elizabeth when expecting the birth of her child, the promised Messiah. They are, however, from a letter by Gordon Craig to his friend, Martin Shaw, the composer, and are but a prelude to even more extraordinary language which reads like Nietzsche – in which Craig describes his vision of the Theatre of the Future.

The place is without form – one vast square of empty space is before us – and all is still – no sound is heard – no movement seen . . . . Nothing is before us –
And from that nothing shall come life – even as we watch, in the very centre of that void a single atom seems to stir – to rise – it ascends like the awakening of a thought in a dream –
No light plays round it, no angles are to be seen, no shadows are visible – only the slow, deliberate inexorable ascension of a single form – near it, yet further back, a second and a third atom seems to have come into a half existence –
– and while they grow the first atom seems to be disappearing – a fourth, a fifth, a sixth, and seventh . . . slowly shapes continue to rise in endless numbers – to rise

and fall while still the folds unfold and close, mounting
one higher than another, others falling until there stand
before us vast columns of shapes, all single yet all united
– none resting
  Until
     like a dew it settles – no more – enough.
     And may my love beginning, have no end.

Craig dreamed of a theatre that would appeal to the
emotions through movement alone. There would be no play or
plot, but simply the correlated movements of sound, light and
moving masses. The audience would have a kinetic experience.
The Bauhaus in the 1920s was to experiment with a similar
theatre, plays whose 'plots' consisted of nothing more than the
pure movement of forms, colour and light.

Influenced by certain illustrations in Serlio's *Five Books of
Architecture*, Craig began to have ideas for a machine, rather
like an organ, which would operate great cubes, such as he
had once seen in Fingal's Cave, causing them to rise or fall at
any speed while, from above, similar cubes would descend and
ascend. Upon these moving cubes, combined with his famous
screens, light would play continually.

And the actors? Craig wanted to remove them. 'The actor is
for me only an insuperable difficulty and an expense.' If actors
were to be used then they 'must cease to speak and must *move*
only, if they want to restore the art to its old place. Acting is
Action – and Dance is the poetry of Action.'

Craig's small book, *The Art of the Theatre*, caused him to
become the spokesman, prophet and leader of the revolution
against realism. He protested that the theatre had become
overburdened with words, its origins being in dance and mime.
He defined the good dramatist as one who knows that the eye
is more swiftly and powerfully appealed to than any other
sense, and in *Towards a New Theatre*, he quoted the derivation
of the word theatre from the Greek (θεατρον) meaning a place
for *seeing* shows.

It was after seeing puppets used by the German director
Jessner that Craig conceived the idea of doing away with
actors altogether and substituting what he called 'über-
marionettes'. The Bauhaus, which set out to employ modern

science and technology for artistic ends, was also to experiment with 'plays' in which pieces of machinery or sculpture would whizz or glide across the stage, while actors were dressed to look like robots. Of course a theatre such as Craig conceived of would cost millions of pounds since robots, elaborate machinery, electronic devices and complex engineering were necessary to realize his abstract visions. But is a theatre without actors any more theatre? Does it not then become a kinetic art?

> To save the theatre we must destroy it [wrote Craig]. We shall build the Theatre of the Future . . . while we are about it, let us measure for an art which will exceed in stature all other arts, an art which says less yet shows more than all.
>
> I prophesy that a new religion will be found contained in it. That religion will preach no more, but it will reveal. It will not show us the definite images which the painter and the sculptor show us. It will unveil thoughts to our eyes, silently – by movement – in visions.

Norman Marshall records how in his old age Craig admitted that the theatre of which he dreamed was still to come.

> I once said that there are just two kinds of theatre, the old theatre of my master, Henry Irving, and its successor which I once called the theatre of tomorrow. I have changed my ideas. The old theatre has been effectively destroyed. In its place we have a new kind of theatre which is infinitely better but is, in fact, no more than a re-edit of the old model, brought up to date, stream-lined and improved. The *real* theatre, the theatre which is an art in its own right like music and architecture, is yet to be discovered and may not come for several generations.

As a person Craig would appear to have been too paranoiac, irresponsible and immature to carry the weight of his own genius. His fame rests less on his actual work in the theatre than on his writings and designs. Even here his head was in the clouds for, as Lee Simonson has demonstrated, his designs for the theatre were often totally impractical because of his complete disregard for the principle of relativity. Scenic design is governed by the relation between the unchangeable size of the human figure and the height of the proscenium arch. A Craig drawing of a six-foot figure is very impressive because of the relation of the figure to the soaring lines of the arch; but when the height of the arch is reduced to twenty feet – which is about as high as it could be in a present-day theatre – the figure of the actor still remains six-foot high, with the result that the size of the arch in relation to the figure standing beneath it is no longer particularly impressive.

Craig's famous screens, his Thousand Scenes in One, are an example of his infectious, yet impractical, ideas. In place of painted scenery he visualized scenery made of screens with two-way hinges, which could be composed in any shape and made in any size, and lit in any colour, according to the mood of the scene. The Abbey Theatre in Dublin was the first to use Craig's screens. W. B. Yeats was a great admirer of Craig, and it was for him that Craig made a miniature set of them which he used to have before him while writing his plays – the different arrangements providing him with all the backgrounds that he required.

It was after reading Craig's article on 'The Artists of the Theatre of the Future' that Stanislavsky invited him to Moscow to design and direct *Hamlet*. For this production Craig decided to use his screens. At first he wanted them built of metal but, as Stanislavsky drily comments, the sheer weight would have necessitated rebuilding the entire theatre and installing hydraulic machinery. The technicians of the Moscow Art Theatre workshops experimented for many months with various metals, wood, even cork; all were too heavy. 'At each appointed cue' Craig had announced, 'a single or double leaf of my screens moves – turns and advances – recedes – folds and unfolds.' But he had no idea how 'those terrible and dangerous walls' – as Stanislavsky described them – were to be operated. Eventually they were made of timber frames and canvas.

With endless patience – the entire production took two years to prepare – Stanislavsky rehearsed the stage-hands so that the screens should seem to move of their own accord. Then, only one hour before the first performance, when Stanislavsky was sitting in the auditorium, having rehearsed the scene-shifters for the last time and sent them off to have a tea-break, suddenly one of the screens began to topple sideways. It fell on the next screen and then, one after the other, like a house of cards collapsing, the whole set crashed to the stage. There was the sound of canvas ripping, timber snapping, and a mass of broken and torn screens lay heaped on the stage. The audience was already entering. The front curtain was lowered while the stage hands endeavoured to salvage the wreck. Instead of the screens being moved in full view of the audience, as Craig had intended, the curtains had to be closed for every scene change.

Although Craig was an able craftsman, draughtsman and a brilliant artist, none the less there was in his life and in his work a basic lack of discipline. He spilled over in too many directions, failing to relate to simple practical realities. It was because of this temperamental weakness in his character that his School of Theatre foundered within a few months of starting, and not because of the outbreak of the war as some have claimed. He was so filled with the general concept of a school that he failed completely to consider the practical details of organization needed to realize his schemes. If, however, many of his ideas seemed impracticable at the time, they were still to have a profound influence upon succeeding generations of designers. Josef Svoboda, Robert Edmond Jones, Norman Bel-Geddes, Wieland Wagner, Isamu Noguchi and many others, benefiting by modern technological advances, have been able to give form to many of his ideas. When Isamu Noguchi designed *King Lear* for John Gielgud in 1955, not one critic recognized that his huge screens, gliding about the stage as though of their own volition, were a superb realization of Craig's concept of mobile screens. 'Instead', Noguchi relates, 'I was deluged with an avalanche of abuse from the press.'

It was Craig's cardinal belief that all great plays have an imaginative décor of their own. When designing Ibsen's *Rosmersholm* for Eleanora Duse, he created not a drawing room, but a dark, greeny-blue space with an opening at the back looking out to a misty distance. In the programme he included a note to explain the idea behind his design.

Ibsen's marked detestation of Realism is nowhere more apparent than in the two plays of *Rosmersholm* and

Ghosts. The words are the words of actuality but the drift of the words something beyond this. There is the powerful impression of unseen forces closing in upon the place: we hear continually the long drawn-out note of the horn of death . . . .

Therefore those who prepare to serve Ibsen, to help in the setting forth of his play, must come to the work in no photographic mood, all must approach as artists . . . . Realism is only Exposure whereas Art is Revelation; and therefore in the mounting of this play I have tried to avoid all Realism . . . .

Let our common sense be left in the cloak room with our umbrellas and hats. We need here our finer senses only, the living part of us. We are in Rosmersholm, a house of shadows.

. . . the birth of the new Theatre, and its new Art, has begun.

If, however, many of Craig's later designs became too grandiose to be successfully translated into theatre reality, it is important to record, as Norman Marshall points out in *The Producer and the Play*, that in his early days Craig worked in inadequate halls and with limited resources with remarkable results. His very first opportunity to put some of his ideas into practice came with a production of Purcell's *Dido and Aeneas*, which he designed and directed for the Purcell Operatic Society, founded in Hampstead by his friend Martin Shaw, who rehearsed and trained the singers. The production was presented at the Hampstead Conservatoire of Music (later to become the Embassy Theatre) in 1900. To W.B. Yeats who was present it seemed like the dawn of something great – 'the only good scenery I ever saw'.

In staging his first production Craig had learned much from the articles and lectures of Hubert von Herkomer, who had a school and theatre at Bushey in Hertfordshire, where he wrote his own plays, composed incidental music for a concealed orchestra and, with his pupils, acted, danced and sang. Herkomer used effects of misty glens, sunrises, moonlight, waterfalls – all achieved by the use of gauzes and electric light.

Many theatre people went to pick up ideas and Craig was taken to Bushey by his mother, the actress Ellen Terry.

In 1901 Craig worked again with Martin Shaw on *The Masque of Love*, which was presented at the Coronet Theatre. For this he used three walls of light grey canvas and a grey stage cloth. The costumes were black and white, with occasional touches of colour. This grey box was filled with pools of coloured light in and out of which moved white-frocked children.

His next production, in 1902, was *Acis and Galatea* at the Penley's Theatre. It is important to stress that for these productions he had little or no money to spend. The singers of the Purcell Operatic Society were gifted amateurs, and neither Craig nor Shaw received any payment for many months of work: everything had to be done on a shoe-string budget. For this production Craig spent hours rummaging through wholesale houses in the City in search of cheap materials. He found masses of upholsterer's webbing (the kind used for supporting sofa springs), and with this he constructed a huge white tent through the lattices of which the light would shine. The costumes were made from yards of ribbon which, as the actors moved in and out of the slits in the tent, floated out behind them.

In spite of the success and importance of each of these productions, the Purcell Operatic Society had to close. Brokers' men arrived at the theatre on the last night, while Ellen Terry, as so often where her son was concerned, was left to pay the bills. 'I send cheques to pay *half* the amount of five *pressing* bills you tell me about – "Old bills", you say! Why, I have been paying your "old bills" these ten years!'

Among those who saw *Acis and Galatea* was Laurence Housman who wrote to Craig, inviting him to design and direct a nativity play he had written, called *Bethlehem*. The play had music by Joseph Moorat who was prepared to finance a modest production. For it, Craig created one of his most evocative effects. When the curtains opened, the audience saw an indigo night sky in which stars were twinkling; in the centre of the stage sat the shepherds in a sheepfold full of sleeping sheep. Edward Craig, in his excellent account of the life of his father, describes how the scene was created. The stars were crystals taken from an old chandelier and suspended at different heights on black cobbler's thread against an indigo backcloth, which sparkled as they caught the light. A few sheep hurdles were placed in an irregular formation, and the sheep were simply sacks filled with wool with the corners tied off at the top to suggest the ears of the sleeping sheep.

Gordon Craig's most memorable and perhaps best known designs are those for the Moscow Art Theatre production of *Hamlet*. In the first scene the stage, with its towering screens, seemed full of mysterious corners, passages, deep shadows, shafts of moonlight, the passing of sentries. Strange unfathomable underground sounds, the howling of wind, and distant cries, could be heard. From among the grey screens there emerged the Ghost, scarcely visible in his grey costume against the grey walls, his long cloak sliding softly behind him. Suddenly the Ghost, caught in a shaft of moonlight, startles the guards, but the Ghost at once fades into one of the apertures in the screens and disappears. The later scene of Hamlet's meeting with his father's spirit, Craig placed high up on the battlements, against a reddening sky, so that the light, shining through the diaphanous material of the Ghost's cloak, made him seem about to dissolve with the approach of dawn.

For the Court of Denmark, Craig covered the screens with gilt paper – the kind used for Christmas decorations. The King and Queen were seated on a high throne, wearing gold costumes. From their shoulders there stretched an enormous gold cloak covering the entire stage. In this cloak were holes through which appeared the heads of the courtiers. The scene was dimly lit so that the gold glimmered against the surrounding darkness. It was at such moments that the genius of Craig was seen in action. Such moments, however, were few. He was a man caught in an archetypal dream, of whom Bernard Shaw was to write,

> If ever there was a spoilt child in artistic Europe, that child was Gordon Craig. The doors of the theatre were wider open to him than to anyone else. He had only to come in as others did, and do his job, and know his place, and

accept the theatre with all its desperate vicissitudes, and inadequacies, and impossibilities, as the rest of us did, and the way would have been clear for all the talent he possessed.

The use of darkness, of shadow, as a counterpoint to light, combined with architectural masses, was not original to Craig. Indeed, many of his ideas had already been anticipated by the Swiss artist, Adolphe Appia, who, in 1891, had published a small pamphlet, *Staging Wagnerian Drama*, which included a complete scenario of *The Ring*. In 1895 he wrote his most important work, *Die Musik und die Inszenierung*, in which he set out in detail his proposed reforms for the revival of scenic art. It was in this book that he advocated a theatre of atmosphere rather than of appearance, remarking that in *Siegfried* 'we need not try to represent a forest; what we must give the spectator is man in the atmosphere of a forest.' Although Irving and the Duke of Saxe-Meiningen were the first to use shadows on stage, Appia was the first to work out a complete theory of stage lighting based on the possibilities of moving lights upon simple, non-representational sets painted a neutral colour. Therefore, in *Siegfried*, rather than cut-outs of trees, Appia proposed to cast the shadows of green leaves upon the actor walking on the stage. As Lee Simonson remarks in *The Stage is Set*, 'the first hundred and twenty pages of Appia's volume are nothing less than the text-book of modern stage-craft.' It was Appia who first demonstrated the necessity of visualizing the mood and the atmosphere of a play; the important of suggestion completed in the imagination of the spectator; the effectiveness of an actor stabbed by a spotlight in a great dim space; the significance of a 'space-stage' (such as Wieland Wagner was to develop at Bayreuth); and the more abstract forms of scenic art. He foresaw not only the possibility of spot-lighting but also of projected scenery, something Craig had never imagined.

Light to Appia was the supreme scene painter; light alone defined and, at the same time, revealed. The very quality of our emotional response can, as we now know, be established by the degree and quality of light used on the stage. Appia used to demonstrate this by the scene from the opera of *Romeo and Juliet* in which the two lovers meet at Capulet's ball. By merely taking down all the lights on the stage and focusing on the two lovers, the designer can help to emphasize the intensity of the moment in the same way that the score does. In Wagner's *Tristan und Isolde*, which he designed for the Scala, Milan, instead of setting the second act in moonlit darkness (the scene is a garden at night) he had the stage bathed in a warm, almost supernatural light, as though night did not exist for the lovers, so radiant was the light within them. For Appia light served not merely to illuminate what was happening on stage but to highlight the emotional mood of a scene from moment to moment. This called for an elaborate lighting plot which would stand in relation to the production as a musical score does for an opera. Today all this is standard practice, but in 1897 it was highly experimental.

One of the first people to experiment with light on the stage was the American dancer, Loie Fuller who, when she danced in Paris in 1892, was hailed by critics and artists alike; Rodin referred to her as a woman of genius. Today she is largely forgotten, yet she inspired many of the creators of *l'art nouveau*, while the director of the Comédie Française wrote, 'it is certain that new capacities are developing in theatrical art, and that Miss Loie Fuller will have been responsible for an important contribution.' Central to her performance was a moving image made animate by the projection of coloured light and slides. The movements of her costume, made from hundreds of yards of fine silk, lit from many directions, created an extraordinary effect. Of all her dances perhaps the most popular was the Fire Dance. For this, fourteen electricians were required, directed by means of gestures, taps of her heel and other signals worked out between them. The effect of flame and smoke was produced by the play of light on the whirling folds of material, especially from below as she danced on a glass floor. A theatre was built for her; she formed a company and a school, and was the first to create performances out of doors in 'found' spaces. She invented lamps and reflectors, and with the aid of magic lanterns and scrims turned the stage into a continually shifting landscape. In many ways she anticipated some of the creations of Alwin Nikolais. Stripping the stage bare of scenery, she created décor through combinations of light, colour and motion. Like Craig she dreamed of a theatre of the future that would be called the Temple of Light. In this theatre the dancers would be abstract forms, the music coming from the invisible orchestra. It would be a theatre of pure illusion, providing that suggestive atmosphere of which Appia also wrote, which would provoke the imagination of the spectator.

> I consider my work to be the point of departure of the great light symphony [she wrote], which will transform the theatre of the future. We don't know enough about the infinite resources of light, and how many treasures are enclosed in the simply ray of a projector.

Perhaps because music was his chief inspiration, Appia did not seek to impose his abstract sets upon realistic plays, but limited his ideas to opera and to Shakespeare. Unlike Craig, he insisted upon the importance of the actor. It was because he considered painted scenery two-dimensional and the actor three-dimensional that he opposed the traditional form of scenery. His designs, consisting mainly of rostra, columns, flights of steps, and ramps, provided, with the aid of lighting, an environmental and three-dimensional use of space in which the actor could feel at ease.

In 1911, at Hellerau near Dresden, a modern theatre was built for Émile Jacques Dalcroze, in accordance with Appia's ideas. The result was an absolute unity of amphitheatre and an open stage within an enclosed space. The unframed stage with its variable stairs and flexible lighting equipment, made it possible in 1912 for Appia to stage the second act of *Orpheus and Eurydice*, which created a sensation in Europe and America. In 1926, Appia designed a huge multi-level stage representing the entrance to Tartarus, while for the Elysian Fields he produced a design with people walking against a wide sky on straight and inclined surfaces. Craig considered this to be Appia's most beautiful design.

In 1914 Appia and Craig shared the place of honour at the International Theatre Exhibition at Zurich. At that time they did not know each other. Craig went to meet Appia at the station. They recognized each other almost by instinct and, while Appia was still some way off, Craig held out his arms in a gesture of welcome which was magnified by the folds of his cape, like the wings of a bird.

Although Appia could not speak English, and Craig knew no French, they carried on a lively conversation over lunch, covering the tablecloth with drawings and diagrams. At one point Craig wrote his name on the tablecloth and next to it that of Appia, over the top of which he wrote the word 'music', and then drew a circle around it. As Jean Mercier comments, it was a perfect symbol of the difference between the two artists. 'The reform of Appia was dominated and directed by a major force – music. Hence the circle which circumscribed and limited the name of Appia, while that of Craig had a freedom which spread to the limits of the cloth!'

Like Craig, Appia mounted less than a dozen productions in his lifetime. A perfectionist, he was continually frustrated by the structure of most existing theatres. He realized that dramatic art could only be reformed by first reforming the place where that art develops.

> The arbitrary conventions of our auditoriums and stages placed face to face still control us! [he wrote] Let us leave our theatres to their dying past and let us construct elementary buildings designed merely to cover the space in which we work.

People came from all over the world to visit Appia, yet Craig was to steal much of the limelight because he was the better draughtsman as well as a writer with a more infectious style. Craig was an extrovert, Appia an introvert. Craig was also an actor and therefore dramatized everything he did or said. In a sense, his meeting with Appia, when he lifted his arms like a great bird and enveloped Appia in his wings, is a very apt image of the two men. Craig is remembered more than Appia by the general public – yet, in most of his ideas, Appia had already anticipated him. But among such artists there is no question of competition. As Stanislavsky observed, 'In different corners of the world, due to conditions unknown to us, various people in various spheres sought in art for the same naturally born creative principles. Upon meeting they were amazed at the common character of their ideas.'

In his old age, Appia was able to see how his ideas were

taking root everywhere. Jacques Copeau, who called Appia his master, wrote after his death,

> He has led us back to the eternal principles. Now we are in possession of a scenic principle and are at peace. We can work on the drama and the author's meaning without having to bother with more or less original formulas for stage sets or new systems. Everything that comes after him has sprung from him and has changed.

When in 1928, Appia died, Craig made a pilgrimage to his graveside.

> I am sorry that you are not here [Craig had once written to Appia]. You, my dear, are the very noblest expression in the modern theatre . . . to me there is far more vivid life and drama in one of your great studies for scenes than anything else known to me in our theatre of Europe.

8 Copeau – Father of the Modern Theatre

At the beginning of the twentieth century Gertrude Stein and Eric Satie were seeking for a freshness and a childlike simplicity in their work. Gertrude Stein, who spoke of 'beginning again and again', explored the relationships of words, parts of speech and the use of the present tense. Satie went back as far as medieval and Greek modes of musical composition, eschewing sonorities, and attempting to make every note audible. Brancusi, the sculptor, was also seeking for a greater simplicity in his work. He would take a single form, such as the egg, as the basis of his sculpture, and try to find the essential form behind the recognizable exterior. These three, united by a common search for the primal in art, became close friends.

In Paris at the same time there was a theatre critic who dreamed of going back to the beginnings of theatre. Jacques Copeau came late to the practice of theatre. For many years a drama critic, he was thirty-five when he began to direct. André Gide, in his Journal for 10 July 1905, had written, 'Copeau, at twenty-seven seems ten years older; his over-expressive features are already worn out by suffering. His shoulders high and firm like those of someone who takes much upon himself.'

It was in 1913 that Copeau founded the Théâtre du Vieux-Colombier. Intent on freeing the stage from cumbersome machinery and showy effects, he was also rebelling against the artificial rhetoric of classical productions at the Comédie Française, as well as against the excessive naturalism of Antoine at the Théâtre Libre. Yet his *Essai de Rénovation Dramatique* is curiously unlike the usual manifesto written by someone launching a theatre. Modestly he set forth his ideas:

> We do not represent a school. We bring with us no formula in the belief that from it there must inevitably spring the theatre of tomorrow. Herein lies a distinction between us and those enterprises that have gone before us. These – and it can be said without offence to the best known among them, the Théâtre Libre, and without belittling the achievements of its director, André Antoine, to whom we owe so much – these fell into the imprudent and unconscious mistake of limiting their field of action by a programme of revolution . . . . We do not know what is to be the theatre of tomorrow but in founding the Theatre of the Vieux-Colombier we are preparing a place and haven of work for tomorrow's inspiration.

Almost the symbol of Copeau's point of departure, of going back to first sources, was his theatre, startlingly simple, without footlights or proscenium arch. Décor was used sparingly, the atmosphere for each play being created almost entirely by lighting and the addition of one or two properties. Copeau revolutionized the avant-garde. He gave it an austere and scrupulously disciplined beauty. He was, as Harold Hobson aptly remarked, the Jansenist of the French theatre. Granville-Barker, a close friend and admirer, wrote to Copeau, 'The art of the theatre is the art of acting, first, last and all the time. You very soon found that out.'

The acting in a modern play at the Vieux-Colombier was, Norman Marshall recalls, at first sight completely realistic, yet business was reduced to a minimum, each gesture was used selectively and thereby gained in significance. Copeau achieved a reality beyond the naturalism of Antoine or that of the early productions of the Moscow Art Theatre. When, in 1920, Copeau staged a realistic play by Charles Vildrac, Antoine, who was then a drama critic, was astonished by the kind of reality he saw depicted on the stage. The action took place in a seamen's café. There was a door at the back through which the sea was suggested by means of light. There was a counter, three tables and ten chairs. That was all.

The atmosphere [wrote Antoine], is created with an almost unbearable intensity . . . . The public is no longer seated in front of a picture, but in the same room alongside the characters. This extraordinary impression has never before been produced to this extent, such a complete elimination of all 'theatrical elements' makes for detailed perfection in acting.

In 1913 Copeau had ended his manifesto with these prophetic words – '*Pour l'oeuvre nouvelle qu'on nous laisse un tréteau nu!*' A bare stage, an empty space: fifty years later the search was to continue in the work of Peter Brook and others. And in one of his most famous productions, Molière's *Les Fouberies de Scapin*, the action was set on a bare platform built of wood, isolated in the centre of the stage and violently lit from above by a large triangle of lights hung in full view of the audience. As in the Kabuki Theatre, the platform could represent the inside of a house, a palace, a battle-camp and the area around it, a garden surrounding a house, a lake surrounding an island, or a lower level of the house. Again, as in the Kabuki, such a setting called for movement and speed from the actors: acting of a really physical kind.

Copeau had a strong sense of choreography but it was not imposed from without, as the invention of a dazzling showman, but developed organically from the text. 'The one originality of interpretation which is not anathema', he would tell his students, 'is that which grows organically from a sound knowledge of the text.' He was deeply sensitive to the underlying rhythms of a text, the intervals of time, and those elements in drama which were similar to music. Again, there is a parallel with Kabuki where music, in some form or another, underlies and sustains the rhythm of the play. Even in silent pantomime in Kabuki there is a basic underlying beat. For each of his roles Nakamu Baigyoku would set a basic regularity of pulse and, with almost metronomical precision, maintain it by his acting and movements. Michel Saint-Denis, who succeeded Copeau, his uncle, at the Vieux-Colombier, inherited this sense of musical structure in a play, and would rehearse certain scenes with a stop-watch.

The existence of the Vieux-Colombier under Copeau was

very short: seven months from 1913–14; then, during the First World War, a period of two years in New York at the Garrick Theatre, presenting the company in over fifty productions; and finally, five years from 1919–24. This brief period was none the less to have a profound influence upon the French theatre – 'Copeau was the seed from which we all grew,' commented Jean-Louis Barrault on the occasion of Copeau's death – and upon theatre in Europe and America.

It was Gordon Craig who sparked in Copeau the idea of *commedia dell'arte* as the basis for a new dramatic form to work toward. Copeau's letters to his actors, especially to Louis Jouvet and Charles Dullin, after his visit to Craig in 1915–16, are full of references to this improvisational form as vital to the training of the actor. He visualized such study leading to the creation of a modern comedy form capable of bringing people together in a communion of laughter and recognition. It was a form of theatre that Peter Brook was finally to realize in his production of *The Conference of Birds*, in 1980. An important feature of *commedia dell'arte* is the use of masks to establish allegorical figures and character types that are larger than life. Copeau began to use masks in Molière comedies while on tour in America in 1917 and 1918. Their use was to become a vital part of his actor training programme. Similarly, in *The Conference of Birds*, Brook's actors made brilliant use of Balinese masks.

Copeau left Craig to visit Émile Jacques-Dalcroze in Geneva and through him he also met Adolphe Appia. Copeau returned to France full of plans for his theatre and school. The period from 1921–4 represents the fullest realization of Copeau's school for actors. There were courses offered for the general public, courses for actors and other theatre artists wishing to learn more about their craft, and courses for young people who had no previous stage experience but wanted to devote themselves to a life in the theatre. By the end of the 1924 season, Copeau was becoming increasingly involved with the work of these young actors, and estranged from his actors. And so, in 1924, he closed the Vieux-Colombier and withdrew to Burgundy with his young actors because he felt they must renew their strength by 'kissing the soil'. There they worked on themes without texts, improvised with masks, rehearsed a

Japanese Noh play – because, as he said, 'it is the most disciplined form we know', – and, in contrast with this, studied in
greater depth the spontaneous skills required by the *commedia
dell'arte*. He laid great stress upon the physical and technical
expertise of the actor, and wanted his students to feel free
to use mime, dance, acrobatics, improvisation, as means of
dramatic expression. He wanted, above all, radical change, a
more communal theatre and a more communal society. He saw
his role as being that of a spiritual guide, 'to filter, choose,
explain, balance, harmonise'. Their lives were to be dedicated
to theatre through playing – celebrating birthdays, homecom-
ings, and other festivals, with improvisations, songs, games,
dancing and the presentation of new works.

In 1922, before their retreat to the country, Stanislavsky
had come with the Moscow Art Theatre to the Théâtre des
Champs-Elysées in Paris. All Copeau's students went to see
the famous Russian troupe, 'a little ready to laugh in advance',
Michel Saint-Denis recalls.

> We were going to see those realists, those naturalistic
> people, the contemporaries of Antoine! We saw *The
> Cherry Orchard* that night and we stopped laughing very
> quickly . . . . The visit of Stanislavsky and his company was
> of incalculable importance to us. For the first time our
> classical attitude towards the theatre, our efforts to bring
> a new reality to acting, a reality transposed from life, were
> confronted by a superior form of modern realism, the
> realism of Chekhov.

In 1929 Copeau shocked everyone by suddenly announcing
his retirement. He was still young, only fifty-three, but, increasingly, the need to be away raising funds meant that the
troupe of young actors was without leadership. Unable to
supervise their work, he was, at the same time, temperament-
ally incapable of allowing them to develop on their own.
Painful though this decision was for him, it may well be that,
deep down, he recognized that his work was done. Michel
Saint-Denis was now ready to take 'Les Copiaux' (as they had
been nicknamed among the vineyards of Burgundy) and form
them into the Compagnie des Quinze. Saint-Denis rebuilt the

stage at the Vieux-Colombier, showing an even greater disregard for ordinary theatrical illusion than Copeau.

The Compagnie des Quinze opened at the Vieux-Colombier in 1931. They had worked together for ten years under Copeau. They were mimes, acrobats; some could play musical instruments and sing; all could invent characters and improvise. They brought to the Parisian stage a specialized repertory of plays, most of them created by André Obey in collaboration with the company. The plays dealt with broad popular themes, the plots of which did not depend upon the psychological development of characters. In performance, as one critic wrote, they seemed to bring 'nature' back to the artificial theatre world of Paris at that time. London they took by surprise – and by storm. Audiences were captivated by the clear speaking of the company and even more by their brilliant miming. Norman Marshall describes a scene in *La Bataille de la Marne* in which a whole army in retreat was symbolized by a little group of exhausted soldiers dragging themselves across the stage, so conquered by fatigue that victory or defeat are equally meaningless to them. Of this production James Agate wrote,

> On the stage nothing save a few dun hangings veiling the
> bare theatre walls, and the floor artificially raked to
> enable the actors to move on different planes. Off the stage
> an immense distance away a military band is playing,
> and in the wings the armies of France go by. We see them
> through the eyes of five or six peasant women clothed in
> black and grouped as you may see them in the fields of
> France on the canvases of Millet.

Agate described the acting as the kind

> which begins where realism ends . . . the whole cast played
> with a perfection of understanding and a mastery of
> ensemble beyond praise. This is great, perhaps the greatest
> acting, since on a bare stage the actors re-created not the
> passion of one or two, but the agony of a nation.

The staging of the Quinze, like its method of acting, dated back to the Molière who toured the towns and villages of France, playing in a tent or *en plein air* on a bare trestle stage. It was this *tréteau nu*, as Copeau called it, which was the basis of the setting used by the Compagnie des Quinze – a light, collapsible rostrum which could divide into four if required, to make smaller stages, or be piled one upon another to represent, with the aid of a ladder, the prow of Noah's ark. Sometimes one or two pieces of scenery were added, as when, in *La Bataille*, a village was represented by some roofs and a church steeple, modelled in miniature and set upon a small platform in one corner, supported on four poles. The background to the action was formed by a kind of tent suspended from the flies in a ring, which removed the necessity for a cyclorama or wings. In Obey's *Don Juan*, the market scene was created by setting up the porches of the houses only and connecting them by gangways with openings in the tent.

> And these porches [observed Ashley Dukes], flimsy and fantastic as they are, contrive to suggest houses much better than the elaborate façades of the scene-painter . . . . If they have rather the air of toys, that is fitting because the artists using them have preserved the spirit of children. It would never occur to them that their porches should be taken seriously – as the contructivists, for instance, take their machines and platforms.

It was characteristic of the company, and in the tradition of Copeau, that in 1934, in spite of having had a striking success with *Don Juan*, feeling stale and repetitive, they decided to withdraw to the country. They rented an estate at Beaumanoir in Aix-en-Provence, and planned to spend four months of the year there studying and rehearsing; four months doing open air productions in Provence; and four months touring France and abroad. From July to September they also planned to take ten professional pupils. This ideal life, however, was marred by human frailties, the company disbanded, and Saint-Denis departed to start a new career in England. It is virtually impossible for actors to live and work under the same roof, which is why Grotowski, learning from the failure of past artistic communities, insists that his actors come to work each day and return each evening to their separate abodes and private lives.

The theatre's debt to Copeau can be measured to some extent by looking through the list of the Vieux-Colombier's offspring:

in France alone, Louis Jouvet ('I owe him everything,' said
Jouvet), Charles Dullin, Gaston Baty, Étienne Decroux ('If
there hadn't been those exercises at the Vieux-Colombier,
probably I would never have chosen the path I have.'), Michel
Saint-Denis, Jean Vilar, Marcel Marceau, Jean Dasté, Georges
and Ludmilla Pitoëff, Suzanne Bing.

The group of actors in Burgundy, under Copeau's leadership,
took with them their own stage when they travelled, which
allowed them to play in any setting. Setting up the stage and
preparing themselves for the play was seen by Copeau as an
essential part of the act of performance.

> The actors could be seen stopping [he describes], and
> singing in a village square, making a game of mounting
> their portable stage. And the comedy, or rather the
> mystery, took place with masks, a little music, ghosts, an
> old peasant, a witch, a princess, assassins and demons.
> Finally, the dream dissipated, the little company would
> roll up its curtains, gather up its props, put out its lanterns,
> and then move on.

Vincent Vincent, a Lausanne critic, wrote of their work at
this time,

> they have definitely detoxicated the theatre of its lyrical
> verbiage, they have done the work of surgeons. They have
> enlarged the field of expression, all in knowing how to go
> back to the sources of convention . . . like wise children,
> the Copiaux have known how to prune, to simplify, to
> clarify.

The search for a poor theatre was begun by Copeau. It is a
journey that has taken Eugenio Barba and his actors through
the mountains of Sardinia and the villages of southern Italy;
Peter Brook and his actors through Africa with nothing but a
carpet for a stage, a few musical instruments, some bamboo
poles, cardboard boxes, and a pair of shoes. The search is also
a quest, like the quest of the Holy Grail. How can one refine
anything down to its most powerful source, essential action,
essential sound, essential emotion? asks Brook. It might take
a lifetime, it is so difficult. Group after group have set out on
this quest and failed. Copeau himself realized that an organic

theatre group must be also a way of life as well as a way of work. The actors must undertake the most intense life of self-exploration. They must strip away their outward personalities, mannerisms, habits, vanity, neuroses, tricks, clichés, and stock responses until a higher state of perception is found. All of Grotowski's exercises, all of Brook's exercises, and those of Barba, and the many other groups in search of a poor theatre, have as their real aim a spiritual rather than a physical goal. The search is for the effortless art which requires that the actor must lose his ego.

'Copeau', says Jean-Louis Barrault, 'was in our eyes the Father of the whole modern theatre.'

9 Reinhardt, Piscator and Brecht

If naturalism had as its apostle in Russia Constantin Stanislavsky; in France André Antoine; in England J. T. Grein; in Germany it was a theatre critic, Otto Brahm, who, inspired by the work of Antoine, became a director and trained a company of actors in the new naturalistic style. As with Stanislavsky and Antoine, his actors were at first amateurs. Brahm helped to clear the German stage of outmoded productions and bring it into the main line of European drama.

One of his most gifted actors at the Deutsches Theater was Max Reinhardt who, in 1905, at the age of thirty-two, succeeded Brahm as artistic director. Here he inaugurated a series of productions which very rapidly caused Berlin to become one of the outstanding theatrical centres of Europe. Realizing that different plays require different environments for their staging, he outlined a plan for three theatres; an intimate house for the modern psychological dramas; a larger auditorium for the classical repertoire; and a huge amphitheatre suited to epic scale productions. This three-fold plan he was to achieve long before the National Theatre in London with its three theatres under one roof had been envisaged. The small chamber theatre was built first, alongside the Deutsches Theater. Seating four hundred, it opened in 1906 with a production of Ibsen's *Ghosts*. In the intimacy of this theatre, audiences could feel that they were in the same room as the characters of Chekhov or Strindberg or Ibsen.

What established Reinhardt, however, as a world famous figure was his work at the Deutsches Theater. Influenced by the ideas of Craig and Appia, he dispensed with painted flats and introduced solid, three-dimensional sets. In 1910, he staged *Oedipus Rex* at the Circus Schumann in Frankfurt, in an attempt to recapture that fusion of actor and spectator which had belonged to the classical Greek theatre. Basil Dean, in his autobiography, *Seven Ages*, describes the experience.

> The Circus held nearly five thousand people and was crammed to the doors. I was completely carried away by the emotional impact of that stupendous production as I listened to the powerful German voices and watched the vast arena filling with the well-drilled crowds chanting 'Oedipus! Oedipus!' under the coloured searchlights.This was an arena production at full stretch. Thus modern experiments in this type of staging were ante-dated some fifty years by Max Reinhardt.

This production, and that of the *Oresteia* the following year, produced on an arena stage backed by a broad flight of steps, topped with huge columns, were a powerful demonstration of the ideas of Craig and Appia. Reinhardt had tried to persuade Craig to design for him but the latter was so unreasonable in his demands and so jealous of his designs that all Reinhardt's hopes were aborted.

Reinhardt so enjoyed working in the Circus Schumann that he decided to make it the third cornerstone of his theatrical empire. The Grosses Schauspielhaus (Great Spectacle House) as it was called, was opened in 1919 with a performance of the *Oresteia*.

It was Reinhardt's hope that this theatre would contain modern life as once the great arena had contained the Greek community. But, without a traditional way of life, or a shared creed, such a theatre was doomed to failure. What successes it did have in its brief existence under Reinhardt were the successes of a director who played on very general emotions through the theatrical devices of light, colour, mass movement and music. Ironically, tragically, as Helen Krich Chinoy points out, Reinhardt's vision was most superbly realized in the massed Nuremberg rallies when the German people were at last fused by a common ideology and a very potent myth.

Like Meyerhold, whom he resembled in so many ways – although Reinhardt was by far the more finished, the more

accomplished director – he borrowed freely from the other
traditions. Perhaps all great artists do this.

> I am a thief [exclaims Martha Graham in her *Notebooks*],
> and I am not ashamed. I steal from the best wherever it
> happens to be – Plato, Picasso, Bertram Ross . . . I steal
> from the present and from the glorious past – there are
> so many wonderful things of the imagination to pilfer – so
> I stand accused – I am a thief – but with this reservation
> – I think I know the value of that I steal and I treasure it
> for all time.

The greatest genius, wrote Emerson, is the most indebted
man. It is not what is taken from other traditions and sources
but the uses to which that borrowing is put. The theatre in
this century has been immeasurably enriched by its increasing
contact with other cultures and traditions.

It was Reinhardt's avowed intention to free the theatre from
the shackles of literature. He offered theatre for theatre's sake
and, as one English critic, Ashley Dukes, drily remarked, 'If
Reinhardt is not giving us Greek drama, what is he giving
us? – The reply is – Reinhardtism – an essence of drama of
his own distilling.' As eclectic as Meyerhold or Brook, he ran
the whole gamut of theatrical invention, directing every sort
of play in every sort of way. 'There is no one style or method,'
he affirmed. 'All depends on realizing the specific atmosphere
of the play, on making the play live.' He could be intensely
theatrical, or he could take realism and charge it with poetry,
thereby adding to it an extra dimension. Martin Esslin, in
'Max Reinhardt, High Priest of Theatricality', has written one
of the most vivid accounts of Reinhardt.

> Reinhardt's supposed eclecticism was, it seems to me,
> merely an expression of the universality, the breadth of
> his range. Being besotted with the art of acting, every
> manifestation of the acting instinct, trade, craft or
> sublime spiritual activity fascinated him. He wanted to
> carry the theatre into every nook and cranny of human
> life: from the private performance for a handful of invited
> guests to the spectacle in town squares and exhibition
> halls that could be watched by thousands.

5 Jacques Copeau

6 Olympia transformed into a medieval cathedral for Max Reinhardt's production of *The Miracle*, 1911

LIMELIGHTS WORKED FROM 9 GALLERIES SUSPENDED FROM THE ROOF

ENTRANCE EXIT

ORCHESTRA

GREAT BACKCLOTH USED WHEN THE DOORS ARE THROWN OPEN

ENTRANCE FOR PERFORMERS

EXIT

SECTION TAKEN OUT OF FLOORING TO SHOW THE UNDERGROUND ARRANGEMENTS TO RAISE AND LOWER STAGE

POSITION OF HILL AND TREES WHEN IN THE ARENA

LESSER SLIDING DOOR WHICH FITS INTO THE GREAT DOOR

GREAT SLIDING DOOR

RAILS ON WHICH THE HILL AND TREES MOVES INTO THE ARENA

PLAYERS MAKING READY IN THE CORRIDORS

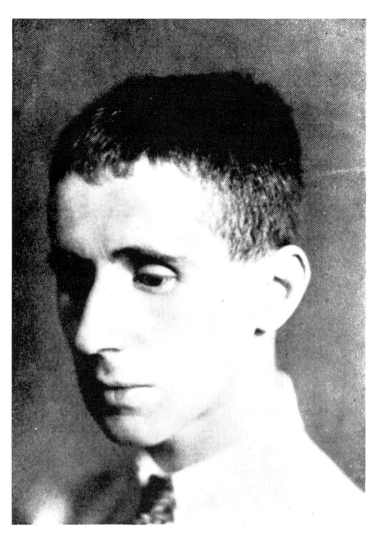

7 Bertolt Brecht, 1959

He delighted in the magical effects of colour and sensational stage machinery as much as in the most austere manifestations of pure acting against blank walls or draperies. Reinhardt was both Teutonic and titanic. He was a brilliant organizer of effects, planning a production down to the smallest detail. His innovations in lighting – and he inspired technical development by giving the electrical industry the most demanding specifications – were copied all over Europe. It was Basil Dean, for example, who went to Berlin to learn from Reinhardt how to light his famous production of *Hassan* and how to use the revolve. Productions like *The Miracle*, which toured the world, transformed stage technology wherever they were seen. Reinhardt was the Cecil B. de Mille of the theatre. Everything was carefully noted and illustrated with diagrams in the *Regiebuch*, the prompt copy, which was even more detailed than the shooting script of a film. It was, in fact, the master plan. Under Reinhardt, the director became the head of a team of artists and technicians.

For Reinhardt the world was a stage. Long before Luca Ronconi, he was staging productions in squares, streets, by lakes, cathedrals, and in private houses. If, for his production of *The Miracle*, theatres in Berlin, London and New York were converted into cathedrals, this was nothing in comparison to his production of *Everyman* in the cathedral square of Salzburg, or of *Faust* on a mountainside at Salzburg. For *Everyman* he enlarged the scope of theatre by involving the whole town. Actors were stationed on the towers of churches throughout the city, calling the name of Everyman; and at the end, as night fell, when Everyman's soul is finally received into paradise, the interior of the cathedral lit up, its massive doors opened, organ music resounded, and choirs sang, while all over Salzburg the bells of the many churches began to peal. Today, in the work of the German director Peter Stein, and of the Italian director, Luca Ronconi, it is possible to see the continuing influence of Reinhardt.

If Reinhardt directed productions on an epic scale, it was a disciple of his, Erwin Piscator, who invented the phrase 'epic theatre' in the 1920s, and pioneered what has come to be known as documentary theatre. He created a sensation in Berlin with a series of expressionist productions in which he made ingenious use of elaborate and expensive machinery. At the Volksbühne in Berlin he installed a conveyor belt on the front of the stage and a cantilever bridge in the centre which could move up and down. Sections of the stage could rise and fall, revolve or slide. Above the proscenium arch blazed Communist slogans; searchlights played on the audience; motor bikes roared onto the stage; loudspeakers blared, drums reverberated, machines throbbed, stage armies tramped, crowds roared and machine guns rattled shrilly. With his inventions, innovations, and new production techniques; the use of scene titles, photo montage, projection of photographs, a split level stage on a revolve, the global stage, the transparent stage floor (first introduced by Loie Fuller) and the use of film, Piscator vastly enriched theatre technique. Startling as so many of these techniques were, they were employed solely to one end: to depict reality in a more exact and authentic manner, to give drama the authority of a documentation of events. He saw theatre as an integral part of the media, the aim of which was to disseminate information. 'The starting point of the work at the Piscator Theatre', he wrote, 'was not, as hitherto, an aesthetic evaluation of the world but a conscious will to change it.' A new society must needs create a new theatre. To this end the old bourgeois theatre had to be destroyed. Theatre was to become a part of the social struggle, a means by which the working class could define its self-awareness.

Bertold Brecht, who worked first under Reinhardt, and then from 1919-30 with Piscator at the Volksbühne in Berlin, described Piscator's as the most radical attempt to endow the theatre with an instructive character. For Piscator the theatre was a parliament, the public a legislative body. He did not want merely to provide his audience with an aesthetic experience but to stimulate them to take a practical stand in matters concerning their own welfare and that of their country. All means to this end were justified. Epic theatre was the name Piscator gave to this new form of drama because of its broad focus and its extensive references to the everyday world beyond the footlights.

Piscator's ideal, possible only with vast subsidy, was a theatre machine as inherently technical as a typewriter, with a use of technology that was to be symbolic of twentieth-century consciousness. 'What we need is not a theatre but a huge assembly shop with a mobile bridge, hoists, cranes, practicable traversing platforms with which weights of several tons could be shifted around the stage at the press of a button.'

Although Piscator sought a theatre that would be scientific, rational, and objective in its documentary approach, the irony was that his work often had the very opposite effect. In his production of *Rasputin*, which he considered his most successful work of the 1920s, the audience became not merely spectators, but participants in this great drama of the collapse of imperialism, so that at the end audiences joined in spontaneously with the massed actors on stage singing the International.

Piscator, like Reinhardt, Brecht and many others, left Germany in 1933 and went to America. For almost a generation avant-garde theatre in Germany ceased to exist. Throughout this period Piscator was without a theatre. Then, in 1962, for four years until his death, he was director of the West Berlin Volksbühne, and identified with a new wave of documentary playwrights, each of whose works he directed: Hochhut's *The Representative*, Kipphardt's *In the Matter of J. Robert Oppenheimer*, and Peter Weiss's *The Investigation*. Without Piscator *The Representative* would never have been staged. Once again people began talking about Piscator's courage. 'Courage?' he replied. 'I don't know what it is. All I've always done is what is necessary.' The work he did in the last four years of his life again showed the reason behind it all. He was, what he had always been – a searcher. 'Hard, difficult plays, steeped in reality, plays that have never existed, are what I must find.' Indeed, he called his new theatre 'a theatre of search'.

It was in 1930 that Brecht, basing his ideas on Piscator's theories, began to develop his own form of epic theatre. Piscator was right when he said 'the epic theatre was invented by me primarily in production and by Brecht primarily in the script.' Whereas Brecht went back to the story line, Piscator returned to documents. But Brecht too approached drama as a form of serious practical sociology, he aimed to transform society by subjecting ideologies to close scrutiny. 'The truth is concrete,' he once said, and his plays, although stories, are based on fact. In, for example, *The Mother*, actual figures and statistics were projected onto the back of the stage so that the audience could measure the private 'invented' lives of the characters against the 'authentic' recorded facts of history.

Bertold Brecht, who died in 1956 – ten years before his master – was one of the most influential figures in the theatre since the 1930s. His company, the Berliner Ensemble, founded in 1949, was a post-war phenomenon. 'Once in a generation', wrote Kenneth Tynan, in 1956, 'the world discovers a new way of telling a story. This generation's pathfinder is Brecht, both as a playwright and as director of the Berliner Ensemble.'

Brecht rejected the naturalism of Stanislavsky or Reinhardt, as it portrayed only the limited picture of man's relationship with particular elements of his environment, such as his family or his place of work, and failed to portray man within a more general landscape – that of the whole of his society. The replacement of the painted backdrop by the blank screen symbolized a more universal and less specific setting. Once again the fourth wall theatre was seen to be lacking, for, as Virginia Woolf observed of the naturalistic novel, from it 'life escapes'.

For Brecht the purpose of drama was 'to teach us how to survive'. Instead of audiences feeling, they were to think. Brecht wanted to stimulate a reaction rather than encourage the kind of passive acquiescence found in the old bourgeois theatre. Once in production, Brecht would often rewrite a play depending on the audience's response. The play thus became an 'encounter' and an 'experiment', with the audience functioning both as interpreter and critic. Like Piscator, Brecht did not believe in the autonomous writer or director. He worked always with a team of assistants who not only researched into historical details but also were encouraged to voice their own opinions during rehearsals. In this way the script was always 'provisional' as no final version could be fixed. Brecht's technique both as a director and as a writer is truly 'reformist' and his plays, which he termed 'experiments' or 'efforts', are like all experimental theatre in their attempt to redefine, improve and advance.

The actors in the Berliner Ensemble were expected to

present the idea of a character rather than to identify emotionally with it as Stanislavsky had advocated. The actor was therefore not to 'be' Galileo but to 'demonstrate' him. To achieve this Brecht insisted that during rehearsals his actors should prefix their lines with the words 'he said' or 'she said'. It was what Martin Esslin has called 'acting in quotation marks'.

Like Meyerhold, Brecht wanted a form of theatre where the audience never forgets that it is in an auditorium watching a re-enactment of the past. To this end characters step out of their roles; a scene is terminated before its emotional climax; at appropriate intervals slides are projected, bearing a message which serves to underline the scene; at the end of each scene, low white curtains are drawn across the action. Brecht's aim was to 'alienate' the audience, to create an effect of distancing so that the audience would not become emotionally involved in the drama. The word 'alienation' is an unfortunate translation as it implies a lack of sympathy with the play. The German 'Verfremdung' refers to the making strange of familiar objects or ideas, thereby enabling the audience to see them in a new light, from a different perspective. By means of such 'estrangement' or 'alienation' the spectator, Brecht maintained, would be enabled to ponder the dramatic action, draw his own conclusions, and so become a more useful member of society. Already in 1921, at the première of *Drums in the Night*, Brecht attempted to make the audience aware that when they went to the theatre they were conditioned to adopt idealistic attitudes which bore no relevance to real life; the auditorium was hung with placards saying 'Gotzt nicht so romantisch' and an artificial moon glowed every time the 'hero' entered. By using traditional theatrical motifs in this ironic mode Brecht's plays became a personal assault on the bourgeois audience who found their expectations being openly flouted.

It is ironic and also, as Ernest Bornemann observes, the ultimate paradox that Brecht's theatre remained to the last a delight for those who were susceptible to his lyricism. In one performance of *The Threepenny Opera*, which Brecht had written as a satire on the conventional, purely 'culinary' opera, it was obvious that his intentions had failed when the audience became totally absorbed in the plot, left the auditorium whistling Kurt Weill's tunes, and even found themselves identifying with Polly Peachum. Every device which he used to destroy the 'magic' of theatre became magic in his hands. The exposed stage lights, far from alienating the audience, communicated all of Brecht's love for the stage. The very rhythm of interruptions became a poetic pattern and destroyed the purpose for which they had been conceived.

> The tragedy of Brecht's life boils down to this simple fact: he gained the admiration and respect of those whom he professed to despise – the poets, the intellectuals, the West; and he failed to gain the one audience in the world for whom he claimed to write: the working class, the Party, the East.

Peter Stein, who made his directorial début in Munich in 1967 with a startling production of Edward Bond's *Saved*, has been described as Brecht's true successor. Like Brecht, and Piscator before him; like Joan Littlewood and her Theatre Workshop in London, Stein has failed to create a working-class audience. In an interview in the American journal *Performance* he observed,

> If we want to play for the workers then we have to be clear about the fact that, the way things stand now, the theatre is not being used as an immediate weapon, as agitation; the other media do it much better. If we want to play for the people we must find how this theatre, as it now exists, can be used. But the working class in itself is not ready or willing or even interested in having a theatre, it doesn't need one; while the middle class thinks it *must* have a theatre. Thus my primary point of departure is an existential survival; one works for and with the audience.

Rather than develop a cynical attitude towards the audience that actually comes, Stein addresses himself to those in that audience who do not feel completely happy in the status quo and who are open to change.

Like Brecht in his treatment of the classics, Peter Stein has been concerned not with 'period revivals' but with a confrontation with the text, not in the mystical or archetypal manner

of Jerzy Grotowski, but seeking to find a political relevance for a contemporary audience. Thus, in his production of *Peer Gynt* (spread over two evenings, and with six actors portraying the various stages in Peer's story) he had no hesitation in cutting, editing and rewriting Ibsen's text so that it could become a parable of the Marxist argument that only by letting go of the bourgeois concept of individuality and entering a collective can man fulfill himself and create those conditions in which self-fulfilment becomes a possibility for all, not just the privileged few.

Ironically, Stein and his ensemble of actors are theatrically among the privileged few within a capitalist society. Committed to only four productions a year, and able to devote three to four years in the preparation of a production, his theatre is without parallel in any other part of the Western world. Stein's production, at the Schaubühne Theatre in Berlin, of Shakespeare's *As You Like It*, hailed by many as the most significant production of Shakespeare since Peter Brook's *A Midsummer Night's Dream*, grew out of a four-year period of research into the whole background of Elizabethan England, including a visit to England by the company: similarly, the company took a trip to Russia as part of their research for Gorki's *Summerfolk*, and a trip to Greece when working on *The Bacchae*. *As You Like It* was staged in an enormous film studio on the outskirts of Berlin. The production carried to an extreme the staging concepts of Okhlopkov, executed with all the bravura of Reinhardt. The first part of the play was presented in a narrow hall with stages all round the perimeter and the audience standing in the middle, after the fashion of Ariane Mnouchkine's famous production of *1789*. Indeed, the production employed many of the techniques she had pioneered, rather in the same way that the Royal Shakespeare Company, in its production of *Nicholas Nickleby*, employed a technique of story-telling that had been pioneered by Mike Alfreds and his *Shared Experience* company. Again, after the manner of Okhlopkov, Stein put all the early court scenes together and had them dove-tailed, often overlapping or even played simultaneously, so that information was telescoped dramatically.

The audience was then led along a corridor and admitted,

one by one, – as in André Gregory's *Alice in Wonderland* –
into a vast studio converted into an entire woodland environment that would have delighted Reinhardt. Again, as in
Stein's celebrated production of *Summerfolk*, real trees were
planted, real corn, a pool, and rural activities of every kind
surrounded the now seated audience. The action was played
above, below, in the middle of, and behind, the audience. Here
was environmental theatre at its most extravagant, a veritable
wonderland of visual distraction.

Provocative and deeply thoughtful as each production of the
Schaubühne is, it is perhaps Stein's major achievement that
he has attempted and, in large measure, succeeded in changing
the basic structure of theatre. In Germany each state or
municipal theatre is run by an Intendant, a super-bureaucrat
appointed by the state who is, at best, a benevolent autocrat
and, at worst, a dictator. Stein, as an informed Marxist, was
convinced that the best theatre could come about only within
a democratic and cooperative structure. It was at the Schaubühne Theatre in Berlin that he and his company of young
actors were enabled to put his ideas into practice, ideas that
were calculated to ensure a proper participation, at all levels,
in decision-making. Salaries were re-assessed, participation
was sought both in the appointment of new staff and in the
casting of plays, while extensive memos were circulated daily
to all staff. Finally, all employees were expected to attend
regular Marxist seminars so that all might 'contribute to the
establishment of a consensus of political and artistic opinion
as the basis of a true working ensemble.'

However, as other such experiments have shown, the added
burden of regular meetings and the unending flow of memos
proved too much so that certain compromises had to be made.
None the less, what has remained is the practice, unique in
any state-subsidized theatre in the West, of involving everyone
in those decisions relating to a production, so that the actors
are consulted about casting, design and overall conception. As
Michael Patterson, in his study of Peter Stein, observes, this
form of participation depends on the willingness to question
and be questioned at each stage of the rehearsal process. It
also takes time but 'where such willingness exists, the results
can be staggeringly impressive.'

Like Piscator and Brecht before him, Stein has had to make compromises with the system. He does not agree with those left-wing groups who regard 'poor theatre' as being more valid than costly productions made possible by state subsidy.

The Schaubühne represents the partial achievement of a socialist ideal, but one that is unlikely to be followed elsewhere, being dependent upon colossal subsidy from public funds. Stein himself recognizes this, but believes that it can act as an inspiration to other theatres elsewhere, in its committed approach to collective theatre.

It was in 1940, when he was in Finland, that Brecht gave a lecture to students in Helsinki on the subject of experimental theatre. What he had to say on that occasion shows how profoundly aware he was of his place in the tradition of Western theatre and of the direction in which he was travelling. They are sentiments that would be acknowledged by Stein and by most of the key figures in experimental theatre today. In reviewing the experiments of Antoine, Brahm, Jessner, Stanislavsky, Craig, Reinhardt, Meyerhold, Vakhtangov and Piscator, he showed how each had enlarged the possibilities of expression in the theatre. Against this general background, and within the particular framework of his experience with Piscator, he went on to explain his own ideas which had begun to be developed in Berlin and were only to be fully realized in the work of the Berliner Ensemble after the war. As he demonstrated, the heterogeneous experiments of half a century were seen at last to have found a common base.

> Is this new style of production *the* new style? Is it a technique which is complete and which can be conveyed as such, the definitive result of all these experiments? The answer is: no. It is *one* way, the way in which *we* have gone. Experiment must continue. The same problem exists for all art, and it is a gigantic one.

10 The Theatre of Ecstasy – Artaud, Okhlopkov, Savary

If people are out of the habit of going to the theatre [wrote Antonin Artaud], it is because we have been accustomed for four hundred years, that is since the Renaissance, to a purely descriptive and narrative theatre – story-telling psychology.

It was in 1925, the same year that Peter Brook was born, that Artaud began to be involved with the Surrealist movement. In 1927, with Roger Vitrac, he founded the Théâtre Alfred Jarry, where for two years they did experimental productions. In 1931, at the Colonial Exhibition in Paris, Artaud saw the Balinese dancers who were to have a profound influence upon his concept of theatre. In 1937 he was certified insane and was not released until 1946. Upon his release, public homage was paid to him at the Théâtre Sarah Bernhardt; among those present were Charles Dullin, Colette, Roger Blin, Jean-Louis Barrault and Jean Vilar. He died two years later.

Some of Artaud's ideas were, of course, not original to him; they had already been pioneered by Appia, Meyerhold and Reinhardt, each of whom had been concerned with breaking down the barrier between audience and actors, while Meyerhold had demonstrated again and again that theatre was a creative act in itself, and not simply the illustration of a dramatic text. The point is, however, that Artaud was discovering these things for himself and for the French theatre. As Ionesco says, 'I think one discovers more than one invents, and that invention is really discovery or rediscovery.'

It is important to stress this. So often the work of a director

is hailed as being original; an 'experiment' is described in the press as an important breakthrough to new forms; or a young director talks about the use of a particular technique, such as the use of film, as though this were for the first time. Truly experimental work, that has an organic, and not merely a spasmodic growth, can only be arrived at in the light of what has already been achieved by other workers in the field. In order to move forward one must first be able to look back. A knowledge of what has been achieved at different times in different parts of the world strengthens a sense of tradition, of one's creative and cultural roots. Truly creative minds, such as Grotowski or Brecht, acknowledge their debt to the past. Such men build on what they find. We cannot escape our debt to the past even when it is necessary to break with it.

A sense of history creates a sense of humour, a sense of humility; we are less inclined to appropriate to ourselves the credit for certain techniques or discoveries. In the 1950s happenings were all the rage, fathered at that period by John Cage who, in 1952, gave one of his first Happenings during which, with the audience seated in the middle, various activities took place simultaneously: David Tudor played the piano, John Cage lectured from a rostrum, Robert Rauschenberg played a victrola, Charles Olson talked and Merce Cunningham danced. Yet this was by no means the first Happening: already in 1916–21 the Dadaists were exploring similar territory. At one such Happening in Zurich, tin cans and keys were jangled as musical accompaniment; someone placed a bouquet of flowers at the feet of a dressmaker's dummy; Arp's poems were declaimed from inside an enormous hat; Huelsenbeck roared out his poems, while Tzara beat time on a packing case. Huelsenbeck and Tzara also waddled about inside a sack, yapping like bear cubs, their heads pushed into a pipe.

If in the 1930s Artaud was announcing that 'the theatre will never find itself again except by furnishing the spectator with the truthful precipitates of dreams,' Stanislavsky at the turn of the century was already seeking a theatre that would 'picture not life itself as it takes place in reality, but as we vaguely feel it in our dreams.'

Artaud's vision of a theatre which would be something more

than mere spectacle had already been crystallized by Appia –
'How can we once more live art instead of merely contempla-
ting works of art?', and by Craig 'The theatre of the future
will be a theatre of visions, not a theatre of sermons nor a
theatre of epigrams.'

It is important to remember that Artaud, writing a quarter
of a century later, was rebelling (like Copeau) against a
particular kind of rhetorical acting then fashionable at the
Comédie Française. He was attacking a French theatre
particularly dominated by words and by reverence for the
author. In place of the poetry of language he proposed a poetry
of space, employing such means as music, dance, painting,
kinetic art, mime, pantomime, gesture, chanting, incantations,
architectural shapes, lighting.

> I am well aware [he wrote] that the language of gestures
> and postures, dance and music, is less capable of
> analysing a character, revealing a man's thoughts, or
> elucidating states of consciousness clearly and precisely
> than is verbal language, but whoever said the theatre was
> created to analyse a character, to resolve the conflicts of
> love and duty, to wrestle with all the problems of a topical
> and psychological nature that monopolize our
> contemporary stage?

He attacked a docile subservience to the script.

> We must apply ourselves to the text (he said), forgetting
> ourselves, forgetting theatre, and lie in wait for the
> images that are here in us, naked, excessive, and we should
> go to the end of these images.

In 1935, before setting off on a journey into the interior in
Mexico, he wrote,

> I am leaving in search of the impossible. We shall see
> whether I can nevertheless find it. I believe that in Mexico
> there are still seething forces which pressurise the blood
> of the Indians. There the theatre which I imagine, which
> I perhaps contain within myself, expresses itself directly.

So might Peter Brook have written, forty years later, when
setting off on his journey, in search of a new theatre, into the

interior of Africa. Artaud was attacking the kind of minority culture that depends on the printed word and has lost contact with the primitive sources of inspiration. He saw that the dualistic rift between mind and body, intellect and feeling, must be healed. The links here with the work of the Living Theatre, the Open Theatre, the Performance Group, the Roy Hart Theatre, the Grand Magic Circus, the Odin Teatret, and the work of Peter Brook are obvious. 'What to do to be truly sincere?' Artaud wrote to a friend. It is the same question that obsesses Brook.

In 1921 Artaud was already arguing that dramatic art was, above all, the art of life which could be expressed without buildings, without sets, since time and space are enough. That Brook's actors should perform on a carpet in the middle of the desert, or in a quarry outside Adelaide, is a living proof of Artaud's vision. In order to emphasize his break with the contemporary stage Artaud proposed 'abandoning the architecture of present-day theatres. We shall take some hangar or barn, which we shall have reconstructed according to processes which have culminated in the architecture of certain churches or holy places, and of certain temples in Tibet.' In this he was following in the steps of Appia who had already foreseen that the dramatic art could not be reformed without first reforming the place where that art takes place. 'The arbitrary conventions of our auditoriums and stages placed face to face still control us!' Appia had written. 'Let us leave our theatres to their dying past, and let us construct elementary buildings, designed merely to cover the space in which we work.'

It was working on this principle that, in 1920, Jacques Copeau started his School of the Vieux-Colombier with the most rudimentary equipment. In 1924 he closed his theatre in Paris and left for Burgundy with his young actors. Their workroom there was a large hall used normally for storing surplus barrels of wine. No distinction was made between stage and auditorium. The floor was given a coating of cement on which was drawn a vast network of lines forming geometric patterns necessary for their work, providing a play of directing lines which helped to maintain a perfect harmony in the various groupings. When, in 1929, the company returned to

Paris under the leadership of Michel Saint-Denis, the first thing they did was to erect a similar studio at Sèvres.

> Working in such a scenic space [commented Appia, who followed the work of the company with great interest] gives the material a malleable form. It makes it a play of areas of varied dimensions, carefully measured, based upon rectangular forms in opposition to the rounded contours of the body and the curving trajectories of movement.

Although Copeau created the simplest form of stage at the Vieux-Colombier, Michel Saint-Denis felt that he had not gone far enough, and he even contemplated taking over a boxing ring in Paris and putting his actors on the central platform with the audience all round, as Jean-Louis Barrault was to do in 1969 with his staging of Rabelais's *Gargantua and Pantagruel*. Artaud's proposed theatre, with the audience in the centre, was to have platforms in the four corners, and a gallery all round, so that the action could be pursued from one point to another.

Artaud was writing this in the 1920s, although his *Theatre of Cruelty* was not published until 1938. Yet already in the 1930s, experiments on these lines were being carried out in Moscow by Nikolai Okhlopkov.

> We are trying to create an intimacy with the audience [he told Lee Strasberg in 1934], and with this in mind we surround the audience from all sides – we are in front of the spectator, at his side, above him, and even under him. The audience of our theatre must become an active part of the performance.

Okhlopkov, after studying under Meyerhold, was appointed director of the tiny Realistic Theatre in Moscow in 1930. His first act, like that of Peter Brook in the 1970s at his Théâtre des Bouffes in Paris, was to strip out the stage and seating. Joseph Losey, the film director, recalls visiting Moscow in 1935. 'That year Okhlopkov was breaking down the proscenium and presenting theatre in the round and the rectangle and the hexagonal, as it had never been dreamed of before.' Since then there have been many experiments in the

use of theatre space, from the pioneering of theatre-in-the-round by Stephen Joseph in England, to that of end-stages by Tyrone Guthrie at Stratford, Ontario; as well as more elaborate explorations by many others. Ariane Mnouchkine, for her production of *1789*, created a circle of stages surrounding the audience who stood in the middle. In 1966 Luca Ronconi was acclaimed for his startling production of *Orlando Furioso*, and in each production since, the problem of space has been at the centre of his dialectic; while in America, Richard Schechner of the Performance Group, is perhaps the most articulate exponent of what is termed 'environmental theatre'. The first scenic principle of environmental theatre, says Schechner, is to create and use whole spaces.

> Literally spheres of spaces, spaces within spaces, spaces which contain, or envelop, or relate, or touch all the areas where the audience is and/or the performers perform. If some spaces are used just for performing, this is not due to a predetermination of convention or architecture but because the particular production being worked on needs space organized that way. And the theatre itself is part of larger environments outside the theatre. These larger out-of-the-theatre spaces are the life of the city; and also temporal-historical spaces – modalities of time/space.

However disparate the aims of Meyerhold, Taïrov, Vakhtangov, Evreinov and Okhlopkov, all had one goal in common: to shatter the static realistic stage of the nineteenth century. But although Meyerhold broke down the naturalistic staging, using scaffolding and abstract shapes, his productions remained centred on the stage, while the spectator was always aware of being at a theatrical performance. It was here that Okhlopkov departed from his master. 'The theatre must do everything to make the spectator believe in what goes on in the play.' By having a multiplicity of stages he was able to cut from scene to scene, sometimes freezing the action in the middle of a scene while he cut to another and back again. Thus, instead of scene following scene in logical sequence, he was able to develop the use on montage in the theatre.

It is to André van Gyseghem that we owe a vivid picture of one of Okhlopkov's productions, showing how the barriers

between audience and actors were broken down and both shared in a common experience. Van Gyseghem is in the crowded foyer of the Realistic Theatre, waiting for the auditorium doors to be opened. Suddenly,

> the doors are opened from within and we flood through them into – what? Babel. A theatre more full of sound than was the crowded foyer. Women shrilling across at one another – babies crying – men shouting orders – lovers quarrelling – a group of men singing to a harmonica. The savoury smell of cooking assails our nostrils as we stagger dazedly into this hubbub, looking for our seats. Seats, did I say? We can't see any seats – anyway, they're looking the wrong way, surely? – pardon, madam, was that your child I stepped on? There are some seats – but a rocky promontory has first to be navigated; we dodge under the muzzle of a gun that is being cleaned by a young man singing lustily as he polishes, only to find our heads entangled, as we come up, with a mass of washing hanging out to dry.

They discover there is no stage. The whole of one side of the long hall has been built up into a rocky, uneven bank, rising to about five feet, with promontories jutting out into the centre of the hall. In between these promontories sit the spectators. The production is *The Iron Flood*. 'When the spectator enters the theatre for this play', said Okhlopkov, 'he finds all the actors already playing. He walks into *life*. A picture of a revolutionary camp. Out of this scene grows the opening of the play proper.' The play itself is concerned with a band of partisans which has got itself separated from the main body and is now in the middle of a long trek across hostile country to find and link up with their comrades. Eventually, after a brush with the enemy, the main body is sighted.

> The excitement mounts as the news spreads, the whole company pour onto the rocky steps, shading their eyes, peering into the distance. Yes! – it is our friends, our comrades – and crying and laughing they rush forward to greet – US! We, the audience, represent their comrades, and the actors flood the theatre, the iron flood breaks over

us, our hands are clasped by the gnarled hands of bearded
peasants, woman greets woman with a warm embrace
and the children dart in among the seats, throwing
themselves at us with cries of delight. Actors and
audience are still one – and we applaud each other.

The plays staged by Okhlopkov, however, were in the main
naturalistic in style and socialist in content so that, although
realizing independently many of the scenic reforms proposed
by Artaud, they remained, none the less, exercises in naturalism. What is of interest today is to compare the designs for
the lay-out of each of Okhlopkov's productions with the
sketches for each of the productions directed by Grotowski for
the Polish Laboratory Theatre. The difference between the
two is that where Okhlopkov sought for a greater illusion of
verisimilitude, Grotowski has concerned himself with an
overall concept or image that would condition the attitude of
the spectator for each separate production.

Nearly half a century later in Italy, Luca Ronconi began to
experiment with some of the same techniques Okhlopkov had
used, except that, like Grotowski, Ronconi consciously broke
away from realistic representation. For many years now he
has been preoccupied with exploring concepts of space by using
a multiplicity of stages and depicting scenes with no logical
progression. But Ronconi goes a step further than his predeces-
sors by inviting the audience to a performance which can never
be a communal experience as each spectator is only able to
witness specific episodes from the entire event.

In all Ronconi's productions there is no *one* way of seeing
an event, of absorbing the totality of the whole action, for this
would be a lie, since, in reality, there is no such thing as
complete knowledge. Instead, the audience witness events
from one viewpoint, aware that there are many options and
several activities going on simultanously.

In 1969 Ronconi's *Orlando Furioso* made theatrical history
with a new kind of theatre which set traps for the audience
by not letting them see the full picture, or allowing them to
follow a sequence of events. They had to follow the actors
around and were only shown certain selected fragmentary
scenes. Based on the sixteenth-century epic poem by Ariosto,

Ronconi was determined to create for the spectator, through a series of impressions and isolated episodes, a sensation similar to that experienced by the reader of the poem. The linear structure of the original narrative, which could be coherently followed from beginning to end, was divided into separate 'closed' units. Each action was to be seen in isolation with no aggravation or development of events, and the spectator could choose whatever portion of events he wished to follow. Nor was there any sense of continuity in style, as the costumes from nineteenth century melodrama were deliberately intended to contrast starkly with the overall appearance of sheet-metal and raw wood sets. The actors who stood on movable wooden floats, frequently placed the audience in a potentially dangerous position by obstructing their paths and forcing them to move suddenly away. In this way a spirit of initiative was created among the audience who participated in the action by attempting to push the floats apart, or assist the 'dead' soldiers who were strewn all over the stage.

In the final scene, gauze cages were moved together from both ends of the stage forming a labyrinth of metal netting which imprisoned both the audience and spectators and it was from this final image that Ronconi's *XX* (1971) took its shape. In *XX* the auditorium was made into a two-storey house consisting of twenty rooms and the audience were divided into small groups and herded into different rooms so that the play did not start at the same time or at the same point for any two groups. Having only a vague impression of what was going on in the other rooms, the audience were made to feel uncomfortable because they were ignorant of the complete picture and could not make sense out of the bizarre happenings.

If each episode were to be viewed in succession, the performance would last eight and a half hours but as it is the production only lasts just over an hour. The play is about the arrest and interrogation of a revolutionary who threatens the success of a fascist regime and from whatever point of view the audience is watching the play each member will witness the climax of this success as the partitions are raised in the final scene to make one huge space for all to see. To the critics who accused him of producing a fascist play, Ronconi had this answer:

> Showing one more time how fascism came about isn't at all interesting. Everybody knows how it happened. One must make it live, plunge the spectator into it. In other words, not into a precise historical situation but into the confusion of all conditions that could, at present, make fascism possible.

Ronconi approaches all his productions as a structuralist, isolating events from their historical setting. His stage, usually full of mechanical invention, is of labyrinthian proportions displaying all the inconsequential otherworldly qualities of a nightmare.

'The theatre will never find itself again except by furnishing the spectator with the truthful precipitates of dreams.' In this one remark Artaud anticipates the whole movement of experimental theatre from the 1960s onwards.

> I say that there is a poetry of the senses as there is a poetry of language. And this concrete physical language to which I refer is truly theatrical only to the degree that the thoughts it expresses are beyond the reach of spoken language. All true feeling is in reality untranslatable. To express it is to betray it. That is why an image, an allegory, a figure that masks what it would reveal, have more significance for the spirit than the lucidities of speech and its analytics.

One of the groups that has most closely followed the spirit as well as the letter of Artaud's famous manifesto is the Grand Magic Circus, under the direction of Jerome Savary, which began life in the 1960s in Paris under the name of Théâtre Panique. In 1968 they brought their first production to London which contained in embryo all that they were later to become. *The Labyrinth*, based upon the play by Arrabal, was staged at the tiny Mercury Theatre. The seating was arranged sectionally so that the actors could move freely among the audience, sometimes crawling under the chairs or, at one point, inviting the audience to dance with them. The 'labyrinth' consisted of criss-crossing rows of blankets hung on lines of ropes about the stage and the auditorium. The production was improvised each evening under the energetic direction of Jerome Savary. There was generated at each performance an atmosphere of extraordinary tension and excitement. A girl appeared to have a real orgasm and at one performance a youth masturbated. There was a great deal of near-nudity and, at one moment, a young man tore off his loin cloth and, holding his penis in one hand, swung out on a rope over the gasping audience, as drums beat and lights flashed. Sometimes the near naked actors spilled out through exit doors onto the rain-wet London street, startling passers-by. Throughout the action there wandered a small boy, the son of one of the company, his face made up like a clown, and one arm in plaster. A procession entered through the auditorium; voices chanting, crying out; drums beating and instruments twanging. At the rear of the procession walked a tall negro in a long sheep-skin, carrying a live goat garlanded for sacrifice. Smoke bombs of sweet-smelling incense were hurled among the audience by the omniscient director. By means of a rope on a pulley in the roof, a young man was hauled up, upside down, playing a flute, suspended above the audience. The singing, chanting, the ascending smoke and incense, the youth playing the flute and the small boy watching brilliantly captured the extraordinary purity that is at the heart of Arrabal's writing, especially his memories of his own childhood. And the audience, caught up in the exuberance of what appeared to be part fiesta, carnival, cabaret, fairground, dance-hall, orgy and revivalist meeting, came again and again. In London the production was attended by shop girls, boys who did newspaper rounds, and the kind of people who normally never go to the theatre. It also attracted actors, writers and critics. Like Sarah Bernhardt, the Grand Magic Circus managed to be both an *édition de luxe* and a best-seller. Their productions released, exhilarated, and liberated, achieving at times the immediacy of a Chagall painting.

Chagall will depict people flying round a room, or show a person with his head turned almost off the neck. In his autobiography he describes how as a child, sitting at the table, he would smell the fish being prepared in the kitchen and his head would fly off, as it were, to the kitchen to take in the

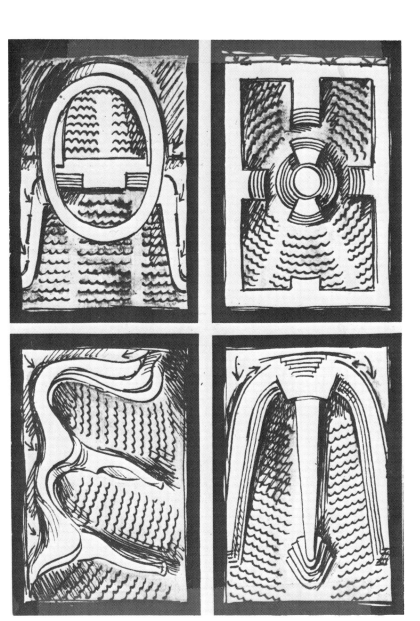

8 Designs by Jacob Schtoffer showing playing areas (white) and audience areas (grey) for various productions of the Realistic Theatre under the direction of Okhlopkov

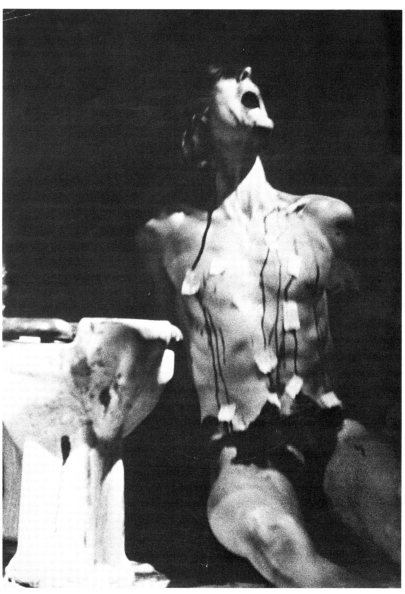

9 Moment from the Grand Théâtre Panique (later the Grand Magic Circus) production of Arrabal's *Labyrinth*

smells. Of his painting of the bride and the bridegroom flying round the room he says that they are in the room and yet not in the room; their thoughts are flying round the room because, for the first time, they have transcended poverty and are in heaven in each other's thoughts. Chagall, like Picasso, gives us what his inner eye sees. It is a question of seeing with the immediacy of a child seeing a cherry tree for the first time, before a label has been fixed, saying 'cherry tree', and the experience codified.

The Grand Magic Circus has been one of the most colourful and popular of the avant-garde theatre groups. From the start Savary chose to work with non-professional actors, and to set up his entertainment in boxing rings, tents, in the streets, rather than in a conventional theatre building.

> I believe the theatre to be a communal project, a celebration. It is a form of expression that will become more and more of a necessity as society becomes increasingly mechanical and organised. Theatre is a way to get people to communicate with each other, to destroy the walls which make separate.

Similarly, John Heilpern remarks that the line in *A Midsummer Night's Dream* which is most meaningful to Brook is Bottom's 'The wall is down!' and which led him to send his actors, at the end of his production of that play, sweeping like a wave into the audience.

It is not surprising that at the centre of one of his most startling productions, *Robinson Crusoe*, Savary should reveal his message to be about loneliness. Crusoe, when offered the chance to leave the island, decides to remain behind, preferring the solitude to the blandishments of civilization. It is towards the end that Savary, as the master of ceremonies, produces from a suitcase a white rabbit. 'What can be more lonely than a rabbit in front of 800 people?' he asks.

> Loneliness cannot be resolved in a few hours. Yes, death is a problem. Five people are going to die tonight. Death is a problem when we think about it. So, tonight, when you return home and stand in front of your mirror, you can do your own magic circus. When you smile into the

mirror (here he bares his teeth in a grin), you will see a part of your skeleton. When you smile, death is already there! This story of Robinson Crusoe, *c'est l'histoire de la solitude.*

At the end of the production Savary instructs the audience to shout 'death'. At first everyone is self-conscious and the word is hardly audible but eventually a thunderous clamour for death bursts from the auditorium. At this point Savary beckons the band to play and within seconds everybody has miraculously started to dance. Savary's Theatre of Ecstasy has quite literally succeeded in banishing death!

Savary is pre-occupied with the problem of the isolation of modern man faced with an over-complex society. For that reason, from the moment of their arrival at the Grand Magic Circus, the audience is made to feel as though it is taking part in a colourful carnival. 'People are sad', he says, 'because they have lost their animality, their sense of play. With modern civilisation man has become a spectator. Theatre should be a feast, a joyous occasion, a festival' – words that echo those of Peter Schumann of the Bread and Puppet Theatre who says, 'Theatre is like bread, more like a necessity. Theatre is a form of religion. It is fun.'

Savary uses fireworks, ropes, pulleys, magic, live music, vaudeville, ballet, animals and always he encourages audience participation. Once, in a nativity play, he handed out sparklers to the audience, as they stood around the manger, in a celebration of light.

Theatre is not and should not be a literary form of expression. A theatrical celebration can take place anywhere: out of doors, in a garage, in a stable. The problem with avant-garde theatre today is that it is absolutely intellectual. You have to be cerebrally inclined to understand what is going on. We, on the contrary, try to appeal to everyone: the illiterate as well as the intelligentsia.

When asked by Bettina Knapp, in an interview for the *Drama Review*, if he would call his theatre symbolic, he replied, 'Everything which emanates from the unconscious is symbolic. Those who do not react emotionally to our antics are cold and calculating, certainly wrapped up in some intellectual framework. They are incapable of enjoying life'. It was Barbara Hepworth who remarked that in order to appreciate art it is not necessary to be able to write an intellectual analysis.

I know by the way people walk round my garden, and touch the statues, whether or not they have responded to them. The experience must come first. Analysis comes later. The difficulty is that the professional critic too often by-passes the experience and ends up by projecting his own expectations onto a work of art. He does not respond to what is there.

There is here an undeclared war between the intellectual and the intuitive, each fearing the other. The intellectual clings to the concept of a literary theatre because he regards words as man's highest achievement; where, then, does he place music, painting, dance, and sculpture? Ultimately, of course, there is no war between the two for, as Fritjof Capra observes, 'both are different approaches. Both are necessary and supplement one another for a fuller description of reality.' Day after day we live far beyond the bounds of our consciousness, wrote Carl Jung.

Without our knowledge, the life of the unconscious is also going on within us. The more the critical reason dominates, the more impoverished life becomes; but the more of the unconscious, and the more of myths we are capable of making conscious, the more of life we integrate.

At the same time in France as Savary's Grand Magic Circus was exploring new ways of creating an immediate theatre through festival and celebration, Ariane Mnouchkine's 'Théâtre du Soleil', also working as a communal group and using similar methods of improvisation, were seeking more specifically to destroy the preconceptions and prejudices of their audience by demystifying traditional concepts of theatre and history. In Limon in 1916 Copeau had anticipated the work of 'Théâtre du Soleil', claiming that the theatre could only be reborn through methods of improvisation. 'Leave literature', he wrote, 'create a fraternity of players ... living, working, playing together ... creating together, inventing together their games, drawing them from themselves and from others.' Like the Living Theatre the company members live and work under one roof as a co-operative receiving a small fixed wage based on box office profits. The company comprises amateurs, professionals and teachers who are all dedicated to the ensemble conditions of work, including daily improvisations and group research projects.

The work of 'Théâtre du Soleil' can be described as the kind of political theatre which seeks to advance the role of theatre through awakening the audience to the conditions of their existence, and to the possibilities of change. Drama is a tool with which to fight bourgeois society, and since theatrical awareness leads to political awareness, the audience must be conscious of theatrical techniques. Through research, improvisation, and experimenting with various theatrical idioms, they aim to portray the complete and complex picture of an event. In an interview Mnouchkine once explained that

> what we want to do is to take some trivial happening and make it concrete, bring it to life, not merely do a play about the opinion we hold on some political problem. Though the temptation, of course, is always there: to show, for instance, that the police are 'pigs'. No, what we must do is try to show how, after all, a man who may have been the son of a vinegrower can become a policeman, and how this changes him.

In some of her early productions Mnouchkine did in fact tackle established scripts aiming to resuscitate the past by using new techniques and new interpretations. In a pre-Brook production of *A Midsummer Night's Dream* the play was acted out on a vast expanse of white rug in a circus ring. Mnouchkine called it 'the most violent and savage play anyone could ever dream'. Puck was cruel and revengeful and the terrified lovers demonstrated their frustrated passions in high-pitched hysteria.

Possibly the most successful creation by the 'Théâtre du Soleil' was the historical spectacle *1789* which in 1971 came to the Roundhouse in London. The play lasted two and a half hours without an interval and was a re-interpretation of the

French Revolution from the point of view of the common people. The production used a variety of theatrical techniques: song, dance, mime, fable, fairground brawls, as well as microphones, fifteen-foot dolls, and blasts of Mahler and Beethoven. The traditional seating arrangements were reversed so that the audience were placed, standing, in the middle of the stage and the performers acted on platforms all around them. At the climactic point of the Storming of the Bastille, the actors came down to harrass the audience, treating them as if they were part of the mob who had just witnessed the event. Undoubtedly, by seeing the Revolution from the 'popular' viewpoint and not concentrating on historical figures like Robespierre or Danton, the play both depicted what bourgeois history books consider irrelevant and also was a source of stunning theatrical originality and vitality.

After the long run and success of this production, the company retired for an eighteen-month period of hard work and self-analysis. As a result of this emerged *The Golden Age, First Draft*, a production which concentrated on portraying the issues of present social reality – focusing intentionally on local and national problems rather than on world-wide problems of famine and war. In order fully to comprehend certain situations and events beyond the actors' experience, such as factory occupations or instances of strikes, the company had to do a great deal of fieldwork. This involved discussion groups with workers at mines, hospitals and schools and then performing and improvising certain factors that had emerged from these discussions. Just as Brecht had done several years earlier with a group of farmers belonging to a co-operative, Mnouchkine and the company not only gained useful information from these discussions and improvisations but, by depicting an objective account of the workers' situation, they stimulated in them a desire to initiate change. As Brecht had pointed out, this was yet another way in which art could influence life.

The work was entitled 'First Draft' because it was only provisional. 'We may well find', Mnouchkine observed, 'the second draft will consist of everything we are trying not to say now,' and in the Socialist weekly paper, *'L'Unité'*, she defiantly declared that in this production, as in all her productions, their aim was to attack before having protected our flanks. To expose what we have but begun, what little we have yet said, to show that much remains to be said. To show a play for what it is: a moment in the inquiry of theatre in the present tense.

The warcry of Artaud was, 'Theatre must be thrown back into life.' Martha Graham used to tell her students that *how* they danced, the state of mind in which they approached a performance, was what determined whether or not they were good performers. 'Dancing is a state of becoming. The Balinese dance to restore the cosmic balance of the world.' Artaud understood this well and it permeated his whole thought.

In a spectacle like that of the Balinese theatre [he wrote], there is something that has nothing to do with entertainment. The Balinese productions have in them something of the ceremonial quality of a religious rite, in the sense that they extirpate from the mind of the onlooker all idea of pretence, of cheap imitations of reality. The thoughts it aims at, the spiritual state it seeks to create, the mystic solutions it proposes, are aroused and attained without delay or circumlocution.

Artaud stands like a beacon fire signalling to the surrounding countryside. The great quality of a visionary, whose sense of the ideal often exceeds his sense of what is practical, is that he is continually setting before us the possibility of a new direction in our work. Men like Appia, Craig and Artaud are the seers, while men like Stanislavsky, Copeau, Brecht, Grotowski and Brook are the guides whose wisdom and practical experience enable them to charter these new territories.

11 The Contribution of the Modern Dance – Martha Graham and Alwin Nikolais

Miss Graham looked like a fanatical prophetess. Everything indicated that she was above the old-fashioned conception of beauty and grace and had a complete contempt for it. I thought barking girls . . . this is not only a suit of grief but a suit of hatred as well. I began to pity the young girls who were distorting not only their bodies but also their souls. All that I saw was ugly in form and hateful in spirit. The feet were placed in any way at all, the toes usually turned in. Miss Graham suddenly turned to me and said, 'You don't know anything about body movements' . . . . After much discussion, John Martin who presided, looked at his watch. 'Mr Fokine,' he said, 'we cannot continue this argument. Ballet has had its chance of saying what it had to say during three centuries, so the modern dance has a right to talk for three weeks.'

As a dancer, as the inventor of a technique of dance which has irrevocably changed the art, as a choreographer, as an actress, as a dramatist, Martha Graham was to become the first woman in the history of theatre to contribute a huge and amazingly varied body of work to the theatre. As Dame Margot Fonteyn has written,

Martha Graham's secret seems to lie in her combination of emotion and intellect, of feminine and masculine – the feminine star with masculine creativity, and her combination of ego-centric artist with unselfish pedagogue. She knew how to give modern dance its own vocabulary of movement, its own technique, making it a coherent art form . . . undoubtedly she is the only one who merits the title, Mother of the Modern Dance.

We have seen how Craig dreamed of a theatre which would appeal to the emotions of an audience through movement alone. In the 1920s the Theatre of the Bauhaus experimented with plays whose 'plots' consisted of nothing more than the pure movement of forms, colour, and light. It was the modern dance, however, especially in the work of such choreographers as Martha Graham and Alwin Nikolais, which was to open up new avenues of expression, in collaboration with sculptors, painters, and composers. It is significant that Martha Graham always refers to her works not as ballets but as 'plays', while Alwin Nikolais uses the expression 'theatre-pieces'. Theatre critics, bound by the fixed idea of theatre as word-play, have failed to realize that modern dance has been one of the most important contributions in the twentieth century to the development of the theatre.

It was Isadora Duncan who first related movement to emotion; hers was the discovery of the power of movement to evolve its own forms when given an emotional impetus. For her, dance was 'not a diversion but a religion, an expression of life. Life is the root and art is the flower.' Duncan cleared the way for an exploration of the inner man, what she called 'the soul', so that by the 1930s dancers such as Mary Wigman were developing individual techniques in order to create psychological dramas. The subjects all dealt with the conflicts within the individual; movement was given a motivation from within. During this period, at its worst, the modern dance became an outpouring of self-indulgent self-expression. Martha Graham was able to transcend all this, her works depicting modern man in search of a soul. Hers is the largest repertoire by a single choreographer in the history of dance, numbering more than one hundred and fifty works. 'I am interested only in the subtle being,' she wrote, 'the subtle body that lies beneath the gross muscles. Every dance is, to some greater or lesser extent, a kind of fever chart, a graph of the heart.' To this end she was to create a technique that would give expression to her inner visions.

It is of the essence of classical modern dance that the

movements flow out of the idea, motion from emotion. The modern dance seeks to convey the most intangible experiences through movement. It is not interested in spectacle as such but in the communication of these experiences, intuitive perceptions and elusive insights. This is not to say that it cannot be devastatingly theatrical, as Martha Graham has demonstrated. Where the ballet is concerned primarily with line and pattern – the external aesthetic – the modern dance is concerned with the basic primal experience itself.

There is a moment in Martha Graham's *Appalachian Spring* when the young wife rolls about on the threshold of her new home. When I first saw this work in 1954, Cyril Beaumont, who was then the elder statesman among ballet critics, said to me, 'But why does she roll about on the floor at that point? It breaks the line.' In this remark lies the essential difference between classical ballet and modern dance. Movement is a fundamental element of our behaviour. When we jump for joy or rock with grief, our movements spring from an emotional state and, though they may seem irrational, they contain the essential nature of the original experience, even though they may not be in any way representational. The modern dance seeks to convey, through the medium of movement, that which lies too deep for words; it explores new ranges of possible, and even impossible, movements in response to whatever demands may be put upon the body by the creative imagination. In looking for an external aesthetic, the ballet critic fails to respond to the inner rhythm of the movement, expressive in the example from *Appalachian Spring* of the young bride's joyous and intimate identification with the virgin prairie and the crossing of the threshold of her new home and life. Strangely enough, it is something Nijinsky would have understood. 'Any imaginable movement is good in dancing', he wrote, 'if it suits the idea which is its subject.' He demonstrated, to the initial scandal of the world of classical ballet, that what might be thought at first to be ugly or primitive could in fact have its own beauty.

Whereas ballet sought to conceal effort, Martha Graham considered that effort was important, reflective of life, especially of life in this century. Thus she evolved techniques of leverage, balance and dynamics that form the greatest single contribution to the idiom of the modern dance. Another of her departures lay in the use of percussive movement, of sharp accent and rebound, as of the down-beat of bare feet at the moment of shifting weight; of the off-beat, as of accented leaning of the body in different directions; of short, broken movements that look unfinished yet complete themselves in space.

In her work she has proved as varied and unpredictable as Picasso. Each season, as John Martin observed, her entire style changed as she discovered new subject matter: dances of revolt and protest; religious ritual and American folk-lore; satire; works exploring the role of woman as artist, as woman; and perhaps her richest field of discovery – a Jungian approach to Greek mythology. Yet she has not sought out these subjects for their superficial attraction as possible vehicles for herself as a dancer. An intensely private person, the works have grown out of her inner voyaging, as her remarkable Notebooks reveal.

Virginia Woolf, in her novel *The Voyage Out*, makes one of her characters ask another, a young writer, what kind of books he wants to write. He replies, 'Books about silence ... the things which people do not say.' Similarly Martha Graham has said, 'There is a necessity for movement when words are inadequate. The basis of all dancing is something deep within you.' And if people are sometimes distraught at the imagery in many of Graham's works, it is because they are so ill-prepared to face the psychological reality which is the basis of her art. 'It is rather like lighting an enormous bonfire in the middle of an ice-house in which everyone is comfortably frozen. To their distress, the subject of Graham's dances is not dancing.'

Above all, in the work of Martha Graham, the theatre redis-covered its religious origins. When, in *Errand into the Maze*, Graham, as Ariadne, came face to face with the feared Mino-taur, she was doing battle with the darkness that is also our darkness (as in *The Tempest*, Prospero says of Caliban, 'This thing of darkness I acknowledge as my own'); she comes to terms with it on our behalf, and emerges triumphantly from the maze that is also our maze. In so doing, she was enacting the sacred mysteries of our own times, the ritualistic purgation of our darkness and the revelation of our innermost selves. It is theatre on its deepest level.

With each new work a point of departure for her questing spirit, Graham has always been The One Who Seeks (to quote the name of her protagonist in *Dark Meadow*); delving below surfaces for the 'why' underneath; agreeing with Picasso that a portrait should not be a physical or a spiritual likeness, but rather a psychological likeness, what she herself has described as 'a graph of the heart, a blue-print of the soul'. It was not surprising, therefore, that London in the spring of 1954 was disturbed. There were many who hated her work or ridiculed it, perhaps because it cut so keenly to the bone. As Craig Barton, her manager, once wrote to me,

> Martha's dancing is about something. It does not entertain or provide distraction. One sees a visual masterpiece in which the dancers move in a masterly and special way, but the reaction of the spectator moves on to another plane of inner revelation, of excited unrest. Even a lyrical abstraction like *Diversion of Angels* has a radiation that shakes one's interior. One has had a serious experience.

With the exception of a few works such as *Diversion of Angels*, *Secular Games*, *Canticle for Innocent Comedians*, and some of her earliest solos, Graham has always worked in terms of a story line so that, unlike the work of more recent choreographers such as Alwin Nikolais, Merce Cunningham, or the 'post-modern' dancers such as Lucinda Childs and Meredith Monk, it is possible to convey something in words of her art. For those who have never seen the Theatre of Martha Graham, it is perhaps worth describing a section of *Ardent Song*. Anthony Tudor told me that for him, in this work, Martha Graham had transcended all her other works; while John Martin, the most distinguished dance critic in America, commented, 'It may well be the richest and the most consistently beautiful of all her rituals.'

With a score by Alan Hovannes (Graham has consistently commissioned work from the leading modern composers and designers) *Ardent Song* had its world première in London in 1954 and took as its inspiration certain lines from a poem by

St John Perse, words which have always had a deep significance for Graham:

– and we have so little time to be born to this instant . . .
The cry! The piercing cry of the god is upon us! . . .
O you, whom the storm refreshes . . .
Freshness and the promise of freshness.

The central figure is the goddess Aphrodite, and the work is divided into four sections, each depicting a different phase of the moon, from moon-rise to dawn.

At the beginning of the second section, shafts of light fall from the wings like moonlight through the pillars of an eastern temple. Three women enter, bound by a single black scarf which frames their heads and is laced under their arms. They move like a constellation in the night sky. One sits and the other two drag her slowly, heavily. They sit and she drags them. The mood is one of grief and lamentation, the weight of darkness. The women then loosen the scarf and, while one of them stands on the material, centre stage, the other two women, each taking an end of the material, unroll it across the stage so that it forms a path of blackness across the sky. The light from the wings shines more intensely now, falling along this path, while the women lie full length along it, looking towards the light, waiting expectantly.

Slowly a shape appears, bright, glittering and scarlet. With arms held out in front, it advances with majesty across the night. The dancer's long hair hangs loosely, while on one side of her head is a twisted, horn-like hat. About her neck and in each hand is a two-headed snake – it has a head at each end of its body. With a drunken lurch the dancer flings it to the ground and stares at it in fascination. As she contracts from the stomach, so her hair swings wildly (Graham has always exploited her dancers' natural equipment as a choreographic extension), her mouth sags; hand, arm and body outlining the curve of the serpent. Facing front, and rising on one leg, the other leg extending sideways, the arms reaching upwards, she falls and lurches with sharp staccato contractions.

Thus contracting and releasing, rising and falling, the figure of Aphrodite lurches about the stage like a wild, possessed Bacchante. It is a lurid, sickening, erotic, drunken and unclean movement. As she gathers up the serpent, holding a head in each hand, so the music quickens and the serpent heads begin to convulse. The body of Aphrodite seems shaken by their violence, the climax of the ejection of the serpent's poison coinciding with her own orgasm. Now the stage is filled with light – it is moon-high – exposing this obscene ritual. Aphrodite crawls limply to a corner where she crouches with bowed shoulders, gazing numbly at the twin-headed serpent, the instrument of her own ecstasy. The sense of thralldom to lust, of the dark night of depravity, the terrible, relentless and inexorable impetus of passion, have rarely been so sickeningly and superbly portrayed in the theatre. Only Jean Genet and David Rudkin, as writers, have been able to articulate this, the dark poetry of perversion.

At the end of this section, the lights dim and the goddess reappears, once again traversing her dark passage across the sky, the serpent once more held in front of her. As she goes, so the three women follow her, the last one rolling over and over in the black material – gathering up the darkness – becoming cocooned, shawled, in the dark memory of ancient grief and lust.

At the back of the stage, figures can be glimpsed dimly, their heads upraised, looking off-stage expectantly. Fingers of light hover over them, touch them and are gone. Suddenly, in a pool of light downstage, there is a flash of green like that of young grass after a storm. It vanishes; the people wait. Again it appears, farther down stage, and it is seen to be the figure of a young girl in green, dancing teasingly in and out of pools of light. For a moment the stage is empty, and then a youth appears, spinning from between his loins a length of blue cloth which descends, like a shaft of light, from the flies. He kneels and leans back against the material as though resting on the sky. From down-stage right, light shines diagonally and in this shaft the young girl appears, carried by a second youth. Gently she is lowered to the ground. It is as though she had slid down the shaft of light.

From up-stage two more youths appear, spinning out great lengths of blue and mauve material, and the three strands of cloth are woven into the dance with the girl in green forming the focal point. At one moment the veils span the stage like a rainbow, with the girl seated in the centre as on a swing – the shafts of light seeming to pass though her – while at the back of the stage another youth spins out more and more blue veiling. It is as though after the night of orgy and profane love we have emerged into the dawn of a new love, the essence of which is worship. 'O you, whom the storm refreshes . . . . Freshness and the promise of freshness.' As the girl travels downstage toward the audience, the veils streaming out behind her, the men and women, now as couples, all face front with upraised faces and outstretched arms; they are reaching up to the full glory of the new day. As the curtain slowly falls, we have the sense of having participated in a ritual of purification, depicting the emergence of the psyche from the darkness of the moon magic ('The moon she comes more near the earth than she was wont, and makes men mad') into the purity of the dawn.

'In my work', Martha Graham once told me, 'I have always sought to reveal an image of man in his struggle for wholeness, for what one might call God's idea of him, rather than man's idea of himself.'

Totally different from Martha Graham in his interpretation of the fundamental concept of modern dance, Alwin Nikolais, along with choreographers like Merce Cunningham and Paul Taylor, sees the dance as moving on a more abstract or mathematical plane. Already in the 1940s he had begun to have reservations about the psychological approach, feeling that the dance had about exhausted itself on the relation of man to man, needing to find the relation of man to the other elements.

> This is how I want man [he would say at this period], with his arms out in time and space, not folded in on his own aching gut. A dancer doesn't have to emotionalize – he needs to motionalize. He doesn't even have to be a person – he can be a thing, a place or a time.

At the Henry Street Playhouse in New York, in order to get his students away from 'self-expression', he began to assign them various props, masks and sculptural objects, disguising the dancers so as not to look like people, costuming them like shapes, moving them about the stage like pieces of sculpture.

His dances, or theatre-pieces, do not express emotional attitudes, or have any story to tell. 'Don't interpret as mad, sad
or glad,' he said during a class for my actors in London. 'Just
move. The drama exists in action. Don't mug it. Remember
here, the medium *is* the message!' Although he does not make
works about specific issues or problems, he feels, none the
less, that audiences will find much in his work relating to
contemporary life, provided that they are prepared to give
their imagination free rein.

We're drastically concerned about our existence in space
[he says]. For fifty years we explored psychological
relationships. Now we're concerned with environmental
relationships and this leads to an even more primal sense.
We don't trust any one sense any more. We want to
understand by having all our senses co-ordinated to find
a truth. This is why we have multi-media theatre. Your
specific references will come out of your own Rorschach.
Though I'm probably as neurotic as the next one, I have a
free access to associations. Inner visions come easily.
Many people have the capacity for this and have long since
failed to use it.

An audience, faced with a theatre-piece by Alwin Nikolais,
is taken by surprise, caught unawares. The experience is like
that of walking in a new landscape. Each moment brings fresh
discoveries, sequences of astonishing beauty and, above all, a
rare and exhilarating sense of fun and pleasure. Nikolais is
primarily excited by the movement of things, encasing his
actors in long shifts, ballooning silk bags, or providing exten-
sions to their limbs in the form of kites on wires, or yards of
elastic tape that create giant cat's cradles across the stage,
tubular projections, resounding discs on their hands and feet,
cone-shaped tents. In *Galaxy* collapsible towers enter the
stage, the hidden bodies motivating the robot-like costumes so
that they rotate, expand, and shrink. Luminous shapes and
masks move across the stage, propelled by unseen actors.
Uniquely, Nikolais has created his own staging, choreography,
music, costumes, décor, and lighting. Every one of the hundreds of colour slides that are used have been hand-painted by
him. His use of lighting is constantly changing the images on

stage – a possibility first demonstrated by that other American dancer, Loie Fuller. In *Tent* he employs a white silk parachute which, suspended on wires, becomes an enchanted canopy, swirling shapes, pinnacles and clouds, incandescent with colour as it is lit from within, behind and in front. It is not surprising that sculptors and painters have flocked to see his productions. In *Sanctum* there is one sequence in which the dancers move within a casing of material that binds them at head and feet so that they resemble certain statues of Barbara Hepworth suddenly extended into movement, or else they 'stand up, still and white, like mummies lined up in a forgotten tomb'.

But without Martha Graham there could be no Alwin Nikolais, Merce Cunningham, Paul Taylor, or Meredith Monk. The great giants cast the longest shadows, provoke the strongest rebellions, offer the most bracing challenge. In the twentieth century the presence of Graham is to theatre and dance what Picasso is to painting. Like a great matrix, Graham contains within the body of her work and of her writings an endless source of inspiration to theatre and to dance. It is not surprising that so many in the theatre, including Peter Brook, have acknowledged her genius. More than any single figure in theatre, Graham has opened the door to the archetypes, revealing their power, splendour and terror.

> People say –
> How did you begin?
> Well – that is the question
> And who knows –
> Not I –
> How does it all begin?
> I suppose it never begins, just continues.

But one takes up the necessity of one's heritage and in time it may become one's calling, one's destiny, one's fame, one's immortality.

10 Martha Graham

11 Martha Graham as Jocasta and Erick Hawkins as Oedipus in Martha Graham's *Night Journey*, music by William Schuman

12 Martha Graham and Robert Cohan in Martha Graham's *Dark Meadow*

13 Alwin Nikolais

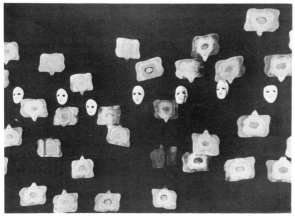

14 (above) *Sanctum*, a Dance Theatrepiece by Alwin Nikolais

15 (left) *Galaxy*, a Dance Theatrepiece by Alwin Nikolais

16 (below) *Triptych*, a Dance Theatrepiece by Alwin Nikolais

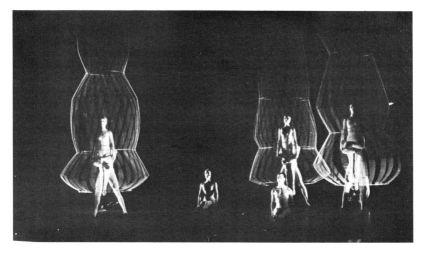

17 Julian Beck of the Living Theatre

18 The Living Theatre's production of *Frankenstein*

12 Further Experiments Today – in America

At her final retrospective exhibition at the Tate Gallery in London, Barbara Hepworth invited the public to touch, strike, caress, become physically involved with her sculptures. She even created a special Walk-Through, an enormous bronze structure which people could step up into, sit in, look out of, walk through. Similarly Isamu Noguchi created a series of Walk-Ons, like crusted turds, providing the feet with a tactile experience of art. Sculpture, they were saying, is no longer an object to be placed on a plinth and admired at a genteel distance. It is through one's hands, through one's feet, through one's body, that these works are to be approached, as much as through the eye. We have a tactile as well as a visual experience. As Pierre Boulez has said of the new music, so also it may be said of the new art, the new dance and the new theatre: that it is like going through a labyrinth. We may get lost but we are being invited to enter into a total experience. After all, we cannot know a tree by merely looking at it. We have to feel the texture of the bark, knowing it at all seasons. So with a work of art.

But Walk-Throughs, Walk-Ons raise the questions, What is sculpture? What is architecture? It is to a sculptor, Isamu Noguchi, that we owe the idea of a new kind of playground, spaces with abstract shapes for children to explore. It is Noguchi who also created for the theatre of Martha Graham some of the most original stage designs of this century. Robert Rauschenberg has created sculptured paintings that also move and speak; John Cage has composed a work entitled *4' 33"* in which the musicians 'perform' four minutes thirty-three seconds of silence, the 'music' being composed of the accidental

Theatre had become institutionalized. All the institutions are crumbling. The Living Theatre had to crumble or change its form.'

The Living Theatre [wrote Peter Brook] are in search of a meaning in their lives, and in a sense even if there were no audience they would still have to perform because the theatrical event is the climax and the centre of their lives. In the Living Theatre three needs become one: it exists for the sake of performing; it earns its living through performing; and its performances contain the most intense and intimate moments of its collective life.

The Living Theatre regarded the traditional theatre as merely a salve for society, enabling the public to return in safety to its bourgeois way of life. 'We feel that our whole culture has to be changed,' challenged Judith Malina who, with her husband, Julian Beck, founded the Living Theatre. 'It has to grow away from what is destructive to what is creative. We have become over-intellectualized, divorced from our bodies, from real feeling.' The same statement was to be made, in varying ways, by other pioneers of theatre in the 1960s: Richard Schechner, Peter Schumann, Anna Halprin, Jerome Savary, Joan Littlewood, Ariane Mnouchkine, Luca Ronconi, Tom O'Horgan, and many more, as well as by such teachers, psychologists, and writers as Carl Jung, Krishnamurti, R.D. Laing, Fritjof Capra, Arnold Toynbee, Theodore Rosjak, Bhagwan Rajneesh, Carl Rogers and Arthur Janov. When so many are saying the same thing, it is no longer an isolated utterance but the symptom of an urgent need in our society.

If we could again become feelingful people and not shut ourselves off from one another [pleaded Judith Malina], then we would not tolerate the injustices in the world. It is part of our process to try to unite mind with body, to heed those intimations within ourselves of immortality.

For Julian Beck it was essential that the Living Theatre, as a living community, should reflect in their lives what they were trying to say on stage: 'We are trying to solve our individual lives as a community.' In many ways the Living Theatre recalled the communistic societies that flourished in America in the nineteenth century – the Harmonists, the Separation-ists, the Oneida and Wallingford Perfectionists, the Shakers. It was easy to imagine the Living Theatre, like the Amish Community today, being exempted from national service and income tax – a people set apart.

Although pacifist by conviction, in their private lives, the Living Theatre carried out the most systematic and violent assault on its audiences. *Frankenstein*, its last mammoth production, was a collage of Grand Guignol, shadow play, yoga, meditation, gymnastics, howls, grunts and groans. As though set in a chamber of horrors at Madame Tussaud's Waxworks, on various platforms erected within the outline of a forty foot high human head, there were presented acts of crucifixion, lynching, guillotining, and heart transplants. What took place on the multiple stages was a representation of yesterday and today, riotings in the streets of Paris and Chicago, bombing in Vietnam. The Frankenstein monster which the actors created was that of our own bestiality let loose and out of control. In holding up their mirror to nature, the Living Theatre was reflecting those restless, wild, daemonic energies that lie so lightly beneath the urban and urbane veneer of our civilization. Audiences were compelled to recognize the truth of what was conveyed, and, confronted with that kind of daemonic energy, were mesmerized. Audiences today, still, are not accustomed to such a totality of performance in the theatre on the part of actors who drove themselves, and sometimes the spectator, into a state of near trance or possession; sweat streaming down their naked bodies, froth flying from their mouths, as they blasted their way through the conventions of nineteenth-century theatre. For four or five hours, audiences would be battered, bored, stimulated, provoked, assaulted. The shocks, assaults, noises, boredom, made it impossible for anyone to remain aloof, or not be involved. No one who saw them is ever likely to forget the impact they made, while their reiterated chants of Fuck for Peace, Free the Blacks, Abolish the State, Viva Anarchy, had a way of sticking like hidden persuaders.

If only we can make the audience feel pain at a public

ceremony [said Julian Beck], this may be the route by
which we enable him to find the way back to his feelings
so that he will never want to commit violence again.

Joseph Chaikin also wanted to make his actors above all
feel and understand. He wanted to free them of their inhibitions and prejudices and create a humanizing kind of theatre.

We have to shake off the sophistication of our time, by
which we close ourselves up [he wrote] and to become
vulnerable again. We realize that life hasn't been too
generous with us, and we've retreated. We've closed off a
great deal of our total human response. But as actors we
must open up again, become naive again, innocent, and
cultivate our deeper climates – our dread, for example.
Only then will we be able to find new ways to express the
attitudes which we hold in common with the outside world
and ways to express the attitudes which we hold as
uniquely our own.

Chaikin believed that in order to perform well, an actor
must not cocoon himself in a social milieu or environment
which was in any way limited or exclusive. He had to experience, and expose himself to, all kinds of people and situations;
he should visit and inspect hospitals and prisons, attend
specialist meetings, and involve himself in situations he would
not normally encounter. If an actor did not do these things, he
was 'simply working off the top of society's crust where very
special advantages are on display.' One of the exercises
Chaikin used extensively in his workshops was called 'worlds'.
This was an attempt to understand certain inner states which
might be outside the actor's range of experiences – such as
paranoia or euphoria. The object of the exercise was to involve
other actors in this world without distorting it.

In 1959 Chaikin had joined the Living Theatre but he left
to form his own group only a few years later because he did
not feel that enough emphasis was being given to the actor's
powers. Nevertheless he claims that it awakened his social
and political conscience and the Open Theatre was clearly
influenced by the Beck's driving commitment and the concept
of living and performing as members of a commune.

The Open Theatre was formed in 1963, initially as a workshop to provide a place for actors who wanted to concentrate on exploring and studying theatre rather than continually breaking this ever-changing and developing process by having to stage a performance in front of a public to the same format night after night. Chaikin called his company the Open Theatre in order to preserve an open form. To categorize is to fix and the structure and direction of this group could never remain static. Chaikin himself described them as a 'laboratory performing unfinished work'.

Like all innovators of a new theatre, Chaikin wanted to break new ground and avoid the limitations of a conventional kind of theatre which undermined true artistic expression. In the opening pages of *The Presence of the Actor* ('Notes on The Open Theatre') Chaikin explains that he goes to a Broadway play, primarily to see the usher, the box office and the environment of the physical theatre – 'This situation has become more present than the situation being played out on stage.' Even in the kind of plays which Peter Brook called 'deadly theatre' – plays which use the old methods and old formulae to a highly reductive end – Chaikin discovered, in a potentially moribund environment, a living situation by looking beyond the immediate action on the stage to the actual experience in the theatre. It was the deadliness of naturalistic mannerisms and realistic representation, and the way in which the established theatre sought to make ultimate definitions which he most loathed. Gordon Rogoff, who worked with Chaikin, describes how the workshop activites created a sense of limitless possibilities, so that everyone believed that they could achieve anything – 'We didn't know it then, but what we were doing was demonstrating that to be theatrical is to be alive, and to be alive, therefore is to be theatrical.'

Chaikin emphasized in his workshops the need to change, to experiment and particularly to take risks. Acting was not simply a matter of putting on a disguise and then removing it, because the actor was himself in some way altered every time he put on the mask. Chaikin saw acting as a 'demonstration of the self', whereas conventional methods encouraged actors to fit into 'typical roles', presenting to the audience a set of stereotypes which also became a recommendation of how the audience should classify themselves. To Chaikin this was yet another factor contributing to the 'moronization' of Americans.

The strength of Chaikin's productions lay in the power of the ensemble: each member had to understand the work as a whole and not just his own limited role. In the workshops which preceded the production of *The Serpent* the problem was to find communal points of reference and a common vocabulary for the group. The Garden of Eden scene begins with a group of people on stage performing certain movements that have been carefully selected out of thousands of other movements. Of this production, Chaikin wrote,

> None of us believe there is or ever was a real Garden of
> Eden, but it lives in the mind as certainly as memory.
> For us it's a gathering of creatures who breathe together
> and are vibrantly alive and become an organized world.

Chaikin never discovered a process of satisfactorily transforming the workshop situation into a live stage performance. Although his whole concept of acting stressed the importance of the mutually stimulating relationship between actor and spectator, he always felt that public opinion put pressure on the actor by concentrating on his expertise, and that an audience ultimately disrupted both performance and player:

> Sometimes the enemy is a production, because in moving
> from the improvisational stage to the production stage,
> there are no handrails. It's very traumatic, all this
> changing. I've learned that the workshop emphasis and
> the performance emphasis are completely different.

Chaikin was always happiest in the workshop environment because he believed that an actor required the discipline of extensive physical and vocal training. Many of the exercises aimed to get away from talking and experimented with words and sounds. After a visit from Grotowski in 1967 the group developed more psycho-physical exercises similar to those of the Polish Laboratory Theatre. Chaikin believed an actor should not only see (that is, 'analyze, criticise and sweep under the rug'), but must also understand. In order to understand he must learn to improvise which in turn will develop his inquiring nature and intuition. It was the 'inside' of a situation which Chaikin wanted to explore through perceptual and non-verbal improvisation and in this way come to a better understanding of the sub-text and the psychological motivations of character.

The Open Theatre, like the Living Theatre, are now no more, but their work has not been in vain. Like yeast it has gone back into the fermentation. In the mid-1960s the continuing search for a greater togetherness tended to centre on the effort to break the proscenium arch. Tom O'Horgan, the director of *Hair*, *Jesus Christ Superstar*, *Tom Paine*, and many productions at La Mama, says of this period, 'It's hard to understand now why it seemed so important then, but there was an incredible urge and need to do it.' Megan Terry, author of the play *Viet Rock*, declared, 'I want my audience to feel rather than to think.' In 1968 she offered a new play, *The People vs Ranchman*, in which Ranchman, an accused rapist in police custody, is depicted dying in the gas chamber, the electric chair, on the gallows, and he goes on being resurrected in order to join in the shouting and heckling with the rest of the cast. As *Time Magazine* reported, the absence of rational content was what was worth thinking about.

> It is not that *The People vs Ranchman* is a bad play. It is not out to be a good one in terms of drama's traditional concern with fate, foibles, and ideas. Like the propaganda plays of the guerilla theatre this play is intended to be a felt experience by the audience.

Today, the greater use of alternative spaces for the staging of plays, the greater flexibility of staging, the greater informality of audiences, and a more subtle realization of the relationship of audience and performers, are all directly the fruit of battles waged so fiercely in the 1960s, as well as of challenges thrown down earlier in the century by Okhlopkov and others. The expatriate Hungarian theatre company Squat has a unique method of exploring the reaction of the audience to performers and to other spectators. One side of its performing space is a storefront window which looks on to a busy New York street outside; this means that for the audience the innocent passers-by become part of an immediate stage action and vice versa. This brilliant technique of shifting the audience's viewpoint originated in Hungary when the company, then considered to be subversive, was only permitted to perform in the privacy of the actors' own apartments. Looking across the street into other people's windows, they found that they were able to watch mysterious dramas unfolding before their very eyes. The object of all their theatre now is to recreate that same sense of mystery.

The name 'Squat' reflects the company's driving independence and nomadic past. Living and performing under one roof, this small company of adults and children aims to transform its members' own lives into art, because theatre has become for them an integral and inseparable part of life. They believe that since Greek tragedy no drama has been able to link the 'cosmic' drama of the characters on stage with the real-life drama of the spectators, and from that time on actors have only been used as mouthpieces for ideas. Living now in an age blinkered by technical achievements and rational thinking, we no longer have any use for the kind of mythology which attempted to explain the 'ways of God' to man and was the basis of all cosmic drama. As a result a great gulf has been created, and it is precisely this gulf which Squat resolutely attempts to present as a phenomenon symptomatic of the company's lives and of its theatre.

Pig, Child Fire! was the company's first American performance and was revived in New York in 1982. It is characteristic of all Squat's achievements. The opening scene presents a cluster of disparate images: a giant puppet figure of a man hangs upside down with the head of a real and identical-looking actor protruding from its anus; a girl sitting on a ledge holding a goat on a string; a woman shuffling to and fro in shoes too large for her. For a long time nothing happens except that the goat tries to eat the script. Passers-by on the street outside peer in or move nervously away – they are as intrigued by the play as we, the paying audience, are by them. The girl then proceeds to read Stavrogin's confessions from Dostoevsky's *The Devils* in a dull, bored, unintelligible manner. The performers do not 'act' but behave like themselves. Everything happens slowly and naturally, at the same speed and with the same lack of efficiency or concentration as would happen in reality. The action, laden with familiar symbols and images, is reminiscent of a Chagall painting since it blends the worlds of dream and reality and seems to take place at various points in space, with the giant puppet distorting any sense of normal perspective.

Like so much of American avant-garde theatre Squat offers no easy answers. Much of the time the spectator cannot understand what is being said or done. Like the theatre of Richard Foreman, Squat therefore requires deep concentration from an audience who are trying to make sense out of what they see. But even if we could make sense out of these strange events, would we be any wiser? The conflict seems to lie in the juxtaposition of the action in the theatre and the action on the street, and also in the fact that the audience cannot easily distinguish the real from the invented action, or the actors from the passers-by. This confusion and the deliberate underplaying help achieve the kind of ambiguity found in the theatre of Peter Schumann and Robert Wilson who both make extensive use of amateur actors. Had the performances been more polished, this effect would have been destroyed by distinguishing the performers from the real life participants.

In the second scene the audience's perspective is further broadened since a recording of what is happening in the street outside is monitored on a video machine which now faces us. In this way we can witness both on the screen and through the storefront window a shoot-out on the street. The video selects and expands the audience's view as it is able to show what is out of our eye line – a wounded man struggling to get up for instance. The violence on the street is then repeated in the theatre as the gunman enters and shoots at the girl on the stage and proceeds to take a knife, sharpen it and hack off the hand of another injured man who lies slumped over the table. The man starts up in pain, the audience gasp, but the man pulls out a false bloody stump and reveals his own undamaged hand. He now fires a gun at his assailant but it is only a toy pistol. Submissively he drops his pants, sticks the gun up his anus and fires. This time the gun goes off. The scene closes with the other man drawing back the curtain and revealing outside a crowd of voyeurs taking photographic shots of the scene inside.

In the third act there is a growing sense of tension among the audience as the video is now pointed not outside but at us sitting in our seats. While on stage a family are gossiping and eating a meal of real food, every one of us in the audience is aware that at any moment our face could appear on the screen and that we too could become a part of that action. When the performance finally ends the stage is left empty. On the street passers-by fill the screen of the store window, while we, the paying audience, file on to the street, to join the bystanders and actors, and merge into one anonymous crowd on West 23rd Street – all aware that we have been shown new ways of seeing and perceiving.

Today the most vital and exciting theatre is mainly to be found at the fringe. For over a decade, Grotowski has doubted that the theatre in our century is an art favoured by a large public. The dreams of a people's theatre, be they the dreams of Brecht, of Rolland, or of Joan Littlewood, have failed. But theatre can and must make itself popular in a new way. That way will be by assuming different forms of theatre to answer the needs of different people. It is by differentiating itself that theatre will extend its audience. Actors (not necessarily professional, for that word itself may become outdated), directors, writers will gravitate towards a particular group to which they feel attracted. It will be a theatre of commitment. People will belong to this group or that, some to Robert Wilson's, some to Richard Schechner's or to Spalding Gray's group, or any one of the innumerable cells of theatre that are springing up all over the world.

It is part of a general movement of the time. It is not so much a fragmentation as that the old structures are breaking up into new cells. The Christian churches are beginning to grasp that here lies the real challenge and potential, while the same pattern is to be seen in other levels of society.

Man has got to change himself. Man has got to evolve himself; he can't wait for this to happen by natural selection any longer. And it seems to me that what is happening right now is that people are trying to help one another to change. People are getting together outside work situations, because science and the reduction of long

19 Scene from *Motel*, from *America, Hurrah!* A play by Jean-Claude van Itallie, produced by the Open Theatre. In the sixties, an era which did not place great value on words, the Open Theatre was unique in its collaboration with the playwright Jean-Claude van Itallie who also wrote for them their most memorable work, *The Serpent.*

20 Founded in 1978, in San Francisco, A Travelling Jewish Theatre 'combine the spontaneity of improvisation with the dazzling language of the mystics' (Susan Griffin). Like Peter Schumann they recognise that the roots of theatre lie in the realm of the mythic, the sacred and the communal; and like Grotowski and Brook, they believe that theatre can be an instrument of healing

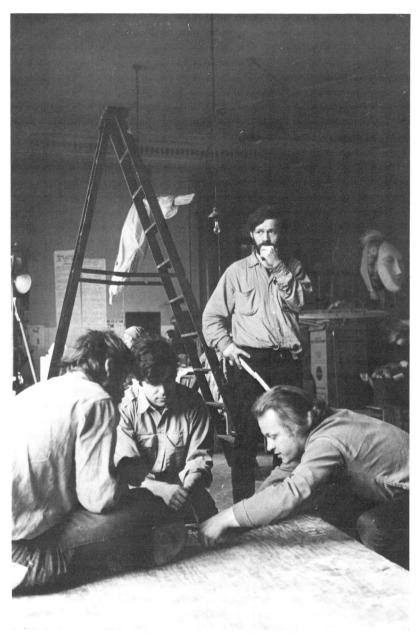

21 Peter Schumann, founder of the Bread and Puppet Theatre

working hours have at last made this possible. And they're using this time and this space to see how they can grow through personal interaction.

So speaks Mike Barnett, author of *People, Not Psychiatry*, and one of the leaders of the Encounter Group movement.

Of those groups in America whose work is an important part of the developing history of theatre in this century, I have chosen to concentrate on those whose commitment is primarily to the non-professional. Leisure which once was a luxury has now become a problem, and how people relate to this challenge of increased leisure is a matter of great urgency. How theatre can relate to the needs of the ordinary individual as a form of creative expression is a question that was to become the prime concern of Jerzy Grotowski in the 1970s. In America the work of, in particular, Peter Schumann with the Bread and Puppet Theatre, and of Anna Halprin with the Dancers' Workshop, may well prove to be among the most important contributions to our society as it approaches the close of the twentieth century.

13 Richard Foreman, Robert Wilson and the Bread and Puppet Theatre

Companies like the Living Theatre, the Open Theatre and Squat owe their existence to the inspiration of one individual, but for their success they depend upon the collaborative efforts of each member of the company who work together to write, produce and perform every production, bringing to life a theatrical event which has involved the labour of the whole group.

Other groups, like the Ontological-Hysteric Theatre, founded by Richard Foreman and Robert Wilson's Byrd Hoffman School of Byrds, and Peter Schumann's Bread and Puppet Theatre, have moved away from the type of experimental theatre which sought to find new means of expression through group involvement, and owe their success to the ingenuity and decisions of their creator. Both Richard Foreman and Robert Wilson, like Peter Schumann, have an entirely autonomous function – controlling every moment of production from the moment the text is registered on paper (or, as in the case of Wilson, stuck onto the wall to form a giant mural), to the careful choreography of each movement and gesture during rehearsal. Foreman even sits in the front row during performances operating the tape recorder and, like the Polish director Tadeusz Kantor, ultimately determines the pace of each production. (To Kantor a theatrical work of art is a form of living sculpture. Objects exist in space like pieces of sculptures bearing no relation to the outside world. Influenced by Craig's concept of the 'übermarionette', Kantor treats actors like objects, frequently substituting them for puppets. Throughout each performance he remains visible to the audience, standing on the edge of the stage conducting the actors with a wave of the hand or a nod of the head. This technique is used not because the actors depend upon his direction to perform, but in order to emphasize the synthetic qualities of performance.)

Both Foreman and Wilson are part of a new formalist tradition in the American alternative theatre which is dominated. by ideas on structure and composition and seeks to make the audience aware of the formal elements in a performance. A new vocabulary has been discovered which aims to disrupt the spectator's viewing patterns by liberating theatre from conventions and set structures. The techniques of stagecraft are exposed, abandoning any attempt to create a fictional illusion on a purely linear format. Theatre has become a ritual of the imagination, no longer concerned with telling a story, depicting character, or voicing social and political polemics, but with portaying visual patterns which can probe deep into the subconscious. This is an abstract and non-literal type of theatre which looks inwards and is concerned with the 'self' and the ways in which people perceive and interpret visually presented images. The technical properties of theatre are revealed for the sole purpose of analysis.

Up until the mid-1970s Foreman's attention was primarily concerned with presenting 'the object' in theatrical terms. He was interested, he said, in 'putting it on stage and finding different ways of looking at it', so that 'the object was there in isolation bracketed from the rest of the world.' Traditionally props have either served the actor or enhanced the setting but Foreman's objects have an independent function and hang isolated in space – they have no logic or purpose but are merely contingent. In an interview with Richard Kostelanetz he admitted that his primary concern was in 'freeing individual elements, freeing the individual word, freeing individual gestures, freeing individual noises, in much the same way modernist poetry since Rimbaud tends to free the word on the page.'

More recently Foreman has concentrated on the realization of fragmented texts. For years he was obsessed with perfection, struggling to build his words into a balanced and harmonic artistic form. It came as a sudden revelation that the clumsy, unfinished, imperfect sentences were not only the truth about his very existence but also symptomatic of the age in which he was living. He had to show what Gertrude Stein called 'the strain of progress'. Foreman's productions all illustrate this point in their 'web of disruptions' and although the setting, the subject matter, and the characters are frequently shifted, there emerges in his drama a pattern of displacements so that the spectator has an experience much like that of watching a television screen which is being switched from channel to channel.

The structure of each play relates directly to the writer's thought processes. Once Foreman has his text, he distributes the lines among his actors and then proceeds to make a recording of the text as the actors read it in a deliberately expressionless tone. This recording becomes the centre of the play around which Foreman 'choreographs' all other aspects of production. When rehearsals are nearly over, he records his own reactions to the production and this is played at various times throughout the actual performance.

All Foreman's plays are made to the same formula, avoiding central themes and depicting a sequence of static and unrelated 'pictures'. In his 1972 production of *Sophia=(Wisdom) Part 3:The Cliffs* the actors move around the stage in extreme slow motion, each one concentrating on his own activity, apparently oblivious to the rest of the group. In the second act, for instance, one actor stands and stares at the audience with a piece of string hanging from his mouth while a girl slowly and carefully marks out a circle with the other end. Another girl sits on a suitcase in front of him looking into a pocket mirror. Other players enter and two crouch either side of him, each clasping a pole with a red boxing glove fixed on the end. This tableau is held for a few minutes until a buzzer sounds and at either end of the stage a highly-stylized boxing match commences in which no physical contact is actually made. Finally Rhoda (the leading actress in all Foreman's plays) crawls across naked. The buzzer sounds again and no one moves. Each visual element is added to produce an elaborate and complex picture.

The way in which words are repeated and reverberated at different tempos and speeds indicates Foreman's use of language which is not primarily concerned with communicating messages but with illuminating the patterns and rhythms of speech. The use of the buzzer breaks both the actions and the words into fragments and also acts as an abrupt intrusion into the play. Foreman recreates the hesitant false starts of the original text in other ways too – the tape of his own recorded commentary keeps breaking into the performance; at varying intervals high-pitched noises blast out of the loud speakers, and performers stare into the auditorium making each spectator slowly aware of his patently voyeuristic role. The audience is not asked to contribute to the performance or participate in bringing about a change in the stage situation, for Foreman distrusts anything that depends upon an audience; all he hopes for is that these repeated interruptions will jolt the spectator into a more acute state of self-awareness. The object is not to think rationally but to perceive the relationships between recurring images and words which are the dramatic documentation of actual thought processes. The audience's consciousness should not be dulled by an easy flow of images or by the slow pace of beautifully orchestrated movements, but rather heightened at the pleasure of discovering these patterns and connections. Even when words lose their meaning and become merely resonant, Foreman is certain that the audience receives what is being said on a semi-conscious level.

Some critics have accused Foreman's work of being a type of transitory theatre in which nothing memorable ever occurs, each performance being a momentary experience which evaporates as soon as one leaves the auditorium. But Foreman has always believed that memory deadens our consciousness. He is certain that his plays have a profound effect on his audience because they are forced to have to try and remember and it is in the struggle to remember that they experience an awakening of consciousness. Clearly it is the kind of theatre that is meant to work on a therapeutic level, though Foreman is aware of the limitations of relying on a group response and has expressed the belief that in an ideal situation a director should work with each member of the audience individually.

Robert Wilson has described his dramatic texts as audio scores 'that can accompany the visual arrangement or can stand independent of it.' As Wilson sets a play to paper he simultaneously creates a collage by sticking each sheet of writing on to his studio wall. The scenes are therefore not segregated but can be viewed as a whole, forming a kind of large architectonic sketch (Wilson was in fact trained both as an architect and a painter). At this point he is both concerned with what the words express and with the actual patterns the words form in relation to each other. In his productions, too, the visual arrangement is as important as the structural patterns made by movements and sounds reappearing, inter-mittently, throughout the performance. Some of his 'plays' which use very little actual music or dialogue have been aptly described as 'silent operas' or 'structured silences'.

Like Foreman, Wilson's theatre is not concerned with a purely linear narrative form, but aims to tell many stories simultaneously. His productions have no beginning or end, since previous plays may be incorporated with the structure of the current play. *The Life and Times of Joseph Stalin*, produced in 1973, was, for example, made up of five earlier plays; it lasted twelve hours and involved 125 performers. The spectator is not expected to stay seated for twelve hours, but is invited to come and go as he pleases since there is no sequence of events to be broken. It is the actual present and not the evolving future that Wilson is concerned with.

Not all his productions are on such a grand 'operatic' scale, involving such a large cast. In *Deafman Glance* (1970) only a handful of performers were used. The opening scene is a tableau held for half an hour with the four characters standing motionless – frozen in time and space. Eventually the actress playing the mother slowly gets up and puts one of her two small children to bed; then she proceeds to slowly and tenderly stab him, while an adolescent deaf boy looks on unable to move. This action is then repeated with the second child. Every movement is performed at snail's pace, dulling the audience's perceptions and shifting their minds on to a lower level of consciousness.

Wilson believes that human beings register sensations on two levels – on an 'exterior screen' and an 'interior screen'. Things consciously perceived are registered on the 'exterior screen', whereas dreams and memories are registered on the 'interior screen'. In *I/Was Sitting on my Patio/This Guy*

Appeared I Thought/I was Hallucinating the whispered voices of the performers are magnified by a loudspeaker so that the audience seems to be privy to their innermost thoughts: this is Wilson's method of showing their sensations and perceptions as they are registered on the 'interior screen'. He believes his work is received on several levels of consciousness which confuses the mind and precipitates the fusion of both screens so that the audience can sometimes believe that they have seen or heard what was not actually there. In his work with brain-damaged children Wilson has shown that while deaf and blind people have veiled perceptions they can still hear and see on their 'interior screen'. In his plays he aims to mesmerize his audience and performers into a similar state of obscured consciousness so that normal means of expression are no longer possible.

Wilson uses many of the same techniques as Foreman. Intermittent sound effects and several tapes running simultaneously shape his productions into a series of individual images and activities which bear no reference to the real world. The disjointed action and the recurring words and motifs which echo throughout the text recreate the sensations of a dream, and the whole performance reflects the architectonic sketch of the text originally drawn up by Wilson. Actions become simply activities performed in a vacuum bearing no relation to a coherent whole. Each element is viewed in isolation, and, as the post-modern dancer Lucinda Childs notes, it is up to the spectator 'to make sense out of what he sees and decide if it's chaos or order, formed or formless, or if that matters.'

Overture to Ka Mountain (1972) is one of Wilson's most ambitious productions. As an environmental theatre performance it even goes beyond Peter Brook's *Orghast*. The performance spread over seven mountains, lasted seven days and nights and included thirty actors and twenty Iranian recruits, much of the acting was improvised and a 'Happening' was planned to involve the whole of the audience. The mountain was covered with mythic archetypes: a fish, a whale, Noah's Ark, a dinosaur, the Trojan horse. Missiles stood ready to defend a cut-out model of the Acropolis, while the skyline of New York was eventually seen to go up in flames. At one point a woman walked slowly backwards and forwards for an hour;

use the space you happen to be in, you use it all – the stairs, the windows, the street, the doors. We do a play anywhere provided we can get the puppets in.

Puppet theatre, he says, is an extension of sculpture. 'Imagine a cathedral, not as a decorated religious place, but as a theatre with Christ and the saints and gargoyles being set into motion by puppeteers, talking to the worshippers, participating in the ritual of music and words.'

I once saw him transform the high, raftered 'medieval' banqueting hall of Brown University on Rhode Island into such a cathedral, for his production of *The Domestic Resurrection Circus*, which portrays the creation of the world and the birth of civilization. By means of vaudeville sketches and mimes, he chronicles man's progress up to the end of the world when the Evil People are cast into Hell – represented by many small dolls falling from a dizzy height into the centre of the hall – while the Good People, who have found Heaven, are discovered seated in a gallery at the back, in giant masks, politely clapping.

After the creation of War, the hall is plunged into darkness. For a long time the audience stands, waiting, to the point of exhaustion. It is like waiting in one of the basilicas in Rome on Easter Eve for the lighting of the great Paschal candle. Dimly we can see that a white carpet is being slowly unrolled along the nave of the hall to the tall doors at the far end. Through these doors we are aware of huge white figures gathering. Throughout the hall, in the waiting darkness, can be heard a reverberation of sound, shaking the foundations. We sense movements in the darkness and high above us in the raftered roof. Something numinous is pending. The one sustained note, from a pipe organ, continues minute by minute, without variation. Finally, the white figures begin to move up the nave. They have long sculptured heads, their elongated hands upheld in prayer, and each is linked to the other by white rope.

How long does all this take? It seems an eternity. Yet we all wait, more than a thousand people in the darkness. Then, suddenly, the organ peals out triumphal sounds and all the lights are switched on. At the same time, up in the organ loft curtains rattle back to reveal, seated in tiers, gigantic masked figures, looking down at us on earth, and slowly, gravely, ironically applauding. The white figures below – who are they? The Twelve Apostles? or the resurrected dead? (Schumann is not concerned with logic or linear narrative, but works intuitively like a poet) – crowd together at the east end of the building. And now, from high overhead, operated by cables and pulleys, a giant figure of Paul Revere comes riding on a bomber, travelling the length of the hall, above the heads of the audience, grey streamers flying. At the moment that the figure crashes into the assembled white figures – some of them twenty foot tall – Peter Schumann rushes in among them, flinging himself to the ground, immolating himself along with the figures of his imagination. All pile up and somewhere, underneath, is Schumann. All that a programme note reveals is 'and finally you will see Paul Revere coming over the mountains, calling us together in this moment of great danger, that we may not miss our domestic resurrection.'

At the end of the evening, the entire audience is led out of the building, as though in the Ark, singing 'The storm is here!' Outside, on the campus, under the stars, joyfully elevating a huge blue sail on a mast, the audience set sail in the ark of salvation. The untidiness, the sheer physical fatigue of the audience, the intervals of boredom – all familiar elements of the experimental theatre scene – are here swiftly forgotten. What remains are the extra-ordinary luminous images of Peter Schumann's imagination, like the illustrations from a medieval missal.

Richard Schechner, in his book *Environmental Theater*, describes an early version he saw of this production in 1970.

For me the most effective scene was when the performers erected a twenty five foot wooden mast, letting billow from it a vast blue and white sail. They unwound many yards of blue and white cloth, about three feet wide. With this about fifteen of them formed the outline of a boat. The sail caught the brisk Vermont wind and this veritable ark sailed across the meadow as the crowd of spectators parted like the waters to let it pass. The players chanted 'The storm is here! The storm is here!' They invited the audience to come aboard. Soon most of the several hundred spectators ducked under the bands of cloth and sailed along within the ark.

Schechner observes how each spectator is given a choice between staying outside or moving inside, between watching and doing, between the society that is going down or those who save themselves in order to start a new kind of world. No one is asked to 'act' or do anything more extra-ordinary than play a little make-believe. As such it provided an example of true audience participation.

When the Bread and Puppet players arrive at a place, after having attracted a crowd, Peter Schumann invites volunteers to help build the puppets and take part in the performance. He will also ask for beds and hospitality for himself and the company. He then proceeds to arrange the performance around the core of regular Bread and Puppet performers with the assistance of many volunteers. In this way, local people are directly involved in the making of a spectacle for their community, whether it is a peace march, a political demonstration, or celebration of Easter or Christmas.

The atmosphere of a Bread and Puppet performance is set well before the play begins. In grubby white pants and shirts, coloured bandanas around their heads, or wearing an assortment of headgear – as if they had all come from a jumble sale – the actors proceed through the streets, beating drums, rattling tambourines, blowing trumpets. Some of them wear giant masks. An actor in a pig's head rolls over on the sidewalk, dances among the traffic, swings from a lamppost, and bows to a terrified dog. Passers-by join in the procession, chatting with the actors, and become the audience. If, as often happens on tour when they are abroad, they have to play in a traditional theatre, Peter Schumann will ignore the protests of the box office and insist that anyone in this procession who cannot afford a ticket, shall be let in free. At the Royal Court Theatre in London, in 1969, even when the house was full, no one was turned away; room was found on stage, creating a secondary audience grouped around the actors.

Casually, often inaudibly, Schumann will announce the programme for that evening. Unobtrusively he dominates the action, his black hair falling across his face, sweat running down into his beard, as he roughly grasps a light attached to a length of cable and holds it in different positions to illuminate the action on stage. It is he who conducts the actors when they sing or chant. Crouching on the floor, he tells us through a hand-mike the simple story of the play as it unfolds. When necessary, he takes part in the action, or accompanies the players on the violin. Literally he stage-manages the show before our eyes and no attempt is made to conceal by conventional stagecraft the untidy seams or unfinished joins. What he is trying to communicate – his essential vision of man and God – is more important than the superficialities of stagecraft. And to observe his actors sitting on the floor when not in a scene, or standing by to make noises and sound effects, to see their faces is to know and experience with them the continuing nature of what they are about. Their gentleness, their humour, their caring, their concern is part of the total action; more – it is the base and ground from which all their work stems.

Schumann's most considerable work is, I consider, *The Cry of The People for Meat*, his re-telling of the Old and New Testaments, prefaced by a burlesqued version of the marriage of the God of Heaven and Mother Earth. For this opening he uses twenty-foot high puppets dancing to raucous music, as at an old-time circus. The birth of Kronos is depicted by a man-sized knight bursting his way through a mass of torn and shredded paper, who then proceeds to slay his father, tossing the giant head into a red sheet where it is bounced up and down. Two screens are now erected on either side of the stage, one marked 'Heaven' and the other marked 'Earth'. Schumann drags on two actors swathed in sheets of polythene. Holding his lamp in one hand, he kneels and blows into the polythene – an image of God breathing life into Adam and Eve. In the background sit the alert, watchful actors. Piled against the walls are the various masks and puppets used in their repertoire. The stage is littered with shredded paper, torn polythene, lengths of cable, and Schumann scrambling for his hand-mike, script and portable light. Yet through all the untidiness and mess, the often blurred effects, he carves his blazing vision of man's ultimate destiny, so that the very mess becomes an image of Chaos out of which God created Order.

It is at this moment that Schumann creates one of his most memorable theatre images. With the announcement of the Flood, he lifts high his portable light to reveal a moving wave of grotesquely carved pigs' heads – the Gadarene swine, an image of mankind at its most bestial. Like drovers at a market, Schumann and another actor move in among them, roughly binding them with ropes as they pile up on top of one another, slithering and sliding forward towards the edge of the stage and spilling over, an avalanche of monstrous heads with huge nostrils and fangs. Kicking at the heads (there are only these heads, the rest of the actors' bodies are clothed with hessian), Schumann moves in among them like one possessed, against a background of twentieth-century traffic noises on tape – the full-throated roar of modern man. At this moment Schumann carves a theatre image that has all the intensity of Blake. At such a moment you cannot but feel he is a 'sent man', a prophet new inspired, one of the few poets in today's theatre. It is as though we were present with the artist at the very instant of creating a work of art.

At the opening of the second half, the company proceed to dress up an actor as the Christus, draping him first with a sheet, and placing in his arm the figure of a new-born baby. Next, they put on his face the mask of a Vietnamese peasant woman. Then, as the Sermon on the Mount commences, the actors proceed to adorn him with various offerings. 'Blessed are they who hunger and thirst after righteousness' and they hang on him cooking pans and offerings of food. 'Blessed are the pure in heart' and they hang about his neck a large red heart. 'Blessed are the merciful', and they hang on him a garland of fresh flowers and weeds. 'Blessed are the peacemakers', and a rifle is slung about his neck. The Christus is thus seen to become a focal point for mankind's projections and longings; literally, they hang their sorrows on him. The actor then mounts a tall stepladder, and now there is drawn up over him, covering his entire body, a giant figure of the Christus, with long hands uplifted in benediction. From now until the end of the play the actor will sit beneath this giant mask, covered with the various offerings, perched on top of the stepladder, suffering the heat and discomfort. In the traditional theatre the actor would either withdraw, unseen by the audience, or his place be taken by another. Here, however, it is as though by accepting all this the actor enters into an imaginative and intimate identification with Christ who took upon him the burden of man's sorrow. One is reminded how, in the Mass, the priest is said to be no longer himself but becomes the representative of Christ. At the end of the play, when the mask is removed, and the actor revealed, his long hair is lank and wet, his face running with sweat and taut with pain; it is seen to be a kind of Passion and, as in Grotowski's theatre, a total offering of that actor in an act of love. To act is to commit oneself.

Towards the end of the play, a long table is carried on, covered with a cloth, and laid with round loaves of newly-baked, wholemeal bread. Peter Schumann and some of the actors take the loaves and, breaking them, distribute the bread among the audience, each person taking a portion and passing the rest on to his neighbour. Schumann crouches by the steps to the stage, chewing bread, and watching with a gentle half-smile, rapt and attentive, as the whole audience break bread and eat. As this happens the Christus slowly lowers its head so that Mary may reach up to caress the sorrowful visage. A deep humming note is heard, like a long, sustained mantra which continues for ten minutes as figures appear in the auditorium, ten feet tall, swathed in hessian, and surmounted by carved heads. These are the twelve apostles. As they mount the stage and take their positions at the table, a second Christus enters, holding in one hand a papier-mâché chalice and in the other a papier-mâché loaf. While the second Christus offers the bread and wine to the twelve apostles, the first Christus, towering above the action, lowers its hands in benediction on the scene below. Throughout all this the houselights are up. Deliberately, at this moment, Schumann eschews a conventional theatrical effect, therby risking laughs – and getting them – but, slowly, the unhurried ritual and the unceasing humming compel silence. The faces of the apostles are very human, yet comic, grotesque, and very beautiful. They are our faces and yet, at the same time, they are archaic visages. The second Christus turns to offer bread and wine to the first Christus and then kneels for blessing. It is at this moment that suddenly, violently, the table is overthrown and the great heads fall as, from above, an aeroplane appears like a black raven, toppling down the towering figure of the Christus. The action is both shocking and clumsy. Conventionally one would say that the effect is bungled and there are more laughs, at first, as the actor portraying Christ struggles out of the burden of masks and hangings. The actors look at us thoughtfully (years later I recall Yoshi Oida, in Peter Brook's *The Ik*, gazing at the laughing audience and asking of the actor playing Colin Turnbull, 'Why do they laugh?'), gently; still rapt in the mysteries they have enacted. Without manifestos, without dogmatic utterances, without aggression, they present a truly poor theatre, a holy theatre. The very materials they use, apart from the superbly made masks – and even they are papier mâché – are the creased and old clothes and lengths of material found in any jumble sale. They dress up in whatever they can find, like the fairies in Arthur Rackham's unforgettable illustrations to *A Midsummer Night's Dream*, improvising with the complete conviction of a child. They make do, pretend. One could not call them professionals in the accepted sense. They bring no conventional skills, sophistication or polish to their performance. There is a deliberate amateurishness about much that they do, and often the action is, intentionally, slowed down so that, at first seeing, it might appear that they have no sense of time whatever. Yet it is easy to see how much Robert Wilson has been influenced by them. The plays are presented with a simplicity that radiates from the inner certainty of Schumann and his followers. One feels that the first Franciscans must have been like this: it is impossible to separate the quality of their life from their work.

In 1973, the year that Joseph Chaikin brought the Open Theatre to an end after nine years of rich experimentation, Peter Schumann announced his intention of disbanding his company. And so, in 1974, after thirteen years, during which the Bread and Puppet Theatre had built up an international reputation, and developed a unique form of theatre, a fusion of puppetry, music, circus and dance, and been hailed by leading theatre critics as one of the most important American experimental theatres, the company dispersed.

Joseph Chaikin chose to end the Open Theatre because he

felt there was a danger of their becoming institutionalized – 'People were doing master's and doctoral theses on the work of the Open Theatre, and more and more Foundations were willing to give grants.' Schumann had never been dependent on grants, he had always steadfastly refused subsidy, but he had found success an increasing burden, with the need to maintain a permanent company and to produce more and more works for more and more tours. Since 1975, therefore, he has been able to enjoy an easier, looser, situation – which has always suited him best. Conducting workshops, living on his farm in Vermont with his wife and five children, and bringing people together whenever he has a show he wants to create. Now he has time to draw, paint, write, sculpt, and relate to the rural community around him. Many of his former company have started their own companies, or joined other groups, but each summer, whenever they can, they come together at Glover, where Schumann lives, for a three-day circus event.

For the past several years, each August, some fifteen thousand people have been turning up to this marathon event, something like a summer fair, which commences at 2 p.m. with a version of *The Domestic Resurrection Circus* in a large gravel pit which provides a natural amphitheatre. Then, between five o'clock and six o'clock, dozens of booth-stages come alive with marionettes, mime and other shows. At half past six, the spectators file into a clearing in the forest for a religious choral and puppet play, based on Bach Motets, *Jesu, Meine Freude*. Finally, at eight o'clock, the day ends with a play that takes in the whole landscape, fields, forests and surrounding hills. It is an attempt at a kind of community celebration and pageant. Peter Schumann thinks that society today has forgotten how to celebrate.

> Celebrations were once the high point of community life [he observes]. Weddings in a European village would last several days. There is something old-fashioned in what we are doing, but in a way it is also new. This is a time when many people feel like getting out of that bag of being organized by others. They want to do it for themselves.

> Out of the darkness emerge enormous white spirit birds, fifteen by twenty-five foot large, suspended above the

ground on poles carried by runners. They circle the camp fires slowly, then disappear into the night. A torch is lit, then another and another, until a torch-light procession is formed. Drums begin in the distance, and the procession moves along the base of the opposite slope towards the fires, drumming as they approach. Swaying gracefully above the torch-bearers in the procession are twelve foot stilt dancers in flowing Red Bird costumes, complete with wings and full bird masks, with long yellow beaks. Smaller red birds dance around their feet.

The ecstasy dance begins. Drums grow louder. The birds shriek and flap their wings in stylized gestures. The dance reaches a frenzied pitch and then the drums ease off and finally cease. Stillness. Humming is heard. Over a nearby ridge appears a procession of colourful, glowing lanterns. The lantern carriers circle the camp fires.

Silently, with the torch-bearers, they form an aisle leading off into the dark. Slowly the bird dancers, the musicians, drummers, puppeteers and audience members begin the mile-long recessional down the lighted aisle and back to the Bread and Puppet farmhouse.

22 Bread and
Puppet Theatre,
Peace Parade, New
York, April 1969

23 Bread and
Puppet Theatre in
Fire

24 The Bread and Puppet Theatre in Glover, Vermont, USA. Chris Braithwaite, publisher of the *Chronicle*, Barton, Vermont, writes 'The Bread and Puppet Theatre which is the source of so much drama, excitement and pride in this town'

25 A play at dusk on the edge of the forest, Bread and Puppet Circus, Glover, Vermont

14 Anna Halprin and the Dancers' Workshop

At the far end of Divisidero Street in San Francisco, in a predominantly black neighbourhood, is Anna Halprin's Dancers' Workshop. For sixteen years she worked with her own company of professional dancers and then they dispersed. It was this company which first brought frontal nudity to the New York stage, long before *Oh, Calcutta*, at one of the Hunter College Auditorium series. Speaking of this group she comments,

> We had evolved such a technique that, were we still working, we'd be another Polish Laboratory Theatre – but who needs that in this country? We have to work with the way the situation is. Here, in San Francisco, I choose to work with non-dancers, and I have to work with the materials they offer.

The Dancers' Workshop has been, and continues to be, an attempt to find a process that unites personal growth with artistic growth, life and art, one aspect feeding off the other and continuously coming together in new ways.

> In my approach to theatre and dance (says Anna Halprin) art grows directly out of our lives. Each person is his own art, just as each community is its own art. Whatever emotional, physical or mental barriers that we carry around with us in our personal lives will be the same barriers that inhibit our full creative expression. It is for this reason that we need to release emotional blocks in order to realize fully our human creative potential in terms of being able to develop effectively as performers and

131

as creators, as well as to participate with satisfaction in our lives. I look at emotional blocks as damaging to artistic growth. When a person has reached an impasse we know something in their life and in their art is not working. What is not working is their old 'dance'. They have to reach out to a new 'dance'.

The thrust of her work is towards unfolding every aspect of the individual within the creative community of the particular workshop, evolving rites, rituals and ceremonies out of authentic life situations.

In 1967 she conducted a series of experiments based upon the idea of myths. These were spontaneous unrehearsed situations of up to fifty people – a cross-section of the community. They were an attempt, the first of a series of on-going experiments, to break down all barriers between aesthetics and the reality of life. For Anna Halprin dance is no longer something to be 'consumed' by the spectator, but something in which he should take part.

I am interested [she says] in a theatre where everything is experienced as if for the first time: a theatre of risk, spontaneity, exposure – and intensity. I want a partnership of the audience and performer. I have gone back to the ritualistic beginnings of art as a heightened expression of life. I wish to extend every kind of perception. I want to participate in events of supreme authenticity, to involve people with their environment so that life is lived as a whole.

Very soon, she noticed that people began to arrive early at her sessions in order to start their own improvisations as a warm-up.

They know they won't be told what to do. They are going to do what they want, or make or allow to happen. People really like to have this kind of responsibility. It gives them a feeling of self-esteem, a chance to use their full capacities. Through group contemplation and discussion the evening can be transformed from a passing turn-on into art, a part of a person's being. It's wonderful to see what happens when you release people's resources.

Typical of the various *Myths* was that based on the image, *Carrying*. For this, people sat on high levels all facing one another for a long time while drums rolled. Finally people were asked to volunteer to choose a person and carry him along the passage. This led to variations such as two people carrying one person, five people carrying two, five carrying one and so on. Gradually the group became aware of the archetypal connotations of the act of carrying: the child carried in the womb, the bride across the threshold, the corpse to the grave, the Pope to the altar, the hero to the crowds.

In *Atonement*, after being briefed and deciding whether to participate in this 'ordeal', the audience entered the studio one at a time and stood facing the wall. The walls and floors of the studio were entirely covered with newspapers from one day's edition. Only one selected page was used, in complete repetition. Each participant chose a position and remained there, silent and still for an hour. A loud continuous roll on a snare drum was played in the centre of the space. Afterwards, the participants returned to the briefing room and were asked to think of two words that best described their experience. They formed small groups and, using these two words, shared their experience.

Her class begins with simple limbering exercises – each person working out according to his or her ability. Her concern is not the usual preoccupation with form. Producing an anatomical chart of the human body she asks the kids to study it. 'We're working with the inanimate body not in terms of style but on anatomical grounds so as to understand our own structures.'

She pauses.

'Where's Mr Bo?'

Someone goes to look for him. Latecomers drift in quietly. One boy has long frizzed ginger hair drawn tightly back and knotted.

Mr Bo is one of three blacks who live on the premises and are the first members and teachers of a new multi-racial group.

We have been too dominated by a white racial culture [comments Anna]. We must allow a symbiosis to take place and you can only achieve this by a company composed of all the nationalities, and minority groups, that we have here, and by living together.

Mr Bo appears, grinning. A big, burly, bearded and bespectacled black, wearing a blue and white spotted bandana round his head, a purple vest, striped coloured shorts, and a gold bangle in one ear, he is an expert on the drums, playing ecstatically, eyes rolling, teeth flashing, as he provides percussion for the exercises. He is also much preoccupied with the idea of death. In an improvisation, which as a group they are developing, based upon animals in a jungle, Mr Bo dies and, as he does so, one of the others who, up to that moment, had been portraying a vulture, swoops down on him and becomes his mate. Throughout this work the performers keep transforming from humans into animals and back again.

> But how to resolve all this material? [ponders Anna
> Halprin]. Death is nature's way of resolving the conflict
> of the jungle and of society, but in this work the solution
> has to be in some archetypal way. It's made me realize
> how in our culture we have so little experience for dealing
> with death. Institutionalism has always dealt with this.
> Can you imagine what form the young today would
> find to honour their dead? We have yet to find new
> rituals.

She comments on Mick Jagger's funeral ritual for Brian Jones's death with the release of several thousand white butterflies.

Every year or every two years the Dancers' Workshop creates a new, different and original full-length work of theatre that is in itself a statement of where they are. Each piece represents the collective effort of everyone involved, and is shared with the outside community. In general, however, Anna Halprin has re-defined the role of the audience. Audience members function both as participants and as spectators at different times during a workshop. At particular moments a group, or an individual, will be asked to perform for the others, who then function as the audience; they change places. All members of workshops conducted by the Dancers' Workshop are united by the common idea of using theatre as a means to undergo certain transformations in their lives, and share in each other's insights into the creative process.

Anna Halprin teaches indirectly. In turn different members create a short movement sequence which the others follow. Then, whoever has set it in motion may be asked to watch the rest and comment.

'Any suggestions to make, Susan?'

Susan analyses what is being done, perhaps demonstrates again.

'How about speed?' asks Anna.

They are encouraged to articulate, each a potential teacher and Anna herself there as an indirect teacher. She takes what they give her and enables them to extend and develop it, assisted by the other permanent members of the Dancers' Workshop.

Now they all sit round Susan who has a project to outline, which turns out to be a street procession. They are to improvise costumes on the spot, and to follow a specific route. The aim of the exercise is 'to zoom, keep up the pace, as we go round the block.'

They begin to make up spontaneous costumes. Susan winds a length of rope round herself; Clint, another of the blacks, drapes a flag over his back, puts a GI's helmet on his head, and a fencing mask over his face. There is great activity and excitement. Then Anna raises her voice.

'You're all ready to go out and do this thing. You know why Susan wants to do it, but what is *your* motivation?'

There is a pause and then, one by one, they throw into the common pile their ideas.

'To see us as a group outside.'

'Every time we work in here I'm conscious of the streets outside.'

'I'd like to make it into a guerilla performance in the streets.'

'A kind of projected energy.'

'Waking people up and sparking the atmosphere.'

'I've a lot of my own energy I have to get out.'

And to top this list Anna adds, 'My motivation is curiosity – just to see what happens!'

They disgorge into the streets, ragged colourful motley band, running, leaping onto walls, racing up flights of steps, encircling cars.

'Make it beautiful!' one of them cries to a startled passerby.

Clint pretends to mow people down with his gun. 'Make love and order – bang bang bang!' he shouts, and at once a mock victim crumples to the sidewalk.

Alicia has a small box full of folded pieces of paper, on each of which she has written a different message – 'First give and then learn to receive,' 'The answer is yes, yes, yes!' 'Soon ye shall receive,' and so on. They swing round streetlamps, run into shops, sweep the sidewalks with a broom, improvise a death scene, while Mr Bo grins broadly, beating away on the big double drum strapped to his chest.

Back in the studio they lie flat, relaxing after this creative outburst. Sherwood, one of the white boys, leans against the furthest wall. The sun splashes on to his face as he leans back his head, eyes closed. His face glows, irradiated from within. The boy with the ginger beard now has his frizzed hair untied, sprung out in a halo, as he sits cross-legged, smoking. Some lean out of the window, some lie flat on the floor of the studio gazing up at the ceiling or along the line of the floor. Everyone is silent, relaxed. All are still, content. They have been allowed the freedom of children – to break constraints – yet without aggression or mischief. They are all aged nineteen to twenty, except for the permanent members of the Dancers' Workshop.

Two black guys, who had followed the procession in their car, enter. One of them, in a black sombrero, white silk shirt, embroidered waistcoat, salt-and-pepper trousers and ochre coloured leather boots, sits on the floor and says with a grin, 'What's all this bull-shit? What's this bull-shit march, man?'

Slowly the others slide forward until they are seated close round the black guy, smiling silently, hemming him in. 'I'm sort of crowded in, man! Hey, these vibrations are pretty warm, man!' There is a silence. Everyone waits patiently.

'Who was carrying the flag? Why was you carrying the flag, man?'

'He got killed for carrying the flag,' comes the answer.

'But what were you doing?'

'If you start to question you miss the point of it all,' someone murmurs.

The black guy sits like a pasha holding court. 'Everybody had their own movement,' he reflects. 'Everybody was doing their own thing, wiggling, dancing – why, man! I wanted to join in! The vibrations you guys was generating – say, could everybody just move back a little? I'm kind of crowded in here!'

The others smile and lie back.

Someone explains that it was a march.

'A march – bum! If you'd run into a thousand guys instead of only two of us, why, man, this room would be *packed!*'

'Do you think people should do that?' he questions and then answers himself. 'You were right. You had to do it. You were bound to do it. You've made it in your minds. No one's going to stop you dance in the streets, walk in the streets!'

Clint, Mr Bo and Sir Laurence Washington Jr – he is the third black member of the company – are getting restless. Mr Bo pointedly asks the time. Anna whispers to me, 'This guy is playing a game called "Dozens" – he's competing for attention, for the chicks. The other blacks resent this.'

Clint remarks, 'We're getting away from our classes.'

'What is the class?' asks the visitor. 'Could you tell me about the classes?'

Quietly he is encouraged to leave. Anna then begins to assess with the group the value of what they have done, what she calls reading the score.

'Did it go the way you wanted it to, Susan? Were the rest of you able to keep pace with Susan's score? The energy and the pace? If you had wanted to use more sound what would you have used? Did you observe how, because Alicia had something to give, this brought people into the game? And everybody felt they were getting something for nothing?'

Some of the group observe how the black community really enjoyed it, but that the white people were either disapproving or pretended it wasn't happening. Gradually Anna begins to draw their comments together.

I'd like to see these episodes on the sidewalk developed. Find specific tasks to do, a particular fantasy. Susan you could perhaps use your rope to draw people in. Then, when you've selected your specific idea you can develop it. Redefine and develop your score and next week, let's do it again. Maybe we could find some particular occasion for perfecting the score.

Now we all withdraw to the second studio which has been transformed into a jungle with huge branches of trees fastened onto scaffolding towers. The studio is dimly lit. The group splits into four animal families and the focal point is the waterhole. Gradually, as their concentration develops, they create primitive relationships, part animal, part human. One moment they are like animals grazing, then suddenly they are a crowd rioting. It turns into a man-hunt with Mr Bo as the scapegoat or sacrificial victim. With only very occasional directions Anna guides the improvisation. Slowly the violence subsides. The darkness, illuminated by pools of green and blue light, is full of chatterings, gobblings, cries, sighs, night sounds. The jungle is quiet at last. Anna opens the studio doors, letting in the daylight. Slowly she exits. The improvisation continues, each still caught up in the mood. One by one they leave the studio, crawling or sliding, continuing the improvisation out into the familiar surroundings of every day. They come down to earth gently. They gather in a circle at the head of the stairs, assessing the value of what they have done.

'What did you think of that, James?' asks Sherwood.

What Anna is doing [I reply] is very important. As people have more and more leisure time, so they are going to want to create their own theatre, their own rituals and ceremonies, to discover a form of theatre that is personally meaningful to them and that will enable them to grow as people.

In the late 1960s the Civil Rights movement in America escalated into a series of riots across the whole country. For Anna Halprin these riots were expressive of the stress and tension experienced by black people. She found herself wanting to use dance and theatre as social tools to bring about healthy changes. When she received an invitation from the director of a black arts centre in Watts to create a performance that would be given in the L.A. Mark Taper Theatre, she responded at once to this opportunity to explore the use of movement and creativity as a way of confronting and resolving the impasse of racial tension

She conducted workshops, developing an all-black dance group in Watts, and all-white group in San Francisco. After nine months the two groups were brought together to spend ten days and nights together in dance encounters before finally giving their public performance. 'We created our production', she says, 'out of the real life encounters, conflicts, prejudices, inhibitions and different life styles of the two groups. We called the work, *Ceremony of Us*! The process of creating the work was to prove as important as the performance itself. During one of the workshop sessions in Watts, one of the men, Xavier Nash, wrote, 'My experience was like this orange that I just finished eating. I was whole, peeled, separated and consumed, and now I am whole again.' Similarly, during the actual performance, another member said, 'I see my life changing in *Ceremony of Us* – thank God!' As Halprin herself has remarked, '*Ceremony of Us* changed all our lives.' In the same way, many who have worked in the theatre of Jerzy Grotowski, Eugenio Barba, Peter Brook and others would acknowledge that their lives have suffered a sea change into something rich and strange.

Sir Maurice Bowra, writing about primitive song and ritual, has observed,

> Above all, it is an art and does what art always does for those who practise it with passion and devotion. It enables them to absorb experience with their whole natures, and thereby to fulfil a want which is fully satisfied neither by action nor thought. In the end, like all true art, it enhances the desire and strengthens the capacity to live.

It is through the exercise of disciplines and skills, however simple, that people grow in an understanding of life and art. People are drawn into theatre workshops such as Anna Halprin's or into encounter groups, – the link between theatre and therapy is very close – because there is in them a hunger for something that they cannot find in their work, their church, school, college, the theatre, not even in modern family life. Especially is this so in America.

It is [as Carl Rogers comments] a hunger for relationships which are close and real; in which feelings and emotions can be spontaneously expressed without first being carefully censored or bottled up; where deep experiences – disappointments and joys – can be shared; where new ways of behaving can be risked and tried out; where an individual approaches the state where all is known and accepted; and thus further growth becomes possible.

But such groups, such companies, require a wise leader if they are not to disintegrate into an ego-stripping trip. And it is precisely here that certain artists will come to play an increasingly important new role, whether among professionals or non-professionals. 'I am coming to see the artist in another light,' says Anna Halprin, 'he is no longer a solitary hero figure, but rather a guide who works to evoke the art within us all.' Peter Brook similarly observes,

a guide who is not a charlatan is necessary if you are not to lose your way. The director does not have to become a ruthless commanding officer. He has to discover ways and means and it is through changing and learning that a group becomes self-aware. Form becomes internal . . . sharing entails discipline.

The role of the director in such a theatre group, or of a facilitator in an encounter group, is comparable to that of a shaman. During the purification ceremonies of the Canadian Eskimo shaman, the aspirant continually cries out, 'All this because I wish to become seeing!' By gaining control of his unconscious imagery the shaman brings into order his own chaotic psyche and that of the community to which he belongs. It is a process of self-healing. The songs and rituals of such a community enable it to master those emotions which might otherwise overwhelm it, enabling each individual, through histrionic means, to understand his own condition more clearly.

Although she acknowledges that she gets a great deal of joy out of being a catalyst for other people, Anna Halprin is uneasy at the suggestion that she herself has become a shaman; rather, she would argue, her task is to enable each individual to become his or her own shaman, to effect their own healing and growth.

This holistic approach has in recent years led her into an area that is almost unique within the performing arts today: the use of performance as a means of healing. As she herself has recorded, 'the healing attributes of dance came to me gradually, unexpectedly and accidentally, through a personal incident that changed my life and altered my dance perspective.'

In the winter of 1972 she was leading a workshop in which she asked each participant to draw their own individual, life-size, self-portrait. The portrait was to be impressionistic, based on a feeling response rather than a naturalistic study. Having done this, each was to use their portrait as the stimulus for creating a dance ritual. She drew her own portrait and observed that what she had drawn was a rear view of her body with an 'X' slashed right through it and, in the region of the pelvis, where the lines of the 'X' met, she had drawn a small circle, as though to say: this marks the spot. Later, in the same workshop, the group decided to draw, collectively, a group self-portrait. As her contribution Halprin drew a dark circular area in the pelvis, the size of a tennis ball. She described it to the group as an embryo to which she was trying to give birth.

The reappearance of the dark area in the group portrait left her feeling uneasy and disturbed. The next day she went to her doctor and asked him to examine her pelvic region. He did so and found a malignant tumour of the same size and shape as she had drawn. A week later she underwent surgery for the removal of the cancer and now has an irreversible colostomy.

Her illness was a turning point in her life and in her work. Since then, in her workshops, she has sought to uncover the natural patterns and movements whereby the body and mind may heal itself. The questions that she now pursues are: what relation does dance (and theatre) have to self-healing, or self destruction? What role do mental images play in the healing and creative process? 'For me,' she says, 'health is the integr-ation, balance and harmony of the physical, emotional, mental

and spiritual dimensions on a personal, social, and eviron-
mental level.'

Three years after her operation she decided to create
another life-size portrait. She chose a sympathetic environment by the sea and spent a week alone in meditation,
dancing, and doing her portrait. When it was finished she
looked at it and felt something was missing. She turned the
drawing over and did a portrait of her body seen from the
back.

> All the time I was drawing I was having internal bleeding.
> I experienced powerful reactions. I had fears of the cancer
> returning. I knew, however, that I had every opportunity
> to confront myself through my portrait and also that I
> had the support of my friends and colleagues.

She returned home, called her doctor to report the bleeding
and was asked to go for tests immediately. Instead she called
her group of friends, family and co-workers, and decided to
dance out her portrait at once.

> Dancing my self-portrait was a marvelous experience for
> me. We have evolved a ritual for approaching this dance.
> No one is permitted to rehearse or plan ahead of time.
> Instead, each person is instructed to stand in front of their
> portrait and wait until the dance within begins to move
> the person and then to follow that impulse and go with
> it, wherever the movement impulse and the feelings take
> one. I did just this. The first part – dancing my back –
> was so full of grief, violence and outrage that I was left
> weak, motionless, feeling used up, finished. Then I danced
> my front – the more hopeful – side. I felt my breath and
> imagined I was water and breath together. I imagined my
> breath was like a river that flowed through my body and
> out of it into a huge sea. My arms and legs, head and
> chest, pelvis, backbone, my hands and feet and face, my
> teeth, nose, tongue, belly, guts, all my insides, seemed to
> flow with this water breath. It began moving with ease and
> smoothness with fullness, increasing in range, turning
> me, sending me spiralling out into space, transforming my
> voice into the sound of chants. My friends and family

joined with me in the chant as if their sounds were those of the sea meeting and blending with my sounds: 'Oh sea, my river runs to thee!' Together we created a spontaneous song that nourished my spirit, that turned me, whirling, like a vortex in space. I felt at one and the same time both totally out of my body and yet deeply within it. I experienced a glorious dance for myself, with the support of the others there with me. Finally we all joined together in a circle. I felt relieved, calm, centred, and knew that I was well again.

Following that experience, she had her tests. The bleeding had stopped. There were no more problems. 'Yet I know that I am not at all finished,' Anna Halprin observes. 'I have more self-portraits to draw and to perform, more visualisations to express on my journey to wholeness.'

Over the past ten years she and her associates have helped to create dance rituals for many different situations. Sometimes they have been for a single person caught in a conflict within a relationship with himself, with a group, or with a community; at other times, as in her City Dance in 1977, when more than two thousand people were involved throughout San Francisco, commencing at 4.30 a.m. with a Fire Ceremony on the hilltops, and ending at dusk by the ocean. She has created rituals for young people moving from one school to another, involving their parents and teachers. She has created dances for four thousand elderly people at a conference on ageing – at which her ninety-four year-old father suddenly got up out of his wheelchair and danced his own affirmation of life. In former times, as she says, communities knew how to celebrate (as Peter Schumann of the Bread and Puppet Theatre says, 'We have lost the art of celebrating') and how to create rituals that would mark the movement from one stage of life to another. A Harvard theologian, Harvey Cox, has commented on the fact that our culture is starved of rituals which will enable people to come to terms with the central crises in their lives: birth, puberty, adolescence, heartbreak, death (and the many kinds of death, not just physical death) and rebirth.

Now in her sixties, the work of Anna Halprin continues and

people come from all parts of the world to join in her search for living myths and rituals.

> People today want to participate in the process of their own lives [she says]. This involves new values on how to become a more creative person in a creative community, having an entire impact on a spiritual, physical and social environment.

In the theatre of today, and most especially in the Third Theatre, an increasingly important part is being played by such shamanistic groups as the Dancers' Workshop, the Bread and Puppet Theatre, the Polish Laboratory Theatre (especially in para-theatrical work), the Odin Teatret, and many more. Such groups see theatre not as a sophisticated entertainment, nor as an intellectual pursuit, but as an experience of life itself.

> There, at the centre [writes John Wain in another context] are the artists who really form the consciousness of their time; they respond deeply, intuitively, to what is happening, what has happened, and what will happen; and their response is expressed in metaphor, in image and in fable.

Philip Toynbee, writing in his journal for 1977, says:

> Last week I reviewed John Heilpern's extraordinary book on Peter Brook's theatrical expedition through darkest Africa: *Conference of Birds*. Never having been a theatre-goer it had never occurred to me that modern theatre could, as it were, rediscover its sacred origins. I now see that audience participation has a real and important meaning; the kind of theatre, I suppose, which is furthest removed from Racine. Furthest removed, also, from Brecht's Alienation Principle, which insists that the play is never anything other than a play
>   The best moments of Brook's strange international troupe in Africa suggest a joyful, as well as a sacred, communication across deep barriers of language and culture.

26 Anna Halprin

27 The San Francisco Dancers' Workshop in a ritual created in 1970 for the Beth Sinai Temple in Oakland, USA

28 Aerial view of the Polish Laboratory Theatre's setting for *The Constant Prince* with the audience placed like voyeurs peeping down on a forbidden act

29 Cieslak, Grotowski's leading actor as the Constant Prince

15 Grotowski and the Poor Theatre

Towards the end of his autobiography, Stanislavsky says that, having tried all forms of experimentation, he has come to the conclusion that,

> for the actor, all these things mean nothing and do not create an inner, active, dramatic art. There is no art that does not demand virtuosity. But, alas, I cannot find for him a true scenic background which would not interfere with, but would help his complex spiritual work. If there is not born a very great painter who will give the most difficult of sets a simple but artistic background for the actor, the true actor can only dream of a simple board stage on which he could come out like a singer or a musician and interpret with his unaided inner and outer qualities, his art and technique, the beautiful and artistic life of the human spirit which he portrays.

That was in 1924 and already there had been Copeau and the Vieux-Colombier. Then, in 1933, the same year that Piscator, Brecht, and Reinhardt left Germany, and the Bauhaus School in Berlin was closed by two hundred police, and Tyrone Guthrie took over the Old Vic Theatre in London, there was born, on 11 August, in Rzeszow in south-east Poland, Jerzy Grotowski, who was to become the most fertile source of new ideas and one of the most powerful influences on world theatre in the twentieth century.

> Grotowski is unique [wrote Peter Brook in his introduction to the English translation of Grotowski's *Towards a Poor Theatre*]. Why? Because no one else in the world, to my

knowledge, no one since Stanislavsky, has investigated the nature of acting, its phenomenon, its meaning, the nature and science of its mental, physical, emotional process as deeply and completely as Grotowski.

When he was sixteen, Grotowski fell gravely ill and for a year lay in a hospital for terminal patients. The experience was to transform his life. In 1951 he commenced training as an actor and went to Moscow to study the Stanislavsky System under the actor, Zavadsky. In 1956, after a journey to Asia, he returned to direct productions at the Stary Theatre in Kraków. Three years later he became director of Teatr 13 Rzedow, in Opole, and committed to experiment. In 1965, when he and his actors moved to Wroclaw, the Laboratory Theatre became officially an Institute for Theatre Research, each production being a working model of current research. From the start the work was uniquely subsidized, albeit modestly, by the government. Grotowski's closest collaborators have been Ludwik Flazen, the theatre's literary adviser, and Ryszard Cieslak, considered by many to be the most outstanding actor in the world, whose performance in *The Constant Prince* most completely exemplified Grotowski's methods.

Working in a small room in Opole, with audiences intentionally limited to forty people, Grotowski seemed, at first, to be fashioning a theatre of exclusivity. Then, in 1966, at the Théâtre des Nations in Paris, *The Constant Prince* was unveiled and although seen only by a few people, because of Grotowski's insistence on limiting the audience, he became world-famous. His work in Wroclaw has since become legendary and has been used as a source of ideas by Peter Brook, André Gregory, Joseph Chaikin and many more. It was Brook who persuaded the Royal Shakespeare Company to invite Grotowski to work with the company. What result did the work have? asks Brook.

It gave each actor a series of shocks. The shock of confronting himself in the face of simple irrefutable challenges. The shock of catching sight of his own evasions, tricks and clichés. The shock of sensing something of his own vast and untapped resources. The shock of being forced to question why he is an actor at all. The shock of being

forced to recognise that such questions do exist and that –
despite a long English tradition of avoiding seriousness
in theatrical art – the time comes when they must be faced.
And of finding that he wants to face them. The shock of
seeing that somewhere in the world acting is an art of
absolute dedication, monastic and total.

Grotowski set out to ask one question only: What is theatre?
In his search for an answer he found that while theatre could
exist without make-up, costume, décor, a stage even, lighting,
sound effects, it could not exist without the relationship of
actor and spectator. This essential act, this encounter between
two groups of people, he called Poor Theatre.

In his writings and in his public lectures – which are capable
of going on all day or all night in Slavonic tradition – Grotowski's style is oracular, allusive, elusive, often difficult of access,
yet lit at times by such flashes of lightning as illuminate an
entire new landscape. No one, since Stanislavsky, has written
of the actor's craft and vocation with such authority, insight
and vision.

For Grotowski, the actor is a high priest who creates the
dramatic liturgy and, at the same time, guides the audience
into the experience. Here, then, is a new element in the
theatre: a psychological tension between actor and audience.
For Grotowski the purpose of theatre, indeed, of all art, is 'to
cross our frontiers, exceed our limitations, fill our emptiness
– fulfill ourselves.' To this end the actor must learn to use his
role as if it were a surgeon's scalpel to dissect himself. 'The
important thing is to use the role as a trampoline, an instrument with which to study what is hidden behind our day mask
– the innermost core of personality – in order to sacrifice it,
expose it.' The spectator, says Grotowski, understands, consciously or unconsciously, that such an act is an invitation to
him to do the same thing. This often arouses opposition or
indignation because our daily efforts are intended to hide the
truth about ourselves not only from the world but from
ourselves.

If Brecht was concerned to make the spectator think,
Grotowski's aim is to disturb him on a very deep level. As

Robert Horan says of Martha Graham, in *Chronicles of the American Dance,*

> If her audiences are sometimes distraught at the imagery of *Dark Meadow* it is because they are so ill-prepared to face the psychological reality which is the basis of her art. It is rather like lighting an enormous bonfire in the middle of an ice-house in which everyone is comfortably frozen. To their distress, the subject of Graham's dances is not dancing.

Grotowski is not concerned with taking the spectator out of himself, in the escapist manner of the naturalistic or romantic theatre, but with taking him deeply into himself. His concern is with the spectator who has genuine spiritual needs and who really wishes, through confrontation with the performance, to analyse himself. If this implies a theatre for the élite, the answer is – yes. Grotowski insists that this be made clear from the start. 'We are not concerned with just any audience but a special one.'

It is his preoccupation with the role of the spectator in theatre that has led him to explore the nature of scenic space, creating a form of staging for each production that would test different aspects of the relationship between actor and spectator. In *Kordian* the action was set in a psychiatric ward. The entire space was filled up with beds so that the spectators found themselves having to sit among the sick. In *Dr Faustus* the spectators found that they were, along with the actors, guests at Dr Faustus's table in the monks' refectory. At the other extreme, however, in *Akropolis*, there was no discernible arrangement of the scenic space, only an attitude on the part of the actors towards the audience – or rather, a non-attitude. These inhabitants of Auschwitz, on their way to the gas chamber, were so deep in their misery, that they did not even see the audience. Already they belonged to the dead. The living spectator had nothing to offer them.

Grotowski's way of working, in the first ten years of Laboratory Theatre, was to take a myth or a situation that had been sanctified by tradition and so become taboo. This the actors would then proceed to attack, blaspheme, confront, in order to relate it to their own experience of life which, in turn, is itself determined by the collective experience of our time – in the case of Grotowski's actors, to the tragic history of Poland, especially in this century. So, in similar manner, did Martha Graham confront the myths of ancient Greece in order to relate their archetypal images to our own comtemporary experience.

In *Akropolis*, Grotowski took a play by one of Poland's outstanding playwrights, Wyspianski (first produced in Poland in 1904) and related it to the experiences of Poland during the Second World War. The original play is set in Kraków Cathedral on the eve of Easter Sunday. The statues and paintings in the cathedral come to life and re-enact various biblical and Homeric themes. Grotowski moved the action to Auschwitz in order to test how far the classical idea of human dignity can withstand our latest insight into human degradation.

The production was set on a large rectangular stage set in the centre of the audience. The platform was piled high with scrap metal. A ragged violinist summoned the rest of the cast who hobbled on in sacks and wooden clogs. The action of the play took the form of daydreams in the breaks between work. The seven actors attacked the mound of rusting metal, hammering in unison, and fixing twisted pipes to struts above the audience. The audience, however, were not involved.

At the end of *Akropolis* there is an ecstatic procession following an image of the Saviour (a headless corpse) into a paradise – which is also the extermination chamber. Irving Wardle, reviewing the production for the Edinburgh Festival in 1968, described it thus,

> What is conveyed is an intensely private sense of what it feels like to be at breaking point. The faces are drawn into rigid masks with eyes that seem to have forgotten sleep; the bodies, held mechanically at attention, seem to have passed the limits of endurance. I can think of few more potent images in the modern theatre than that of Jacob's wedding procession with his scrap-heap bride, and the final singing descent into the ovens. At such moments, even to a foreign spectator, Grotowski seems rather to be creating myth than exploiting it.

Grotowski's actors do not use furniture and props naturalistically, but with the imaginative spontaneity of a child and the sophistication of a disciplined artist. For them the floor becomes the sea, a table becomes a boat, the bars of a chair become a prison cell and yet what they are trying to do is light years away from the miming on a bare stage of Copeau's young actors. For Grotowski, the floor becomes the sea not to advance the narrative, as in the Oriental theatre, but as part of an interior drama. For Grotowski is concerned to expose the spiritual process of the actor. By means of years of training, of daily exercises, and a rigorous physical technique and vocal expressiveness, he brings the actor to such a point of heightened awareness that, as in a trance, he is enabled to be wide open in performance. 'It is', says Grotowski, 'a question of giving oneself. One must give totally in one's deepest intimacy, with confidence, as when one gives oneself in love.' But such a sacrifice on the part of the actor is not the uninhibited abandonment which may be observed in many groups influenced by, but only partly understanding, Grotowski. Grotowski lays great stress upon discipline, technique and training – as also do Peter Brook and Eugenio Barba.

> The actor who accomplishes an act of self-penetration [says Grotowski] is setting out on a journey which is recorded through various sound and gesture reflexes, formulating a sort of invitation to the spectator. But these signs must be articulated. Undisciplined self-penetration is no liberation. We believe that a personal process which is not supported and expressed by a formal articulation and disciplined structuring of the role is not a release and will collapse into shapelessness.

One recalls Stanislavsky's realization that for the new art, new actors and new techniques would be necessary.

> The actor [continues Grotowski] must be able to express, through sound and through movement, those impulses which waver on the borderline between dream and reality. In short, he must be able to construct his own psycho-analytic language of sounds and gestures in the same way that a great poet creates his own language of words.

Grotowski always acknowledges his debt to others: to Dullin, Delsarte, Stanislavsky, Meyerhold, Vakhtangov, the

Kathakali dance, the Japanese and Chinese theatre, and many more. Each has helped him to evolve his own method.

When we confront the general tradition of the Great Reform of the theatre from Stanislavsky to Dullin, and from Meyerhold to Artaud, we realize that we have not started from scratch, but are operating in a defined and special atmosphere. When our investigation reveals and confirms someone else's flash of intuition, we are filled with humility. We realise that theatre has certain objective laws and that fulfilment is possible only within them or, as Thomas Mann said, through a kind of 'higher obedience' to which we give our dignified attention.

16 Grotowski and the Journey to the East

In the name of audience participation in the 1960s, audiences were insulted, sexually groped, manhandled, locked out of the place of performance and kept waiting for an hour or longer, divested of their shoes or other clothing, even thrust on stage during the last act of *Hamlet* (in Central Park, New York) and invited to shoot the King and thus affect the play's direction; yet always the spectator knew that he was being manipulated; he was not genuinely being invited to take part, only to dance to the tune of the actors. With each of his productions for the Polish Laboratory Theatre, Grotowski had systematically explored the relationship of the actor and the spectator by his use of the scenic space. In *Apocalypsis cum Figuris*, he abandoned all attempts to organize the space. Actors and audience, together, without pretence, on equal footing, entered the large empty room that was the playing area. The scenic space in this production was allowed to be fluid, dictated by the movements of spectators and actors. Towards the end there is a scene in which the Simpleton, nearing the end of his torment, gazes around in mute appeal at the faces of the audience. Yet there is nothing that any spectator can do to reach out and assist this silent call for help from a fellow human being in distress. It was this final realization of the ultimate passivity of the spectator in the traditional performance situation that led Grotowski to announce, in the early 1970s, that he and his actors would no longer perform plays, but that their future research would concern itself with the creativity of the spectator rather than that of the actor.

Grotowski, like Brook, is in the business of research; it is his task to ask questions, to experiment. He is not denying

past and present achievements of theatre in other forms. Essentially the participation of a spectator is an interior activity; the spectator responds empathetically to what is happening and, at certain moments of heightened awareness, as Brook says, he is capable of being changed for life.

The book, *Towards a Poor Theatre*, is a logbook of a certain period [says Grotowski]. Reading it carefully you will notice the reflections of different phases which occasionally contradict each other. The Grotowski system has never existed; it is just an abstraction of the learned, drawn from different phases. The book reflects a certain road. I am not saying that it did well or badly, just that it's already a long way off. *The road is a matter of moving forward.* At certain moments people will applaud you. If you stay, perhaps the applause will get louder. But life will be ruined. One must continue. Life is a single task to achieve. Being applauded is pleasant but not essential; it can be useful and give possibilities. But one must not let one's self be imprisoned by the fact of being accepted. Now I have abandoned certain forms of culture where the spectator is passive and the place fixed.

In 1976, at the Théâtre des Nations in Belgrade, he developed his ideas further.

At present my colleagues and I no longer put on shows but we foster, in large or limited groups, certain kinds of process which may last several days in different places, and with people of different backgrounds, but who have, nonetheless, something to share. The details of the action are different each time, depending on those taking part, and who are the actual source of the material that they will live through.

When asked whether these processes can be called theatre, he replied,

All the elements of a certain type of theatre are present: contacts, impulses, movements, improvisations, sounds, music, space. There is also an aspiration to go beyond the mode of communication used in everyday life. But we are

not seeking to create characters as in a play. We are
ourselves. Is this theatre? Or is it something else?

Like Anna Halprin and others, Grotowski and his colleagues
have become increasingly concerned with the creativity of
ordinary people. He has called this work para-theatrical. It
means, in practice, the isolation of a chosen group of people
in a remote place, in an attempt to create a genuine encounter
between individuals who meet, at first, as complete strangers
and then, gradually, as they lose their fear and distrust of
each other, move towards a fundamental encounter in which
they themselves are the active and creative participants in
their own drama of rituals and ceremonials. Grotowski's
concern is to take theatre away from the realm of aesthetics,
critics, box office, the division of actors and spectators, and to
restore to those who seek it a sense of drama and ritual in
their own lives. The Theatre of Sources, as Grotowski terms
it, is aimed at 'bringing us back to the sources of life, to direct
primeval experience, to organic primary experience.'

At first only small groups of people were selected for these
ventures into para-theatre. Much of the approach was similar
in spirit to the experiments of Gurdjieff at Fontainebleau, or
of Roy Hart in London.

For the first few days [wrote one participant] we do
household work. We do not talk about what is to happen.
Habits brought from the city slowly die out. We immerse
ourselves in the rhythm of a different life. Gradually we
become sensitive to each other. The work here is hard. We
dig, grub up stumps of trees, chop wood, carry coal and
stones. We build a large hut that will be our home.

In one of the earliest sessions a group spent two months in
the country building a barn, in which they were eventually to
work. When the structure was completed, Grotowski told them
that all of the objectives that were to have been achieved in
the performances planned for the barn had been accomplished
in its building, and so the group was disbanded.

Gradually the number of those taking part in the para-
theatre workshops was increased until in June 1975, at the
Théâtre des Nations, held that year in Warsaw, the workshops

were opened to everyone. In all some four to five thousand people took part. Appearing at the festival were also Eugenio Barba, Grotowski's disciple, Peter Brook, André Gregory of the Manhattan Theatre Project, Joseph Chaikin of the Open Theatre, and many other key figures in experimental theatre. At one of the public seminars Chaikin said,

> The Polish Laboratory Theatre, to my mind, is passing through an exceptionally creative period. It will enable us to renew our thoughts about theatre, will transform it. Perhaps we shall not be able to call the result 'Theatre'. Theatre today is boring. There is something static, lifeless, about it. This is felt by people who, in the past, enjoyed it. And I genuinely feel that Grotowski is one of the people who in theatre has gone further than any of us. And in that sense he has influenced those who work in the theatre and those who go to it.

André Gregory also observed, 'It is evident that barriers are disappearing between those who are the audience and those who are the artists. It is a development of something at which some of us have worked for the past seven years.'

For Grotowski the concern now is how to bring out the vitality inherent in each person and in this way to enrich their lives so that they may become a source of strength to them. Only in this way, he argues, is a new culture and a new theatre possible. Even in those situations where individuals want to understand each other and live as fully as possible, our culture offers few routes, while in the main the churches have failed to understand the spiritual needs of today. At the same time, however, there are those who question whether para-theatrical work can fill the void. Is there not a real danger, they say, that Grotowski and his colleagues are entering a spiritual region for which he and they may not be equipped? The danger lies, I think, less with Grotowski than with his imitators.

Under the general title, *Holiday*, Grotowski instituted three phases to the para-theatre workshops: *Night-Vigil*, *The Way*, and *Mountain Flame*. The *Night Vigil*, was used as a preliminary means of testing participants for the journey ahead. Jennifer Kumiega has described how it can be seen as an awakening – 'the awakened are recognised and the sleepers, untouched, sleep on.' *The Way* involved a far greater depth of commitment from those taking part. Participants were taken by truck to an unknown destination in the depths of the countryside and there left to make their way on foot.

At this stage, no one knew how long the journey would take or had certain prior knowledge of what to expect. In the event, the Way involved at least one night spent in the forest, regardless of weather, and the possibility of para-theatrical work sessions in the countryside, in addition to the journey itself.

The entire process could take up to forty-eight hours and was very demanding physically and emotionally. Sometime toward the end of the second day, the participants would become aware of the Mountain on the horizon.

The Mountain of Flame lies to the north-east of Wrocaw. Deeply wooded, it is surmounted by an ancient castle. The mountain and the surrounding countryside is the property of the Laboratory Theatre, for their para-theatrical projects. 'The Mountain is something we aim towards, something which demands effort and determination. The Mountain is a kind of test. It is also a real mountain'.

Since a fundamental requirement of the work is security, the need to provide an environment which is not open to the general public and where each person taking part may feel absolutely free is crucial. 'But there is also', remarks Grotowski, 'an urgent need to have a place where we do not hide ourselves and simply are, as we are, in all possible senses of the word.'

Much of Grotowski's para-theatrical work needs to be seen in the perspective of work already pioneered by Anna Halprin and others (not forgetting Robert Wilson's seven-day-long Mountain Project in Shiraz), as well as in the rich tradition of religious festivals that have been going on in Poland for the past four hundred years. These annual festivals attract people from hundreds of miles away and many people journey to them on foot. Some of the celebrations last for as long as a week, and two of them take place on a mountain. One of these, the Transfiguration of Christ, takes place literally on a sacred mountain. At another, the Celebration of the Sufferings of the Lord, which is attended annually by some fifty thousand people, the major events of Holy Week are re-enacted not on a stage, but before a series of twenty-four chapels spread out over a distance of six miles. The events are not compressed into a few hours, but continue for a week. Here, surely, we find the origin of Grotowski's *Mountain Project* and *The Way*. In these religious dramas the central roles are played each year by the same individuals (corresponding to Grotowski's guides), while everyone else participates in, and becomes caught up in, a living drama, enduring the elemental conditions of rain, mud, thunderstorms, high winds, and sleepless nights. It is not surprising, therefore, that in recent years those with an interest in avant-garde have been especially attracted to these festivals, as Marjorie S. Young says in her introduction to *Journeys to Glory*, 'for here they find a drama in which there is virtually no barrier between actor and spectator, an experience which truly engages the audience.'

The out-pouring of art from Poland, and the richness of its theatre with such key figures as Tadeusz Kantor, Josef Szajna, Henryk Tomaszewski (the founder of the Polish Pantomime theatre), Bohdan Gluszczak, and many more, stem from a histrionic genius in the national character. A deeply emotional people, they have retained a close access to their emotions as well as to a rich and varied expression of them. It is not surprising that Karol Wojtyla, when Bishop of Kraków, now Pope John Paul II, improvised many rituals, gatherings, and pilgrimages up into the mountains, nor that in his early years he wanted to be an actor.

The spiritual, archetypal dimension of Grotowski's para-theatrical work meets not only a deep need in many who take part, but is unmistakably Polish in its outward manifestations. Ronald Grimes, in *New Directions in Performing Arts*, has described the experience at length in a meditation upon Grotowski as Pilgrim.

A pilgrimage is a person in motion, a person whose action originates in the deep roots of his own physical, cultural, and spiritual home; who then proceeds to a faraway place – often a mountain – in search of a shared adventure; and who descends finally to a new or re-newed home-space. In short, he is en route to his roots. Though a pilgrim is an ordinary person, he is proceeding through extra-ordinary space – he is in para-ordinary space. Grotowski calls his space para-theatrical. It is para-religious as well. Yet para-ordinary does not mean supernatural. It means very ordinary, very natural, authentically simple and direct.

As the story-teller in Herman Hesse's *Journey to the East* remarks, 'It was my destiny to join in a great experience. Having had the good fortune to belong to the League, I was permitted to be a participant in an unique journey.'

Some people, says Grotowski, define theatre by the existence of a room, a stage, spectators and actors.

> For a long time I have been wary of this definition which is perhaps acceptable if one makes theatre simply as a means of earning money or winning glory, but completely inadequate if you consider life as a land to be crossed once only and fully.

When asked about his own personal role in the para-theatrical groups, Grotowski answers,

> I like being close to people, crossing the frontier at the risk of not knowing how to return. Some people need to stop, others want to go past the limits of effort and fatigue. I don't like to say I control; let's say I analyse, though it's hard to say. One of our experiments consists of crossing a barrier of fire. Someone goes through, then calls another by name, 'Jump through the fire!' and the other person crosses the flame. That might seem banal. But why doesn't the one who is called go round the obstacle? Something invisible intervenes here, something which has passed between the two people before, that makes a person jump through the fire, even if he has never done it before in his life, even if he's never run a risk without controlling himself. The goal to be reached demands the passing of the limits of fatigue, being stronger than one's own strength.

In Herman Hesse's novel, *Steppenwolf* the hero visits a

Magic Theatre and the notice outside reads, 'Anarchistic Evening Entertainment – entrance not for everybody!' The owner of the theatre says to the hero, 'It is the world of your own soul you seek. Only within yourself exists that other reality for which you long. I can give you nothing that has not already its being within yourself.'

Similarly Grotowski and his colleagues recognize that their kind of theatre is not for everyone. As Grotowski himself has acknowledged. 'Poor Theatre is only one possibility among many. It is not meant for everyone. I am not making myself an apostle. I'm simply looking for people who have the same needs as myself.'

Grotowski recognizes that there will always be a need for professional performers and their particular skills and gifts, although his own energies are now directed towards a non-professional form of theatre. By putting people in touch with their elemental and archetypal roots, it is possible that a new kind of theatre, a new kind of art, may be born, one more appropriate to the age of Aquarius, into which we are now moving, than the lingering nineteenth-century literary theatre with its bourgeois trappings of box offices, bars, programmes, intermissions, critics and serried ranks of seats.

Just as the purpose of education is not merely to increase the quantity of knowledge and information, important though this may be, but to deepen and enrich the quality of life itself, so, too, in the arts, the aim must be to bring man into communion with those mysterious sources of vitality and meaning that lie within him. Teilhard de Chardin, in *The Future of Man*, writes,

> We need to remind ourselves yet again, so as to off-set this truly pagan materialism and naturalism, that although the laws of bio-genesis by their nature presuppose, and in fact bring about an improvement in human living conditions, it is not *well-being* but hunger for *more-being* which, of psychological necessity can alone preserve the thinking earth from the tedium of life.

This relationship of art to life is of increasing importance as society moves into a shorter working week and a shorter working life, so that the question of what people will do with their greatly increased leisure time becomes one of the most urgent sociological, psychological and spiritual problems of our day. The majority of people possess, no matter how unused, real creative and imaginative faculties, so that the question is less one of educating people to appreciate the fine arts than of providing facilities and environments in which they can be and are actively encouraged to use their creative faculties. Sir Maurice Bowra, speaking of the origins of primitive art, observed,

> Such arts are indispensable to those who practise them. Because they give order and harmony to their sudden over-mastering emotions and their tumbling, jostling thoughts, because they are so inextricably a part of their lives, it gives them a solid centre in what otherwise would be almost chaos.

So, today, the individual needs to re-discover once again how to give form to his most urgent feelings, so that he may the better understand himself and others: through gesture, through movement, through colour, rhythm, music, ritual and ceremonial; in his living, in his loving, in his dying; in his creation of a home, a garden or a relationship, as well as in a work of craft or art. We have to learn how to respond directly and truly to our deepest impulses and to give them form and rhythm; like the youth Tito who, at the close of Herman Hesse's *The Glass Bead Game*, quite unself-consciously, as though he were a participant in one of Grotowski's para-theatrical workshops, begins to dance on the mountain top as the sun rises. 'Without knowing what he was doing, asking no questions, he obeyed the command of the ecstatic moment, danced his worship, prayed to the sun, professed with devout movements and gestures his joy, his faith in life.'

Richard Mennen has described some of his experiences during 1975.

> I'll describe yesterday's trip to the woods: I was apprehensive, not knowing what to expect, or if I would be able to do it . . . for the next hour, two, three, I have no idea, we walked and ran through the woods, and waded through the streams, ran through the fields with chest-

high grass under a full moon. At one point my feet, which were very sore from stepping on rocks, sticks, etc. were beginning to refuse to move – they were baulking at the pain. I knew if I gave in to my feet that soon I would be crawling. So I didn't, and at one point ran even though I couldn't see. Still I was the last one to reach the bonfire in the middle of this semi-marsh. The fire and all the dancing figures in the wilderness and the sounds echoing in the night.

Felt like I was going to vomit, probably the sun, and couldn't sleep well. Also suddenly had these irrational feelings of panic about what I had just been through. Got scared about it. By the end, I felt a profound connection with the natural world, and that I had begun to search in a very physical way for roots and sources. One of the most memorable moments was when I found myself digging with my hands into the loose earth of a recently ploughed field full of roots and asking the roots who I was. I wrote in my journal:

As I dug deeper into the earth, my whole arm in it and the roots, I felt in my body, with each thrust, something strong, hidden, like birth, like sex, like death; frightening and necessary. I do not know what it was, but it was something. It was also like a source.

The literalness of the metaphor is almost appalling, yet clearly it was not a metaphor for me. It was an action to which I was committed and thus went beyond aesthetic naïveté and became a simple act with reverberations in my organism. It is clearer to me now that I was only at the beginning of a process of exploration that had a vitality and reality born out of the special context. My normal patterns of behaviour were disrupted and my actions bound up with something bigger than my ego. Furthermore, I was not alone.

The work of the Laboratory seems an attempt to provide a context, a spring-board, launching pad, whatever, from which to enter into a relation with the elemental primitive connections between a man and his body, man and his imagination, man and the natural world, man and another man.

A psychiatrist who took part in one of the workshops observed,

> I would like to meet such people all the time, people who
> have been awakened, who are wide open to receive reality.
> People who participate in the drama of life, their own and
> that of other people. It seems to me that this work turns
> passive participants, through action, into actors of their
> fate. It seems to me that this is one of the forms of theatre
> of the future. What matters is to bring out the vitality
> inherent in every man, and once it has been brought out,
> to enrich life itself so that it can become again the source
> of strength for culture and for the theatre.

For Grotowski, at last, the wall is down.

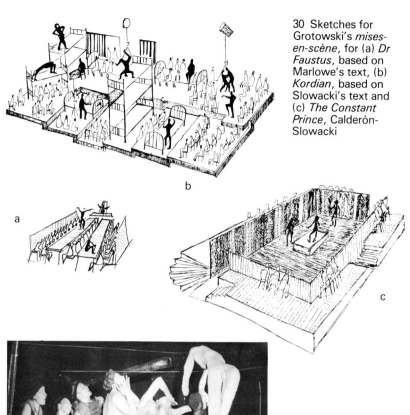

30 Sketches for Grotowski's *mises-en-scène*, for (a) *Dr Faustus*, based on Marlowe's text, (b) *Kordian*, based on Slowacki's text and (c) *The Constant Prince*, Calderón-Slowacki

b

a

c

31 The final procession from the Polish Laboratory Theatre's production of *Acropolis*

32 Peter Brook and Jerzy Grotowski

34 *Min Fars Hus* (My Father's House)

33 *Min Fars Hus* (My Father's House), a theatre work
created by Eugenio Barba and the Odin Teatret

17 Eugenio Barba and the Third Theatre

It is March 1979 in Holstebro, on the far side of Denmark. It is bleak, cold, remote – seas and rivers frozen. On the outskirts of the small town there is a compound of huts and old army buildings. Here a company of actors, Danish, Norwegian, Spanish, Italian, American, English, live and work. They are the Odin Teatret, founded by Eugenio Barba. Their day begins at seven in the morning and continues for ten or twelve hours of training, rehearsal, and daily chores.

In their larger studio they are rehearsing a new work based on the life and writings of Bertold Brecht. It has been in rehearsal for many months and it may be years before it sees the light of public performance. Again, it might not ever be performed publicly. It might be discarded as being merely a stage in the evolution of the company.

The last work that they created in this way, *Min Fars Hus* (My Father's House), revolved around the life and works of Dostoevsky, sieved through the filter of the actors' own truths, experiences and longings. This encounter, in the Grotowski sense of that word, this confrontation between the actors of Odin and Dostoevsky took three years to create and was the most personal, the most autobiographical of their productions, and the one that proved to have the deepest impact upon audiences.

> How I wish I dared to show my face as you do [wrote one spectator]. I am ashamed, safe only perhaps when I am alone. What I loved is what you did with us. For us. I should love to have asked you if you are happy or if you

suffer when you play. To me it seems that I would be happy.

Another spectator wrote, 'Later, during supper, my mother (who had not read anything about you or your work) said, "One can't say what one has experienced, one would discover too much." The hundreds of letters received, and the photographs of this production convey vividly that immediacy and vulnerability in performance about which Grotowski has spoken, which is the goal of Peter Brook and which is the essence of what Eugenio Barba calls the 'Third Theatre'.

The Odin Teatret was founded in 1964 by Barba, who had spent three years studying with Grotowski in Poland. On his return to Norway he began to work with a group of young people who, like him, wanted to create theatre but found the doors of traditional theatres closed against them. Two years later, the Odin Teatret was invited by the civic dignitaries at Holstebro to set up a theatre research centre on the lines of the Polish Laboratory Theatre. In 1968, the Odin published Grotowski's *Towards a Poor Theatre*, edited by Barba, a book that was to exercise a profound influence on theatre everywhere.

Of Barba's original group two came with him to Holstebro, Torgeir Wethal and Else Marie Lauvik. It is the latter who plays Mother Courage in the new work. The rehearsal that I observed took about an hour but seemed much longer because of the concentration of energy and the intricate orchestration of images. The action covers the entire length of the studio, with benches for spectators ranged on either side. Various scenes occur simultaneously in different parts of the space. Central images occur, claim one's attention, then recede, yet continue in the background while new images come into focus. But always, wherever and whenever one looks, each actor is totally present in his or her activity. At my side, a calor gas stove hisses, and an actress in a chef's hat is busy frying onions and making an omelette – the chopping of the onions, the cooking and serving being woven dramatically into the action.

One of the most searing images concerns Mother Courage and her daughter. The daughter, mocked by the rest, climbs to the top of the travelling booth. In each hand she holds one half of a pair of shears; these she brings together in loud clamorous chimes, like the booming of cathedral bells, silencing the laughter of the other actors below. But now she suffers a fresh assault. She is dragged down from the booth by a young soldier who thrusts her to the ground, pulling her skirt over her head. She lies with the material clenched between her teeth, so as not to scream. The actor playing the soldier brings a bowl of water and places it between her thighs, close up to her crutch. He throws himself down and begins sucking at the water noisily. The mother sits by her booth, watching. Later, at the moment of the girl's execution, while another soldier sits reading a girlie magazine, the Cook, who has been watching with absorption, drops a plate which smashes to pieces. The Cook murmurs a soft apology and hands the cooked omelette to the executioner who scoops it into his mouth with the same loud sucking noises as those of the recent sexual assault.

Only occasionally does Barba rise to intervene, quietly discussing a point with the actors. In the main he sits cross-legged, rolling his own cigarettes and smoking continuously. A dark-skinned, curly-haired, vivacious Italian, with a boyish grin and easy charm, but with the shadows of strain under his eyes, it is his energy and talent that constitute a major part of the life of the Odin community. He lives in a converted farmhouse outside the town, on the edge of a river, with his English wife and their two children. Over dinner he talks about the way in which he sees theatre developing. The commercial and subsidized theatre, which he calls the First Theatre, he describes as blooming but deadly. The Second Theatre is the established avant-garde which has abandoned the actor for the director. He cites directors like Robert Wilson and Victor Garcia who are only interested in actors as puppets to be manipulated in their displays of directorial virtuosity.

The Third Theatre he describes as that which confronts an audience with messages of an inner life. These messages are intuited by the spectator at a deeper level of knowing than that of the rational mind. It is a form of theatre that came fully into being with Grotowski, whose disciple Barba is.

If anyone exists whom I can call my master, my teacher

[he says], it is Grotowski. He taught me my craft. His fundamental theories, his work process and his professional consciousness are still a challenge to me. You are a disciple as long as you recognise that your teacher has still something to give you, inciting you to further and personal growth. In this sense I am still Grotowski's disciple and will be so for a long time.

Such a form of theatre speaks directly to the fundamental experience of each person present, to what Jung described as the collective unconscious. It is a theatre of symbols. It will be argued, rightly, that many great dramatists also deal with symbols, from Ibsen to Shakespeare. But what Grotowski and Barba ask of the actor is not that he play the Lady from the Sea or Hamlet, but that he confront these characters within himself and offer the result of that encounter to an audience. Grotowski would have the actor be his own creator and not the servant of the dramatist. In the same way, Martha Graham staged not the story line of the great Greek myths, but her own, deeply personal, autobiographical confrontations with the Ariadne, Jocasta, Phaedra, within herself. The theatre of Martha Graham was forged out of her own conflicts as a human being. 'When I have a problem', she would say, 'I go into the studio, lock the doors and dance my way through it. That is how the works are born.'

The process of Graham's great rituals of theatre can be traced in her remarkable *Notebooks*, and it is a process very similar to that employed by those who belong to the Third Theatre. But with a difference. Martha Graham was her own creator, evolving and teaching a technique that could embody her own unique visions. In the Third Theatre, groups such as the Odin, Brook's company in Paris, the Performance Group in New York, and many more, create their works collectively. The Third Theatre means a collective theatre. Not surprisingly, the process of creation is a very long and arduous one, often taking years to create one work. John Heilpern, writing in the *Observer* on 11 May 1980, observed,

Peter Brook's production of *The Conference of Birds*, which has just opened in New York to rave reviews, was among the first experiments attempted by Brook when he formed his International Centre of Theatre Research in Paris ten years ago. In a sense then, the production of this Sufi fable has taken ten years to complete – but it has been worth waiting for. *The Conference of Birds* brings to the boil – and makes marvellously clear – much of what Brook has been trying to capture over the years.

For the Third Theatre the question is: how can the organic actor (the actor who must create his own material) be his own matrix and, at the same time, shape the results into objective signs whose origin is his own subjectivity? For this is the essence of the new art and the new craft of the actor-creator. For this new actor of the Third Theatre there are, as yet, few signposts. Each group is compelled to carry out its own research. It is an heroic task and Barba says that only those driven by an indomitable need to create will be able to overcome the inertia that is satisfied with superficial results.

Our profession [he says] gives us the possibility of changing ourselves and thereby of changing society. I don't mean that we think of saving society through the theatre. We have no pretentions about unmasking other people. What we are interested in is unmasking ourselves. In our work there are key themes that strike us as vital. You might call them wounds or obsessions that we keep digging into. That's what gives a work of art, and the works that follow it, their original vital coherence. It is obvious that the questions we try to shed a light on strike an echo and a note of kinship in certain people, but not in everybody. The best we can do is to analyse our own personal brand of truth and stage a confrontation between the truth and our own experience. And this sort of confrontation involves change. In our selves.

Many will question whether an actor, or a group of actors, can, in fact, change society. Piscator failed to prevent the rise of Hitler and the Third Reich. People cannot be changed on an intellectual or cerebral level; yet an appeal to the emotions, as Brecht also knew, is not the answer. Theatre-goers are often moved by an actor's performance in a certain role and will compare one performance with another. But no one's life is changed. Deep-rooted attitudes and prejudices remain deep-rooted. So what is it that individuals like Brook, Barba, Grotowski and others are talking about? What is it that each is in search of?

It is that moment when the actor, both as a person and as a performer – the two are inseparable in this form of theatre – encounter the spectator.

> I don't think theatre is to do with communication [observed Peter Brook in a television interview on the BBC], that's journalism. When theatre is true, there is an actual 'moment of truth', and when that happens there is a change of perception. Every one of us, most of the time, is blind to reality; but when life, or some aspect of life, is perceived more intensely, then there is real food for the soul. I personally have need of this. When it happens in theatre, the outward silence of concentration is transformed into a living silence; there is a miraculous moment of grace in the theatre. And when that happens, there is a change of perception and what is received is for life. In the theatre there is a special possibility, for a short time, of seeing life more clearly. Which is why a pallid, an effete audience, is less likely to be the soil out of which this will happen.

Eugenio Barba would maintain that this kind of encounter between actor and spectator is most likely to take place in an intimate gathering of people, which is why the Third Theatre almost always insists on small audiences. What is experienced by forty or eighty people in a small space cannot be extended to eight hundred in a large auditorium. Some critics have said that this makes for a theatre of exclusivity, a theatre for a minority. The answer of such groups is perhaps best expressed by Mother Teresa of Calcutta who, when challenged about how few people she is actually able to help, always answers with a smile, 'I do what I can!' It is not the task of the Odin Teatret or of the Polish Laboratory Theatre, or of the Waseda Little Theatre in Tokyo, or any other group from the Third Theatre (and there are hundreds of them) to play before a large audience in an attempt to open up their work, like a commodity, to the largest number of buyers. They play to and for those who ask to meet them: Brook's actors, like those of Barba, will often give an unscheduled performance for a handful of people. They do what they can, and encourage other groups to follow their example; to fashion their own forms of theatre for their own communities. In the interests of research it may happen in time that they will begin to play for larger audiences but, if that should happen, it will not be within the confines of a conventional proscenium arch theatre, but in something closer to Peter Schumann's gravel pit at Glover, or the quarry outside Adelaide where Peter Brook's actors played *The Conference of the Birds* in 1980.

Like Gurdjieff, or Roy Hart, Barba will allow no distinction to be drawn between the private and the public or the professional. It is the quality of the person that determines the quality of the performer. In the same way, on the journey through Africa, Peter Brook emphasized the importance to the actors of the daily routines within the camp. 'Everything we do on this journey,' he said, 'is an exercise in heightening perception on every conceivable level. Everything feeds the work and everything surrounding it is part of a bigger test of awareness.' Just as Copeau chose his actors not for their theatrical abilities, but for their human qualities (they became excellent actors through the work they did), so Barba says,

> We pick our actors not for their talent but for their inner strength, their outward magnanimity, their perseverance. We are trying to build a theatre where each feels he has his or her own place in our little society, and assumes a share of the responsibility of the entire project, from the physical and technical and administrative aspects to daily chores such as cooking and cleaning.

At the Odin the central concern is to enable each actor to have as much time and the right conditions in which to carry out his own research. The training for Barba's actors, for Brook's actors, for all who belong to the Third Theatre, is continuous and unending. The work is merciless, both in its physical and vocal demands, as well as in its continuing exposure of the emotional and psychological being of the actor. The creative process for the organic creator, as Martha Graham has observed, is remorseless.

The organic actor (writes John Heilpern) takes years to develop. The fully creative actor, creating from nothing as a painter fills a blank canvas – I don't think the fully creative actor really exists. It's why Brook believes it is a crucial area to work on. Why not try? But you need the patience of Job.

Because the work is organic, it means that the actor's training changes over the years. Barba's one test is how much the actor is prepared to give for what he believes and declares. It is nothing less than a daily process calling for the transformation of the individual within the transformation of the group as a whole. Each actor, after he has been with Odin for four years, receives the same salary – which is slightly below that of an unskilled labourer in Denmark.

The actor has to learn how not to be afraid of himself, of the other, until the actors become transparent to one another and to the audience. It is this sharing of their deepest experiences through images of great power, shaped and orchestrated by a living technique, that makes the Odin Teatret so powerful in works such as *Min Fars Hus*.

Now. When I have overcome my fears [writes Dag Hammarskjold in his diary] of others, of myself, of the underlying darkness – at the frontier of the unheard-of. Here ends the known. But from a source beyond it, something fills my being with its possibilities. At the frontier.

Of course there are dangers. They should not be minimized. The creative process claims many victims. Many fall by the wayside. A group, like the Open Theatre, may decide it has reached a cul-de-sac and so cease to exist. Another danger is that a group may become so introverted that it ceases working altogether. It is what happened to the painter Mark Rothko. Is this the danger implicit in all introverted art? The First Theatre has always the stimulus of new writers, feeding in new ideas, demanding new styles, of acting or direction, and providing new challenges. Because the First Theatre is out in the open it can be responsive to seeds blown on the wind. But how can a tightly sealed hermetic group be open? It is the awareness of this danger perhaps that has led such groups as the Odin Teatret, the Roy Hart Theatre, the Performance Group, and others, to sub-divide, developing artistic families within the larger unit; sending out actors to work in different parts of the world to absorb other influences and ideas, returning to share with each other the fruit of their harvesting. In this way the seed of the Third Theatre is sown upon the wind. In 1980, after ten years of working together, Peter Brook dispersed his actors, only to reassemble them two years later, to travel through India and work on a new project.

In its first years the Odin Teatret appeared as a remote offshoot of the Polish Laboratory Theatre, but gradually it became a model for hundreds of other similar groups all over the world and with whom Odin maintains close links. In 1976, at the Théâtre des Nations in Belgrade, Barba organized an international conference of all the representatives of the Third Theatre. Few of them are recognized, few of them are professionals or belong to a trade union. Yet they are not amateurs. Their whole day is filled with training, research, and rehearsing. Throughout Europe, in North and South America, Australia and Japan, such groups may be found. Like the Waseda Little Theatre in Tokyo, which was formed in 1965 by Tadashi Susuki. The twenty members of his company come together four nights a week to take part in a series of rigorous and demanding exercises devised by Susuki. They rarely perform and audiences are always small. Each summer they assemble for two months of intensive training and then give a single performance. Yet their work is influential in Japan and abroad.

Thus in different parts of the world, similar groups are seeking to be present in their own environments and communities through the medium of theatre. Occasionally they are asked, as was the Odin in its early years, as was the Polish Laboratory Theatre – what use is your theatre? But theatre, says Barba, is not just a product. It creates relationships between people; which is why Odin prefers to remain in a place for a period of time, performing, giving workshops and meeting with people. It is not so much that another theatre is being born, as Grotowski says, but rather that other situations are beginning to be called theatre.

Each of the great figures of twentieth-century theatre – Stanislavsky, Meyerhold, Craig, Appia, Copeau, Grotowski, Brook – has had to place himself outside the system, to go out on a limb, in order, as Barba says, to create a theatre that answered their own personal, but not private, needs which, at the time, were unrecognizable and unrecognized.

What Grotowski began in a small room in Opole in the 1960s is now manifesting itself all over the world. Just as there is in the Christian church what Dr Alec Vidler has called the para-church, small, unheralded groups living and working at the fringe, so, too, in the womb of the nineteenth-century theatre that still, Oedipally, dominates Europe in particular, new growth is taking place in these mushrooming para-theatre groups of the Third Theatre.

In 1974 the Odin Teatret went to live for several months in Carpignano, a small but culturally isolated village in Southern Italy. One evening, after they had been living there for a month, they went to call on some friends, taking with them their musical instruments. The people began to follow them out of curiosity. 'Suddenly', says Barba, 'we were in a square, surrounded by people expecting us to do something.' So for an hour they sang and played popular Scandinavian folk songs and did some of their vocal exercises. At the end, the people said, 'Now you must hear our songs.' And they began to share with the actors of the Odin Teatret their own traditional songs of work, love, birth and death.

Out of that incident there developed the idea of a theatre of barter. 'It was as though the people seemed animated by a desire to present themselves to us,' observed Barba. This led to Odin exploring the whole area of clown shows, parades and street theatre. Instead of charging for performance they would barter for a return of entertainment. In this way the traditional roles were reversed and the players, having played, became spectators, and the spectators became the performers.

It was in Carpignano one day that the actors were stopped by an old peasant woman and asked, 'Who are you?' This question pulled them up short. For the peasant woman 'actors' meant actors on television or film, which they were not. And so each asked himself, 'Where are we really actors?' In Holstebro and in all the places where they performed before an audience that had come to see them? But what were they in an isolated village in Italy?

One can work for years [says Barba] behind a door with the word 'Theatre' written on it. All that you do requires a meaning so that your work seems justified. But what happens when the door and its sign is knocked down?

It was this question that led them like Brook and his actors, to ask again the essential question: What is theatre?

18 The Mountain with Many Caves: Peter Brook, Alfred Wolfsohn and Roy Hart

Obviously I don't believe the theatrical status quo is healthy [remarks Peter Brook, as we share a taxi back from London airport]. I don't believe it is even promising. Single events flicker here and there. Different schools of theatre come and go. A new playwright emerges. But I don't see much hope in any of this because I don't believe it begins to grapple with the essential problems. How to make theatre absolutely *necessary* to people, as necessary as eating and sex? Something that is a simple organic necessity – as theatre used to be and still is in certain societies. Make believe is a *necessity*. It's this quality, lost to Western industrial societies, I am searching for.

To this end Peter Brook formed his own company of actors, of different nationalities, in Paris in 1970, under the title of the International Theatre Research Centre. Directly following his sensationally successful production of *A Midsummer Night's Dream* for the Royal Shakespeare Company, approaching fifty, at the height of his fame, he turned his back on commercial and subsidized theatre, in order to concentrate upon a programme of systematic research. Assisted by the English poet, Ted Hughes, he created a new language, Orghast, and created a play of the same name, which his actors performed at the 1971 Shiraz Festival. For many who saw *Orghast* at Persepolis, like the music critic, Andrew Porter, it was an unforgettable experience: 'The playgoer who has entered deeply into *Orghast* has passed through fire and can never be the same again'; while Irving Wardle, in *The Times*, observed that it was the beginning of something which was not only new for Brook but without parallel in theatre history: the creation of a form of theatre comprehensible to anyone on earth.

But Brook was not satisfied. He felt that the result was too narrow, exclusive; theatre, he argues, must encompass the serious and the comic, the spiritual and the bawdy, being both élitist and popular. And so it was that Brook turned to the twelfth-century masterpiece, *The Conference of the Birds*, by the Sufi poet, Farid ud-Din Attar, in an attempt to create a work of theatre that could be accessible to everyone wherever it was played. The poem tells how all the birds of the world, known and unknown, gathered together in order to discuss how to set out on the pilgrimage to the court of the Simurgh – the City of God. Eventually they set forth on their journey and reach the court of the Simurgh, where they finally attain union with him. In the Epilogue, Attar writes,

> O you who have set out on the path of inner development, do not read my book only as a poetical work, or a book of magic, but read it with understanding; and for this man must be hungry for something, dissatisfied with himself and this world . . . my book is at once a gift for distinguished men and a boon for the common.

In 1972 Peter Brook set off with a group of his actors (including some who did not speak any English), a small fleet of landrovers and their crews, a film crew, a journalist reporter, John Heilpern (who has written brilliantly about the experience in his book, *Conference of the Birds*) on a journey that cost 60,000 dollars, was to last three and a half months, and take them through six countries: Algeria, Niger, Nigeria, Benin (formerly Dahomey), Togo and Mali. They had no planned programme but Brook hoped to develop one particular show based on the Sufi poem.

Like Grotowski, Brook is concerned with the question: What is theatre? What is a play? What is an actor? What is the relationship between them all, and what conditions best serve this relationship? Again and again he stresses the transient nature of theatre – as opposed to the repertory principle of repetition. A play for Brook has no reality except *now*.

for weeks and months. It seemed like an awful moment of truth in Agades. The group began to make the sound. The Peulhs were still staring into their mirrors. I watched the actors grow hesitant, uncertain whether to continue. But the sound stretched and grew – and the Peulhs unexpectedly looked up from their mirrors for the first time. The sound took life, vibrating. The Peulhs discarded their mirrors and joined the sound. Oh, it seemed miraculous! It was as if the Peulhs were pulling the sound from them. They pointed to the sky.

Just as the unimaginable sound reached its height, or seemed to, no one would venture any further. Somehow it was frightening. The two sides had met and come together in one sound. And yet it was as if they were stunned and frightened by the discovery. Ted Hughes has written of the sounds far beyond human words that open our deepest and innermost ghost to sudden attention . . . . But now the Peulh offered an exchange and sang their songs. And they told Brook something very precious. He knew at last that he was on the right road in the search for a universal language. Perhaps we were only beginning to understand. But spirits speak there, in invisible worlds.

The Peulh music showed that a universal language might be as simple as one note repeated many, many times. But the right note must be discovered first. The Peulhs could vary and enrich the sound, changing it in subtle ways, but the strength behind the sound is not made through force. 'Somehow, the strength makes itself. With the Peulh everything seemed effortless. Even the sound itself seemed to have a wondrous life of its own . . . we were light years behind their "simplicity".'

Both Peter Brook and Liz Swados, the American composer, had talked of the possibility of one note that could become a source, the purest of essence. So much of the group's work had been based on this, that a sound might somehow be found that would encompass and convey an entire feeling. Of course, the actor has first to get at the emotion, to tap those archetypes that lie dormant in the collective unconscious. It is towards this end that the long discipline of work is directed. And

35 Peter Brook and his actors in Africa, one of many versions of *The Conference of Birds*

36 Hywel Jones in *Deaths and Entrances*

37 Judgment scene from *Deaths and Entrances*

38 Alfred
Wolfsohn and
Roy Hart

39 Roy Hart and
the Roy Hart
Theatre on Paxos,
Greece, July 1973

working on such a level means that one visual image, or one word, can prove more expressive than an entire speech.

In *Deaths and Entrances*, a work that I created with the actors of Stage Two in 1970, over a period of nine months, there was a sequence in which the actor, Hywel Jones, spoke only one word. The work was a meditation on death: on the many forms of death; the death of a love or of a relationship, the death of an ambition, as well as physical death. We die many times in one life-time. During the months of work I came across these words from Carl Jung's *Seven Sermons from the Dead*, which became the theme of the work as it unfolded.

The dead came back from Jerusalem where they found not what they sought. In the night the dead stood along the wall and cried. 'We would have knowledge of God! Where is God? Is God dead?' Now the dead howled for they were unperfected.

The work began with a series of wooden coffins, on one of which lay the actor, Hywel Jones, bound tightly, from head to ankles, in a sixty-foot length of gauze. From within the tombs could be heard the voices of the dead calling out to each other, the actors using their own names: Di! Kevin! Paul! Hywel! On hearing his own name called, the shrouded figure stirred, as though being woken from centuries of sleep, and then began to struggle, trying to break out of the bonds of death. The actor was so tightly bound that the sense of struggle within the shroud was acute, as the actor cried out in terror, breathing heavily, gasping for air, sweat seeping through the gauze like seepage from an open wound. Finally he breaks through and as he gazes intently upwards, as though he had fought his way through the earth and surfaced to the light of day, he begins to emit the sound – 'Lie – lie – lie!'

The terror of being buried alive is still a very real part of the taboo on death – perhaps the only remaining taboo in Western society? – and here the actor's sense of release from the claustrophobia of death (interior death and physical death), the awareness of space and freedom and illumination, finally culminated in a sound that became the word 'Light!' With the final articulation of the word-sound-image, the actor turned to the other coffins and, throwing off their lids, cried out the word repeatedly, like a trumpet summoning the dead to the day of resurrection. Slowly, from within each coffin, an actor emerged, carrying a small ladder, setting out on the stage of a new journey: for the actors, in creating the work, believed that each death leads to a new resurrection, a new journey, a fresh exploration. Life is a journey through many deaths.

Into that one sound the actor poured all the intensity of his own life experience. The image was personal to him, and yet re-explored at each performance. The vibrations of that one sound, charged with the actor's own research and life experience, conveyed to the spectator who had ears to hear something of the essential darkness of death, and of the awe and wonder of being delivered up from this experience into that of a rebirth, a resurrection, as well as the desire to share this experience of awakening with those who have not yet been awakened. In this one sequence the actor, Hywel Jones, earned the right to say the one word, *Light*.

> All that has dark sounds [wrote García Lorca, the Spanish poet and dramatist and director and actor] has *duende*. It is not a matter of ability but of real live form; of blood, of ancient culture; of creative action. To help us seek the *duende* there is neither map nor discipline. All one knows is that it turns the blood like powdered glass, that it exhausts, that it rejects all the sweet geometry one has ever learned, that it breaks with all styles.

There were many who, hearing for the first time the eight-octave voice of Roy Hart, or the sounds created by his company, were disturbed. Such sounds rejected all the sweet geometry they had ever learned; such sounds, they would say (especially critics), are not human. Yet, as Roy Hart once observed, 'Those who can hear without fear know that these sounds which are commanded to come forth are under conscious control.' It was not surprising that composers such as Henze, Stockhausen and others, wrote for this unique instrument, nor that Peter Maxwell Davies especially created for him the music-theatre composition, *Songs of a Mad King*.

It was in the early 1960s that Peter Brook first visited the Roy Hart Studio in London and was much impressed and excited by what he found. In 1966 he returned twice and described the work as 'full of pith and moment', and wrote on behalf of the company to the authorities, urging a grant to support their research. 'What they are doing', he wrote, 'deserves encouragement and support and could certainly be of interest and value both culturally and educationally to the English theatre as a whole. There are no other groups with such aspirations.' He also took Grotowski to see their work. In 1972, Jean-Louis Barrault, always a great supporter of The Roy Hart Theatre, invited both Roy Hart's actors and Peter Brook's actors to take part in a ten-day event, organized in Paris by the Théâtre des Nations.

The Roy Hart Theatre, now based in France, grew out of the work of Alfred Wolfsohn who was born in Berlin in 1896 and escaped from Germany in 1938. He died in London in 1962. Believing that the voice is the audible expression of a man's inner being, he devoted his life to trying to discover why, in most people, the voice is shackled, monotonous, cramped. Through his research he learned that the voice is not the function solely of any anatomical structure, but the expression of the whole personality. Working with a great variety of people he proved that the human voice is restricted only by the psychological problems of the individual and that, conversely, the voice is a way through which all aspects of an individual can be developed. His work with singers and actors and ordinary people led to an increase in the vocal range, irrespective of sex, from two to eight octaves, and even nine. He delivered his findings before astounded, and often disturbed audiences who included such eminent figures as Aldous and Sir Julian Huxley, the music critic Wayland Young, George Steiner, and John Cage. In 1979 Grotowski publicly acknowledged his own debt to the work of Wolfsohn.

Because it was generally considered that the structure of the voice depended on the vocal chords, singers possessing such an extended range were considered to be the result of some freakish development. However, in 1956, an analysis of the voice of Jennie Johnson, one of Wolfsohn's most gifted pupils along with Roy Hart, at the Zurich Laryngological Institute, showed a vocal range of five octaves and six tones. The various tests, X-ray, high-speed film, and stroboscope, demonstrated that the larynx was not affected by the sounds produced from bass C to F 4, but, on the contrary, was healthy and normal. It is important to stress this because many, including theatre critics, often accused Roy Hart, inaccurately, of ruining the voices of his actors. On the contrary, he liberated them.

What Wolfsohn found is that many sounds are produced not by the larynx, but by many different parts of the body, from energy centres in the head, chest and stomach, and are resonated throughout the body. These centres Grotowski has called the 'resonators'. To the listener it appears as though the actor is speaking with different parts of the body. Grotowski has defined about twenty resonators and is convinced that others remain to be discovered. Thus, what has been known for centuries by Tibetan monks and certain tribes in Africa is being rediscovered by the West in the twentieth century.

The range of the human voice, wrote Alfred Wolfsohn, can be expanded to more than seven octaves, even nine, and this possibility proves that the restriction of the human voice to a specialized one is artificial. In other words: there exists in the human voice a common structure which makes it possible that that which is called soprano, contralto, tenor, baritone, or bass exists in everybody, whether child, male or female. 'He believed', writes Maria Guther, 'that to find the voice, work with it, nurse it, dredge it out of your depth, pull it out of your guts, would lead to becoming something like a human being.' It was this link between the voice and the psychological growth of the individual that perhaps marked Wolfsohn's most important discovery. Similarly Anna Halprin, of the Dancers' Workshop in San Francisco, speaks of the links between movement and the psychological growth of the performer:

> Whatever emotional, physical or mental barriers that we carry around with us in our personal lives will be the same barriers that inhibit our full creative expression. It is for this reason that we need to release emotional blocks in order to realize fully our human creative potential, in terms of being able to develop effectively as performers and creators, as well as to participate with satisfaction in

our lives. I look at emotional blocks as damaging to artistic growth as to personal growth.

'The voice is like a mountain with caves,' says Peter Brook. 'Go into all the different caves there are.' It is in this context that the research work of Alfred Wolfsohn and of Roy Hart is important. They demonstrated that by releasing psychological tensions, and by employing the many resonators in the human body, a fuller and richer range of sound and emotion can be tapped; and with this release of primal sound, as Peter Brook's actors in Paris have also found, comes a release of psychic energy. As the English theatre critic, Herbert Kretzmer, wrote of a performance of *The Bacchae* by the Roy Hart Theatre,

> They are not acting in a play, not inviting the audience to lose itself in some fiction. They are people seeking to liberate their tensions – and ours – through sound. The impact and the insight are sometimes stunning. I have never seen actors giving quite so much of themselves.

Philosophically Roy Hart believed that most people live a one-octave life (the philosophical concept of eight octaves occurs in the teachings of Gurdjieff, about whom Brook has made a film, *Meetings with Remarkable Men*), and that their full potential is rarely realized. His concern, like that of Wolfsohn, and of Gurdjieff, was to build a bridge between the conscious and the unconscious, the male and the female, the feeling and the intellect, the dark and the light, within every human being.

> For you I have come out of myself
> To perform life without a mask . . .
> at the deepest level of myself.
> It is the acting of confrontation –
> a whole theatre of irresistible contradictions.

These words by Serge Behar are from a play written especially for the Roy Hart Theatre. They express admirably the goal of the Third Theatre. And it is, above all, these irresistible contradictions that absorb Brook.

Brook is in search of a work of theatre that will make total sense, regardless of language, wherever in the world it is played. Month after month, at his centre in Paris, he found that the most powerful expression in sound and movement always came through shedding more and more outward forms – or masks. His is an attempt to make the greatest impact using minimal means. Brook's training methods are like those of a Zen master rather than a conventional theatre director. This is why he insisted, during the long journey through Africa, that the camp should be seen by the actors as an extension of their work. In their lives as well as in their acting the actors had to strive for the kind of spontaneity which can come only from an arduous and sometimes agonizing process of self-exploration.

> They must strip away their outward personalities, mannerisms, habits, vanities, neuroses, tricks, clichés, and stock responses, until a higher state of perception is found [writes John Heilpern]. To watch a piece of theatre performed truthfully is to see in a different way. Perhaps we awaken. We are shaken out of our everyday condition and we see life differently. Sometimes our lives are changed. But the actor must change first. He must shed useless skins like a snake. He must transform his own being.

In the Invocation to *The Conference of the Birds*, Farid ud-Din Attar writes to the reader,

> Do you think it will be easy to arrive at a knowledge of spiritual things? It means no less than to die to everything . . . . My friends, we are neighbours of one another: I wish to repeat my discourse to you day and night, so that you should not cease for a moment too long to set out in quest of the Truth.

Because Brook is in the business of research, because his work is in the nature of a quest, it means that the moment anything is a success it must be abandoned. If not, it becomes set and closed. But it can be a terrific strain on the actors. 'The bull is different with every fight,' says Brook. 'If you don't see that, it will kill you.'

Above all, it takes time, it takes years. The man who wishes to transform himself or build a group or break with the old cannot take anything for granted. A real beginning again is something so difficult to grasp that it cannot skip one single step, however insignificant it may seem. This is as true of the work of the Odin Teatret, of the Performance Group, of the Polish Laboratory, as it is of Brook's company. The seed takes root slowly and its progress is almost imperceptible. The new that emerges from the old will not happen overnight. Time and time again performances of *The Conference of the Birds* have died the death, or performances of *The Ik* (a play based on Colin Turnbull's book *The Mountain People*) been dismissed by critics as mere acting exercises. Risks have to be taken, failure has to be courted with all the detachment of a Manolete, if there is to be growth. The temptation to play safe, to fall back on proven resources, is always the first temptation in the desert.

> Seeing Brook's new work at its best is to witness that rare happening in the theatre [wrote John Heilpern in the *Observer*], a true and refreshing spontaneity on the stage. It appears to flow naturally, whereas over years and years it has in fact been worked for, like a dog.

So Brook has managed to develop not a highly polished and obviously professional form of theatre, but a theatre of simplicity that is compelling because it functions in a Zen-like stage of artlessness. At one of the first meetings in Persia in 1971 Brook said to the assembled actors,

> We call what we are doing 'research'. We are trying to discover something, discover it through what we can make, for other people to take part in. It demands a long, long preparation of the instrument that we are. The question always is: have we good instruments? For that, we have to know: what is the instrument for? The only good purpose is that we should be instruments that transmit truth which otherwise would remain out of sight. These truths can appear from sources deep within ourselves and far outside ourselves. Any preparation we do is only part of the complete preparation. The body must be ready and sensitive, but this isn't all. The voice has to be open and ready. The emotions have to be open and free.

The intelligence has to be quick. All of these are preparations. There are crude vibrations that can come through very easily; and fine ones that come through with difficulty. In each case the life we are looking for means breaking with a series of habits. A habit of speaking – maybe a habit made by an entire language. The simple starting point we have at this moment, that such a mixture of people meet without even a common language means that a lot of habits are immediately broken. Habits are lazy. In this difficulty the life lies.

Today we begin to prepare. The seed takes root slowly, and its progress is almost imperceptible. You must take every care. The New that emerges from the Old will not happen overnight.

19 Towards AD 2,000

On 28 January 1984 the Polish Laboratory Theatre issued the following statement:

> For some time the company has ceased to exist practically as a cohesive group. We believe that we have accomplished what we set out to do. We ourselves are astounded that we persisted as a group for a quarter of a century, constantly changing, inspiring one another. Each of us remembers that our origins lie in the common source whose name is Jerzy Grotowski. From now on each of us has to meet alone the challenge of his/her own creative biography and the times in which we live.

After exactly twenty five years the company of the Polish Laboratory Theatre were shutting up shop in exactly the same way as had the Living Theatre and the Open Theatre. Other groups have succeeded the Laboratory Theatre, while the former vice-director, Zbigniew Cynkutis, now runs a new experimental project, The Second Studio. Grotowski himself is teaching at the University of California, researching those ancient rituals of the various world cultures which have a precise and therefore objective impact upon their participants quite apart from their theological or symbolical significance. His mind is still questing although whether, uprooted from his own culture, he can, any more than did Bertolt Brecht, survive within the harsher, more alien, climate of the American academic world, is a moot point.

Many of the groups which came into being in the sixties and seventies, both in America and Europe, no longer exist. Even the Odin Teatret has scaled down its operations. In an essay entitled, 'The Decline and Fall of the American Avant-Garde', Richard Schechner examines why the American experimental theatre has declined. Looking back across the century, if the early part represented the springtime of experimental theatre, then the 1960s and 1970s may be said to have represented its summertime. During this period such experimental companies believed that they would come to occupy a central niche and that commercial theatre would be squeezed to one side together with regional and State theatres. That has not happened and, to my mind, it was arrogant to assume that only the Third Theatre (as Eugenio Barba termed this movement) had any lasting value. Commercial and subsidized theatre alike are capable of creating works of imagination, quality and insight, as much as are the radical groups of the avant-garde. It was, after all, commercial theatre which brought 'Waiting for Godot' to England and America. As Peter Brook has written, 'In the theatre the small experiment and the big show both can have quality and meaning. All that matters is that they should aim at capturing truth and life. Captivity kills fast. For this reason there are no conclusions. The method must always change.'

The degree of energy, commitment and sacrifice required for experiment and, above all, group-oriented works, is such that often a group runs out of steam, and creative ideas dry up; or its original members find they want to marry, have children and a home, and this requires earning more money. The cutback of grants and state subsidies is also an added factor. Lastly, the very nature of much of the work created was, predictably, self-defeating. As Schechner points out, such groups as the Performance Group (his own company), and the Open Theatre, failed to develop any sense of continuing tradition: their works were primarily performance scores rather than dramatic texts and so could only be enacted by the groups which had created them. They failed to develop any way of transmitting performance knowledge from one generation to another; unlike Martha Graham who created not only a new form of theatre, but an objective body of technique as a result of which, in 1987, a third generation of Graham dancers was able to revive one of her earliest dances. The recreation of this work, *Celebration*, had an electryifying effect upon its new audience, proving to be as modern as any theatre work by Foreman or Wilson. 'Graham zaps audience with fifty years of stored energy', was a headline in *The Christian Science Monitor.* 'Both times I saw this work,' wrote Marcia B. Siegel, 'I sat stunned. It was as if I had been watching a film with all the pieces cut up and spliced together in different ways and still the ways had hardly been exhausted.' (CSM, 16 Nov. 1987).

But if money is the root of all evil, the lack of it is a severe threat to experimentation in the arts. The rising costs of materials, the increasing stranglehold of unions – all militate against research. With this in mind, in the early summer of 1987, an international conference of arts administrators was held in London with participants from around the world: Australia, New Zealand, Israel, North America, Europe. The purpose of the conference was to discuss the hows and whys of funding the arts. Sir Peter Hall, director of Britain's National Theatre, spoke of the importance of the arts 'particularly in the wild and somewhat barbarous society in which we now live, a society so varied that it doesn't have religion or morality to bind us together.' The conference was organized by Luke Rittner, Secretary General of the Arts Council of Great Britain, the first arts agency of its kind in the world. It was created in 1946 under Royal Charter to serve as a non-partisan go-between for State funds and Britain's many art institutions – museums, galleries, libraries, theatres, as well as individual artists. Its aim was to help the arts flourish and make them more a part of the mainstream of British life. The Arts Council subsequently became a model for similar agencies in the old British Commonwealth, and also inspired the setting up of the American National Endowment of the Arts.

What the conference revealed is that the cash crisis hitting the arts in Britain is one that is shared globally; the key problem facing most countries is a lack of adequate funding in order to keep pace with the growing demand on the part of the public for the arts, and the increasing level of subsidy required by theatres, art galleries, and museums in order to survive. As Luke Rittner commented, 'Everyone is now having to cope with governments that are committed to reducing public expenditure and it doesn't matter if the government is to the right or to the left, everyone is in the same boat; yet at the same time the arts have become of more interest to more people than ever before.' (Interview with Linda Joffee, CSM, 25–31 May, 1987).

The three funding systems represented at the conference were:

1. 'Arm's length', as the Arts Council approach is called, since state subsidies for the arts are provided with minimal government interference.

2. The 'ministry' approach, as seen in France, where there is a Ministry of Culture led by a Cabinet minister, thereby linking policy and state art subsidies directly to central government.

3. The 'endowment' or American approach, where although central government offers grants, the bulk of the arts funding must come from other sources.

According to Luke Rittner all three systems have their strengths and weaknesses. He feels that the ministry approach brings politicians too close to artistic policy and this he says is a mistake: 'Politicians are generally neither artists nor good arts administrators.' On the other hand he feels that the American style of patronage leaves too much to chance. An arts body can easily have trouble raising funds from industry, foundations, or individuals, and the precariousness of the system becomes greater the less prestigious the arts organisation; in other words the bigger opera and theatre houses and galleries tend to get commercial sponsorship because they are a better advertisement for a product or a company, whereas the smaller and more experimental companies fall by the wayside. Rittner is convinced that the most effective combination involves balancing central government money, filtered through a third party such as the Arts Council, to cover the 'bread and butter' of arts expenditure, with local government and private sponsorship.

That an international conference on the funding of the arts was organized by a Briton was no accident. During the last nine years under Mrs Thatcher's government the arts have come increasingly under threat. As Linda Joffee observed, 'hardly a month goes by without news of some opera house, orchestra or drama company having to make cutbacks to keep its head above water,' while others have gone under altogether. A key concern of the conference participants was that of the increasing reliance of the arts on private sponsorship, a policy strongly advocated by Mrs Thatcher; but as Luke Rittner notes, 'if you put pressure on industry and business corporate sponsors to the point that you're saying to them, "you've got a duty to support the artistic life of the country", then you're in danger of killing the goose that lays the golden egg. Business does *not* have a duty to support the arts. Business has a duty to make a profit. I *do* think the government has a duty to support the arts. I don't think business has!'

Rittner insists he would welcome increased state money for the arts but it's just not happening in most Western countries. The basic problem lies, he says, not with the views of Mrs Thatcher or any other leader, but 'that there just isn't the political will to really see the arts as an absolutely central part of national life and to fund them accordingly. And yet, in Britain alone, five million more people go to the theatre each year than to see football. Britain's most popular spectator sport!'

The fact remains, however, that the alternative and experimental theatre, in spite of its successes and achievements, plays but a limited role in the lives of ordinary people, and this is not to ignore the continuing work of many dynamic smaller companies. Andrew Davies in *Other Theatres* (Macmillan, 1987) came to a sombre conclusion at the end of his survey of alternative theatre in Britain: 'If *Other Theatres* is a first history of alternative experimental drama in Britain, sadly it may also be something of an obituary notice too.' The increasing costliness of professional theatre and the cutback of subsidies is inevitably having a crippling effect on much creative work. Even as dedicated a company as the Odin Teatret would not survive without subsidy. There is, however, an additional factor that threatens the experimental in theatre. It is the way in which mainstream theatre tends to absorb and take over the experiments of the avant-garde. It is interesting to ponder how much Bill Bryden in his acclaimed production for the National Theatre, *Mysteries*, may have been influenced by the environmental staging techniques of the

Performance Group in New York. In the same way that the classical ballet has now absorbed many of the techniques of the modern and post modern dance, so commercial and mainstream theatres are quick to harvest the discoveries of others. In the Royal Shakespeare Company's highly successful production of *Nicholas Nickleby*, one wonders again how much the directors were influenced by the specific story-telling techniques evolved by Mike Alfreds and his Shared Experience company in the three years prior to *Nicholas Nickleby*.

It was with their first production of *An Arabian Night* in 1975 (based upon the Sir Richard Burton translation of the stories of the Arabian Nights) that Shared Experience pioneered those story-telling techniques which they were to perfect in their brilliant staging of Charles Dickens' *Bleak House*. Exploring the theatrical possibilities of story-telling, the company set themselves two disciplines: to take the stories from the Arabian Nights straight off the page without adaptation, and to create everything through the actors without recourse to technical effects, scenery, props, costumes, or make up. 'Our premise was that an actor comes into an empty space and says directly to an audience, "Once upon a time there was . . .". From that moment he must use every technique he possesses to recreate the story most vividly.' They rehearsed *An Arabian Night* for nine weeks, exploring the varieties of narrator in a wide range of stories: the narrator as observer, as moralist, as protagonist and narration, shared by all the characters. They worked on the relationship between audience, actor, narrator, and character, moving to and fro between the actors describing their characters, the characters describing themselves, in both the first and third person, as well as acting out situations.

For *Bleak House* (one of the great panoramic novels of Dickens' maturity, with over a hundred characters) Mike Alfreds the founder of Shared Experience, who subsequently moved to the National Theatre, rehearsed his seven actors for nine months, working straight from the page, chapter by chapter, culling not just dialogue but narrative, rhetorical and descriptive passages. In order to cut as little as possible they evolved a four-part, ten-hour production. As with Peter Brook's *The Mahabharata*, or the Royal Shakespeare Company's *The*

Greeks, each part could be seen on a separate night or continuously during a weekend. Apart from seven folding chairs everything was mimed. Imaginary desks were leaned on, imaginary spectacles donned. The sound of storms, carriages, and birdcalls were created by the actors. The use of mime is not, of course, new and we have seen how brilliantly Jacques Copeau and his young actors used a bare stage and mime; but the techniques of adapting a novel for the stage in this way, and as used in *Nicholas Nickleby*, were pioneered by Mike Alfreds.

If at the turn of this century Constantin Stanislavsky was the great patriarchal figure not only of Russian but of world theatre, there is little doubt that Peter Brook will dominate the close of this century when he will be seventy five. Brook is among those who see that deep change is necessary but he no longer believes that conventional theatre can provide such change. 'Since, in the total sickness of the society we are living in,' writes Brook, 'the possibility of affirmation through the conventional theatre is virtually excluded, it is therefore essential to re-discover the roots of both theatre and human experience.' So, at the Théâtre des Bouffes in Paris, he continues his attempt to 're-unite the community, in all its diversity, within the same shared experience', working with a company of actors drawn from different cultures and backgrounds. 'Each human being,' says Brook, 'carries within her/him all the continents, but each of us knows only one of them. So when a person with one known continent and a mass of dark continents meets someone else whose condition is the same, and they communicate, there is illumination for each.' In a production such as *The Mahabharata*, in particular, one can see Brook drawing upon the richness of each cultural tradition within his company: Indian, Persian, African, Italian, French, American, British. If at times the United Nations approach to an acting ensemble produces some over-acting, some poor acting, and, above all, poor diction, so that the text is often unintelligible, it may well be that these faults cannot be rectified within one generation. What Brook is attempting here is so new, and so radical, that the full fruits of this experiment may not be realised for some years.

With this company Brook has created a number of

outstanding productions: *Orghast, Timon of Athens, The Ik, The Cherry Orchard, Ubu aux Bouffes, The Conference of the Birds*, and lastly, *The Mahabharata*. *The Ik* was based on a tribe of hunters in Northern Uganda which had originally existed in relative prosperity on the lowlands until, in 1946, a government order forced them to resettle on the arid mountains above their former homes. This brutal uprooting led to a total disintegration of their social, family and religious structures. Unable to make a living they became no more than beasts. In the story of the Ik, Brook sees a grim parody of Western society *in extremis*; for we are all potential Ik. 'The parallels are alarming,' observes Brook. 'The same sort of situation can be seen in Western life.' The impoverishment of our inner cities, the ever present fear of atomic accidents; the greed of our materialistic society which destroys the resources of this earth while millions die from starvation and disease; men and women's continuing inhumanity to one another; and the ineptitude and arrogance of many politicians do not augure well for the future of our civilization. Like the Ik we, too, as Jung foresaw, are in grave danger of being dispossessed. If we are to survive at all we will have to invoke the deepest strengths of our spirit, as the Rinpoche observes in Andrew Harvey's remarkable book, *A Journey to Ladakh*: 'Within this world and within man there are great powers: powers of love, of healing and of clarity, that can lead a man to liberation. The worse the time – and this present time is Kali Yoga, the Age of Destruction – the more we should look for those powers within ourselves.'

The search today still remains, as Peter Brook expressed it in 1972 in his book, *The Empty Space*, for 'a necessary theatre, one which is an urgent presence in our lives, speaking to a man in his wholeness.' As part of this search, Brook's creation of *The Mahabharata* is its most recent and extraordinary offering. An ancient Sanskrit manuscript, fifteen times longer than the *Bible*, *The Mahabharata* is a vision of society, like ours, in discord, coming to the brink of destruction. Reflecting popular theatre traditions, martial art forms, and Asian dance, it is the most spectacular of all Brook's productions since 1970 and yet, at the same time, represents the ultimate refinement of his use of minimal scenery. The fruit of ten years' work, research and travels, it takes nine hours to perform in three parts. Ideally Brook prefers it played from midday to midnight (as I saw it done), in the manner of some of Robert Wilson's earlier productions. Brook likens the experience to going on a journey to a foreign country.

The central figure of *The Mahabharata* is the god-man figure of Krishna who encourages each person to go to the very end of their own karma, to go beyond every form of limited morality. *The Mahabharata* says, in effect, that there is in all mankind this inexplicable impulse to massacre but, also, there is always a profound interior voice speaking of self-understanding. Its heroes are forced to confront both the impulse to kill and the still, small inner voice. One of the most memorable passages in *The Mahabharata* is a catechism shared between the voice of an unseen questioner and Yudhishthira, leader of one of the opposing functions.

What is quicker than the wind? *Thought.* What can cover the earth? *Darkness.* Who are the more numerous, the living or the dead? *The living, because the dead are no longer.* Give me an example of space. *My two hands as one.* An example of grief. *Ignorance.* Of poison. *Desire.* An example of defeat. *Victory.* Which animal is the slyest? *The one that man does not yet know.* Which came first, day or night. *Day, but it was only a day ahead.* What is the cause of the world? *Love.* What is your opposite? *Myself.* What is madness? *A forgotten way.* And revolt? Why do men revolt? *To find beauty, either in life or in death.* What for each of us is inevitable? *Happiness.* And what is the greatest wonder? *Each day, death strikes and we live as though we were immortal. This is the greatest wonder.*

The production has many moments of great visual beauty, deploying fire and water in a way that is not possible in nineteenth century proscenium arch theatres, while the text is full of profound insights and a rich mischievous humour and earthy comedy. The programme notes, however, make certain unjustified claims for Brook: 'The result of these years of performance and research is that Brook is able to apply the utmost simplicity of means to complex and subtle ends. In *The Mahabharata* a piece of cloth becomes a cloud or a lake, a single wheel a war chariot, a stick a sheaf of magic arrows.' Such a combination of sophistication and simplicity is, however, far from new. Apart from a number of directors in the world already working in this area, there have been those, as this book has shown, from Copeau to Brecht, Martha Graham to Shared Experience, Grotowski to Barba, whose whole search has been for the ultimate image; while the Kathakali dance theatre has been doing this for centuries! In the Kathakali tradition an actor will take a bench, and, by his varying use of it, appeal to our imagination to complete the picture. If he crouches behind the bench, rising up slowly, and finally steps onto it, he has climbed the Himalayas; if he lies down to sleep on it, then it has become his bed; if he sits in lotus position before it, it is his altar; if he turns it upside down and sits in it, he is paddling his canoe down the rapids; if he upends it and climbs it, it has become the tallest tree in the forest. Always it is a bench, but he pretends, and we pretend, that it is a mountain range, a bed, an altar, a canoe, a tree.

The Shifting Point, a collection of Brook's writings over forty years, exemplifies his willingness to follow any likely path, not in a restless pursuit of change like Meyerhold but continually adding to his own store of knowledge. He combines the energies of a Reinhardt with the single-mindedness of a Grotowski. Brook once asked an Indian actor his secret and the reply might have been Brook's own answer to the same question: 'I try to bring together all that I have experienced in my life, so as to make what I am doing a witness for what I have felt and what I have understood.' It is not surprising that Brook should have made a film, *Encounters with Remarkable Men*, based upon the life of that remarkable twentieth-century teacher, Gurdjieff; for Brook himself is not only an outstanding director but, like many great artists, a pathfinder and a master.

Brook, like Grotowski, and countless numbers of ordinary people, is turning towards a re-examination of spiritual values. It is significant that, in the West especially, many more people spend large sums of money attending day and weekend courses on Tibetan chanting, meditation, Tai Chi, and other alternative and holistic practices. Much of this activity reaches loony proportions, spawning religions of ego, but underneath this

40 Eugene O'Neill's *The Hairy Ape*, directed by Peter Stein, May 1987

41 'The war' scene from Peter Brook's production of *The Mahabharata*

42 The 'Exile in the forest' scene from Peter Brook's production of *the Mahabharata*

movement there lies, indisputably, a hunger for and a need of rituals that will enshrine the fears, yearnings and conflicts of people today. This may explain, for example, why many theatre groups are turning towards the East and those myths which the West has abandoned. People are starving for a richness and meaning to life. It seems to me probable, therefore, that the next major development in theatre will be in the area of ritual.

Ritual is one of the neglected forms of theatre. Although certain rituals are timeless, perfected and handed down across the centuries in the form of the great liturgies of the major faiths, others need to be created for a specific time, place and need. They may take the form of major works of theatre such as *The Mahabharata*, using trained professional actors, or they may take the form of 'performance art' which seeks to bring the human back into the visual arts. Thus Suzanne Lacy in America organizes elaborate works, often involving a whole community; for her *Whisper the Waves, the Wind* (1984) she used one hundred elderly people who were seated at tables on a beach in San Diego discussing their experiences of ageing. Linda Montano, a former Franciscan nun, undertook to spend a year of her life in New York tied by an eight-foot length of rope to Tehching Hsieh. The experiment broke down because, ironically, they discovered they were in a continual tug-of-war; quite literally they were pulling each other in opposite directions; he insisting that the work was purely formal, while she wished to explore the personal and spiritual implications. This experiment became in itself a theatre ritual, a very potent metaphor of male/female relationships, the Yin and the Yang.

In past cultures and times there have been rituals for national, communal, social, and personal, events. Increasingly, however, many of these rituals have become fossilized. As Harvey Cox, the American theologian, has written,

> We are dragooned into rituals that mean little or nothing to us, yet, when we need the symbolic deepening of an important experience we somehow lack the necessary gestures and images. No wonder we undergo 'identity' crises until we die. Rituals should mark and celebrate the transition from one phase of life to the next.

Rosemary Manning, an English writer, in her novel, *The Open Door*, has one character make this observation: 'Oh, God, why is there no satisfactory ritual for *parting*? The pain is raw at the edges: no healing balm of sherry.' Today there are no rituals for a woman who has been raped, suffered a miscarriage, or been battered and beaten. There are no rituals for pregnancy, and no liturgies for those who cannot subscribe to orthodox baptismal ceremonies and who yet would like some form of ritual to mark the commencement of a new life. There are no rituals for a broken marriage, a broken relationship, a broken home. What rituals exist for a young woman's first menstruation, and her passage from girlhood to womanhood? What rituals exist for the aged, to celebrate their becoming the elders of our society? Why wait until someone is dead to express our gratitude, our love? What rituals have we for the dying, and for the dead?

Time and again, however, when people are given the responsibility of making their own theatre, creating their own rituals, the results are surprising and unexpected. In the summer of 1980 I taught a six week course on ritual on a campus outside Grand Rapids, Michigan. One of the group, Emily Stuart, a dancer, had to leave halfway through the course in order to return to her work in Indiana. I suggested to the group that it should create a ritual of farewell. The basic structure was agreed upon by the group without Emily (she was left to create her own contribution, unknown to the others), but the detail was left to each individual to create, and not known in advance. On the day itself I acted as Emily's guide. She was blindfolded and led across the campus to where the others were waiting. Emily arrived on that morning with a sack which was enormously heavy. She said it was the burden which she wished to take with her on the journey and that it contained her offerings for the group. The long ritual that followed I have described in *Inner Journey, Outer Journey* (Rider, 1987). Long afterwards Emily Stuart wrote about the experience. 'My arms ached for days with the weight of that burden, but I would not have had it otherwise. It was a burden I chose to carry and what I wanted to give to you all, for I had received so much. I am content.'

The creative process, says Jung, consists in the unconscious activation of an archetypal image, and in elaborating and shaping that image into a finished work. We may choose to journey to some distant part of the world to see a rare perform- ance of *The Conference of Birds, The Constant Prince*, or *The Mahabharata*, and be changed, or we may create our own myths and rituals and so be changed. As the barriers disappear between those who are the audience and those who are the artists, so Grotowski's dream may yet be realized. If I may quote from an earlier chapter in this book, for Grotowski the concern is how to bring out the creativity inherent in people and in this way to enrich their lives so that they may become a source of strength to them. Only in this way, he argues, is a new culture and a new theatre possible. Even in those situ- ations where individuals want to understand each other and live as fully as possible, our culture offers few such routes, while in the main the churches have failed to understand the spiritual needs of today. There is in people today a very real hunger for the things of the spirit and in many a deep need to rediscover within themselves the roots of theatre.

The last time I saw Anna Halprin in County Marin, after a week-long ritual centred on Mount Tamalpais, she remarked to me at breakfast, 'Art is an enduring process for it touches on the spiritual dimension in a way that no other human activity does. In art you are able to give expression to it; you receive back a *vision* which is a *map* by which you can set other goals.' The Theatre of Ritual may well prove to be the last discovery of the twentieth century.

Grotowski, Halprin and others point one way: deeper and deeper into the inner world to the point where the actor ceases to be actor and becomes essential man/woman. For Brook and others their way of theatre leads in a different direction, 'out of loneliness to a perception that is heightened because it is shared. A strong presence of actors and a strong presence of spectators,' as Brook writes in *The Shifting Point*,' can produce a circle of unique intensity in which barriers can be broken and the invisible becomes real.' Then public truth and private truth become inseparable parts of the same experience.

Each of the major figures in this book has opened up a new path, seeming to create, at least for a time, an entirely new theatre. It is only as we look back over the past century that we can see that each is but a different aspect of theatre, each complementing and enriching the others, so that the art and craft of theatre are constantly evolving and maturing. All art grows out of questioning. This book began with the words, 'to experiment is to make a journey into the unknown'. Theatre will constantly renew itself, with or without subsidies, so long as it continues to make such journeys. Let the final words be those of that persistent questioner, Peter Brook:

> Theatre must attempt to create a more intense perception at the heart of our own world . . . theatre only exists at the precise moment when the two worlds of the actors and the audience meet: a society in miniature, a microcosm brought together every evening within a space. Theatre's role is to give this microcosm a burning and fleeting taste of another world, in which our present world is integrated and transformed.

Epilogue

On 6 April 1933, the writer Anaïs Nin attended a lecture given by Antonin Artaud at the Sorbonne on the subject 'Theatre and the Plague'. She sat in the front row because he had asked her to.

Is he trying to remind us that it was during the Plague that so many marvellous works of art and theatre came to be, because, whipped by the fear of death, man seeks immortality, or to escape, or to surpass himself? But then, imperceptibly almost, he let go of the thread we were following and began to act out dying by plague. No one quite knew when it began . . . . His face was contorted with anguish, one could see the perspiration dampening his hair. His eyes dilated, his muscles became cramped, his fingers struggled to retain their flexibility. He made one feel the parched and burning throat, the pains, the fever, the fire in the guts. He was in agony. He was screaming. He was delirious. He was enacting his own death, his own crucifixion. At first people gasped. And then they began to laugh. Everyone was laughing! They hissed. Then one by one, they began to leave, noisily, talking, protesting. They banged the door as they left . . . . More protestations. More jeering. But Artaud went on, until the last gasp. And stayed on the floor. Then when the hall had emptied of all but his small group of friends, he walked straight up to me and kissed my hand. He asked me to go to the café with him . . . . Artaud and I walked out in a fine mist. We walked, walked through the dark streets. He was hurt, wounded, baffled by the jeering. He spat out his anger. 'They always want to hear *about*; they want to hear an objective conference on "The Theatre and the Plague", and I want to give them the experience itself. The plague itself, so they will be terrified, and awaken. I want to awaken them. They do not realize *they are dead*. Their death is total, like deafness, blindness. This is agony I portrayed. Mine, yes, and everyone who is alive . . . . I feel sometimes that I am not writing, but describing the struggles with writing, the struggles of birth.'

BIBLIOGRAPHY

The following are the books, journals and papers that have most helped me in writing this book. 'Beauty being preferable to scholarship' – especially for the ordinary reader – to quote Anthony Burgess, I have avoided disfiguring the text with footnotes, and thus stifled the courtesy of particular acknowledgments. However, I have learned so much in the process of writing this book that I should like to record my especial debt to the following, as well as provide a list of sources that will enable the committed student to do further research.

1 Introduction

Artaud, Antonin, *The Theatre and Its Double*, Grove Press, New York, 1958.
Green, Julian, *Diary 1928-57*, The Harvill Press, London, 1964.
Hesse, Herman, *Steppenwolf* (translated by Basil Creighton), Penguin Books, London, 1959, 1973.
Magriel, Paul (ed.), *Chronicles of the American Dance*, Henry Holt, New York, 1948.
Noguchi, Isamu, *A Sculptor's World*, Thames & Hudson, London, 1967.
Woolf, Virginia, *Between the Acts*, Hogarth Press, London, 1969.

2 Stanislavsky's Life in Art

Komisarjevsky, Theodore, *Myself and the Theatre*, E. P. Dutton & Co., New York, 1930.
Slonim, Marc, *Russian Theatre*, World Publishing Co., Cleveland, 1961, Methuen, London, 1963.
Stanislavsky, Constantin, *My Life in Art*, Bles, London, 1924; Little Brown & Co., New York, 1924.
Stanislavsky, Constantin, *An Actor Prepares*, Bles, London, 1937; Theatre Arts Inc., New York, 1936.

The Quest of the Holy Grail (translated by Pauline Matarasso),
 Penguin Classics, 1969.
Tynan, Kenneth, *Tynan on Theatre*, Penguin Books, London, 1964
 (first published as *Curtains* by Longmans, Green, London, and
 Atheneum, New York, 1961).

3 The School of Realism

Cole, Toby and Chinoy, H.K., *Directors on Directing*, Vision & P.
 Owen, London, 1970; Bobbs-Merrill, Indianapolis, 1964.
Fishman, Morris, *Play Production: Methods and Practice*, Herbert
 Jenkins, London, 1965.
Gyseghem, André van, *The Theatre in Soviet Russia, 1943*, Faber,
 London, 1943.
Hartnoll, P. (ed.), *The Oxford Companion to Theatre*, Oxford
 University Press, 1967.
Marshall, Norman, *The Producer and the Play*, Macdonald, London,
 1957
Moore, Sonia, *The Stanislavski System*, Gollancz, London, 1976;
 Viking Press, New York, 1966.
Roose-Evans, James, *London Theatre – from the Globe to the
 National*, Phaidon Press, London, 1977.
Roslavleva, Natalia, *Era of the Russian Ballet (1770–1965)*,
 Gollancz, London, 1966.
Stanislavsky, Constantin, *My Life in Art*, Bles, London, 1924; Little
 Brown & Co., New York, 1924.
Taylor, J.R., *The Penguin Dictionary of the Theatre*, Penguin Books,
 London, 1966.
The Quest for the Holy Grail (translated by Pauline Matarasso),
 Penguin Classics, 1969.

4 Meyerhold and the Russian Avant-garde

Braun, Edward, *The Theatre of Meyerhold*, Eyre Methuen, London,
 1979.
Braun, Edward (ed.), *Meyerhold on Theatre*, Eyre Methuen, London,
 1979.
Deak, Frantisek, 'Russian Mass Spectacles', *Drama Review*, Volume
 19, No. 2 (T-66), June 1975.
Fisher, David James, 'Romain Rolland and the French People's
 Theatre', *Drama Review*, Volume 21, No. 1 (T-73), March 1977.
Hoover, Marjorie L., *Meyerhold*, University of Massachusetts Press,
 Amherst, Mass., 1974.
Meyerhold, 'Meyerhold orders Music', two letters relating to his
 production of *La Dame aux Camélias,* published in *Theatre Arts
 Monthly*, Sept. 1936.
Nemirovich-Danchenko, Vladimir, *My Life in Russian Theatre*,
 London, Bles, 1968.

Slonim, Marc, *Russian Theatre*, Methuen, London, 1963; World
  Publishing Company, Cleveland, 1961.
'The Soviet Theatre Speaks for Itself', *Theatre Arts Monthly*, Sept.
  1936.
Symons, James M., *Meyerhold's Theatre of the Grotesque*, University
  of Miami Press, Coral Gables, Fla, 1972.
Worrall, Nick, 'Meyerhold's Production of the Magificent Cuckold',
  Drama Review, Volume 17, No. 1 (T-57), March 1973.

5 Taïrov and the Synthetic Theatre

Houghton, Norris, *Return Engagement*, Putnam, London, 1962.
Houghton, Norris, 'Russian Theatre in the 20th century', *Drama
  Review*, Volume 17, No. 1 (T-57), March 1973.

6 Vakhtangov's Achievement

Gorchaikov, Nikolai, *The Vakhtangov School of Stage Art*, Foreign
  Languages Publishing House, Moscow.
Guthrie, Tyrone, *A Life in the Theatre*, Hamish Hamilton, London,
  1960; McGraw-Hill, New York, 1959.
Houghton, Norris, *Return Engagement*, Putnam, London, 1962.
Markov, Pavel, 'The Actor and the Revolution', *Theatre Arts
  Monthly*, Sept. 1936.
Moore, Sonia, *The Stanislavski System*,Gollancz, London, 1976; The
  Viking Press, New York, 1966.
Stanislavsky, Constantin, *My Life in Art*, Bles, London, 1924; Little
  Brown & Co., New York, 1924.
Strasberg, Lee, 'Russian Notebook', *Drama Review*, Volume 17, No.
  1 (T-57), March 1973.

7 Craig and Appia – Visionaries

Buckle, Richard, *Diaghilev*, Weidenfeld & Nicholson, London, 1979.
Cole, Toby and Chinoy, H.K., *Directors on Directing*, Vision & P.
  Owen, London, 1970; Bobbs-Merrill, Indianapolis, 1964.
Craig, Edward, *Gordon Craig: The Story of His Life*, Gollancz,
  London, 1968; Knopf, New York, 1968.
Fay, Gerard, *The Abbey Theatre*, London, Hollis & Carter, 1958.
Goffin, P., *Stage Lighting for Amateurs*, J. S. Miller, London, 1955.
Hartnoll, P. (ed.), *The Oxford Companion to the Theatre*, Oxford
  University Press, 1967.
Lloyd, Margaret, *The Borzoi Book of Modern Dance*, Alfred Knopf,
  New York, 1949.
Magriel, Paul (ed.), *Chronicles of the American Dance*, Henry Holt,
  New York, 1948.
Marshall, Norman, *The Producer and the Play*, Macdonald, London,
  1957.

Noguchi, Isamu, *A Sculptor's World*, Thames & Hudson, London, 1967.

Simonson, Lee, *The Stage is Set*, Dover Publications, New York, 1932.

Sommer, Sally R., 'Loie Fuller', *Drama Review*, Volume 19, No. 1 (T-65), March 1975.

Stanislavsky, Constantin, *An Actor Prepares*, Bles, London, 1937; Theatre Arts Inc., New York, 1936.

8 Copeau – Father of the Modern Theatre

Barrault, Jean-Louis, *Memories for Tomorrow* (translated by Jonathan Griffin), Thames & Hudson, London, 1974.

Bowers, Faubion, *Japanese Theatre*, P. Owen, London, 1975; Hill & Wang, New York, 1959.

Clurman, Harold, *The Fervent Years*, Hill & Wang, New York, 1945.

Copeau, Jacques, 'Notes on the Actor' (translated by Harold J. Salemson) from *Actors on Acting*, Toby Cole and Helen Krich Chinoy (eds), New York Crown Publishing Co., New York, 1970.

Decroux, Etienne, *Mime Journal*, Nos 7 & 8, Etienne Decroux 80th birthday issue.

Dukes, Ashley, 'The Compagnie des Quinze', *Theatre Arts Monthly*, April 1935.

Eldredge, Sears, 'Jacques Copeau and the Mask in Actor Training', *Mime Journal*, Nos 3 and 4, 1979-80.

Heilpern, John, *Conference of the Birds*, Faber & Faber, London, 1977.

Herrigel, Eugene, *Zen in the Art of Archery*, Routledge & Kegan Paul, London, 1973 (a book much read by Grotowski, Barrault and Brook too, I suspect).

Hobson, Harold, *French Theatre since 1830*, John Calder, London, 1978; Riverrun Press, Dallas, 1978.

Kusler, Leigh Barbara, 'Jacques Copeau's School for Actors' *Mime Journal*, Nos 9 and 10, 1979.

Marshall, Norman, *The Producer and the Play*, Macdonald, London, 1957

Saint-Denis, Michel, *Theatre: The Rediscovery of Style*, Heinemann, London 1960; Theatre Art Books, New York, 1960.

9 Reinhardt, Piscator and Brecht

Bornemann, Ernest, 'The Real Brecht', *Encore*, No. 15, July-Aug. 1959.

Cole, Toby and Chinoy, H.K., *Directors on Directing*, Vision & P. Owen, London, 1970; Bobbs-Merrill, Indianapolis, 1964.

Dean, Basil, *Seven Ages: An Autobiography*, Hutchinson, London, 1970.

Dukes, Ashley, 'The Compagnie des Quinze', *Theatre Arts Monthly*, April 1935.

Esslin, Martin, *Brecht, a choice of evils*, Heinemann, London, 1959.

Esslin, Martin, 'Max Reinhardt, High Priest of Theatricality', *Drama Review*, Volume 21, No. 2 (T-74), June 1977.

Graham, Martha, *The Notebooks of Martha Graham*, Harcourt Brace & Jovanovich, New York, 1973.

Hayman, Ronald, *The German Theatre*, Oswald Woolf, London, 1975; Barnes & Noble Books, New York, 1975.

Innes, C.D., *Modern German Drama*, Cambridge University Press, 1979.

Lackner, Peter, 'Peter Stein', *Drama Review*, (T-74), 1977.

Mairowitz, David Zane, '*Summerfolk* by Peter Stein', *Play and Players*, Volume 24, No. 8, 1977.

Mairowitz, David Zane, 'As they like it' (Peter Stein's *As You Like It*), *Play and Players*, Volume 25, No. 3, 1977.

Mairowitz, Charles (ed.), *The Encore Reader*, Methuen, London, 1965.

Patterson, Michael, *German Theatre Today*, Pitman, London, 1976.

Patterson, Michael, *Peter Stein*, Cambridge University Press, 1981.

Rorrison, Hugh, 'Berlin's democratic theatre and its *Peer Gynt*', *Theatre Quarterly*, Volume 4, No. 3, 1974.

Rühle, Gunther (translated by Anthony Vivis), article written for *Erwin Piscator, Dream and Achievement*, catalogue for the Piscator Exhibition presented by the Archiv der Akademie der Künste, Berlin, in co-operation with the Goethe Institute.

Willett, John, *The Theatre of Bertold Brecht*, Methuen, London, 1964.

Willett, John, *The Theatre of Erwin Piscator*, London, Eyre Methuen, 1979.

10 The Theatre of Ecstasy – Artaud, Okhlopkov, Savary

Artaud, Antonin, *The Theatre and Its Double*, Grove Press, New York, 1958.

Capra, Fritjof, An Interview, *Revision*, Winter 1978.

Coast, John, *Dancing out of Bali*, Faber, London, 1954

Gyseghem, André van, *The Theatre in Soviet Russia, 1943*, Faber, London, 1943.

Hayman, Ronald, *Artaud and After*, Oxford University Press, London, 1977.

Jung, Carl, *Memories, Dreams and Reflections*, Collins and Routledge & Kegan Paul, London, 1963.

Knapp, Bettina, Interview with Jerome Savary: 'Beating the Drum', *Drama Review*, Volume 15, No. 1, Fall 1970.

Lenhoff, Gace, 'The Theatre of Okhlopkov', *Drama Review*, Vol 17, No. 1 (T-57), March 1973.

Shorter, Eric, 'Paris – Savary and Brook', *Drama*, Spring 1975.

Stanislavsky, Constantin, *My Life in Art*, Bles, London, 1924; Little Brown & Co., New York, 1924.

Strasberg, Lee and Kingsley, Sidney, 'An Interview with Okhlopkov' and by Strasberg, Lee, 'Russian Notebook 1934', both from *Drama Review*, Volume 17, No. 1 (T-57), March 1973.

11 The Contribution of the Modern Dance – Martha Graham and Alwin Nikolais

Denby, Edwin, 'Reminiscences of a ballet critic', Interview with John Howell, *Performance Arts Journal 11*, Volume IV, Nos 1 and 2, 1979.

Fonteyn, Margot, *The Magic of Dance*, BBC, London, 1980.

Graham, Martha, *The Notebooks of Martha Graham*, Harcourt Brace & Jovanovich, New York, 1973.

Gray, Terence, *Dance Drama, Experiments in the Art of Theatre*, W. Heffer, Cambridge, 1926.

Hering, Doris (ed.), '25 Years of American Dance', *Dance Magazine*, 1954.

Leatherman, Leroy, *Martha Graham, Portrait of the Lady as an Artist*, Alfred A. Knopf, New York, 1966.

Lloyd, Margaret, 'The Borzoi Book of Modern Dance', *Dance Magazine, 1954*.

Martin, John, *The Dance*, Tudor Publishing Co., New York, 1946.

Nikolais, Alwin, letters to the author.

Reiss, Françoise, *Nijinsky* (translated by Helen and Stephen Haskell), Adam & Charles Black, London, 1960.

Schoenberg, Bessie, Interview with John Howell, *Journal 11*, Volume IV, Nos 1 and 2, 1979.

12 Further Experiments Today – in America

Barnett, Mike, *People, Not Psychiatry*, Allen & Unwin, London, 1974.

Bierman, James, 'Three Places in Rhode Island' and Gray, Spalding, 'About Three Places in Rhode Island', both in Autoperformance issue of *Drama Review*, Volume 23, No. 1 (T-81), March 1979.

Bradby, David, and McCormick, John, *People's Theatre*, Croom Helm, London and Rowman & Littlefield, Totowa, N.J., 1978.

Brook, Peter, *The Empty Space*, Penguin, Harmondsworth, 1972.

Chaikin, Joseph, *Presence of the Actor*, Atheneum, New York, 1972.

Frater, Alexander, 'Interview with Joan Littlewood', *Daily Telegraph Magazine*', 2 Feb. 1973.

Hayman, Ronald, *Theatre and Anti-Theatre*, Secker & Warburg, London, 1979.

Houriet, Robert, *Getting Back Together*, Abacus, London, 1973.

Kirby, Michael, *The Art of Time*, E.P. Dutton, New York, 1969.

Lahr, John, *Acting out America*, Penguin, Harmondsworth, 1972.

New York Arts Journal, 25 and 26, 1982.

Nordhoff, Charles, *The Communistic Societies of the United States,* Dover Publications, New York, 1966.

Pasolli, Robert, *A Book on the Open Theatre*, Bobbs-Merrill, Indianapolis, 1970.

Peaslee in A.C.H. Smith, *Orghast at Persepolis*, Eyre Methuen, London, 1972.

The Performance Group, *Dionysus in '69*, Farrar Straus & Giroux, New York, 1970.

Performing Arts Journal, 10 and 11, 1979.

Roose-Evans, 'The Space Within', *The Texas Quarterly*, Vol. XVI, No. 1, Spring 1973.

Schechner, Richard, 'The End of Humanism', *Performing Arts Journal*, 10 and 11, Vol. 4, Nos 1 and 2, 1979.

Schroeder, R.J. *The New Underground Theatre*, Bantam Books, London, 1968.

Shorter, Eric, 'Short and Long Measures in Paris', *Drama*, Spring 1970.

Smith, A.C.H., *Orghast at Persepolis*, Eyre Methuen, London, 1972.

Wesker, Arnold, *Fears of Fragmentation* (outline of the history of Centre 42), Jonathan Cape, London, 1970.

13 Richard Foreman, Robert Wilson and the Bread and Puppet Theatre

Argelander, Ron, *Soho Weekly News*, 19 August 1976.

Barab, Margarita, 'Bread and Puppet – a man and his theatre', *Country Journal*, 18 July 1974.

Blanc, Maurice, 'Clowning with the life force', *Village Voice*, 5 Sept. 1968.

Blumenthal, Eileen, 'Affirmation in the Hills', *Voice*, 4 Sept. 1978.

Braithwaite, Chris, 'The Circus Approaches', *Southern Orleans Chronicle*, 24 July 1975.

Bread and Puppet, *Masaccio*, Centro Studi Teatrali, Ouroboros, 1977.

Clemmons, Nelda, 'Vermont sets aside a cool summer day for revelry and magic', *Tampa Times*, 11 Sept. 1979.

Goldensohn, Barry, 'Peter Schumann and the Bread and Puppet Theatre', *University of Iowa Review*, 1975 (excellent this).

Green, Susan, 'Bread and Puppets', *Burlington Free Press*, 18 Aug. 1978.

Gussow, Mel, *New York Times*, 25 Feb. 1971.

Kourilsky, Françoise, *Le Bread et Puppet Théâtre*, La Cité Editeur, Lausanne, 1971.

Leverett, James, 'Dancing in the Streets', *Soho Weekly News*, 13 Sept. 1979.

Lumpkin, Ross, 'Last Bread and Puppet Circus', *Soho Weekly News*, 22 Aug. 1974.

Roose-Evans, James, 'If only I could be as expressive as my dreams!',
Drama, Summer 1971.

Schechner, Richard, *Environmental Theater*, Hawthorn, New York,
1973.

Sterritt, David, 'Many Sided Bread and Puppet Man', *Christian
Science Monitor*, 9 Feb. 1973.

Thalenberg, Eileen, 'Not by Bread Alone', *Arts Canada*, Dec-Jan.
1970-1.

White, Michael, 'Open ended interview with Joseph Chaikin',
Guardian, 8 June 1973.

14 Anna Halprin and the Dancers' Workshop

Bowra, Maurice, *Primitive Song*, Weidenfeld & Nicolson, London,
1962.

Brook, Peter, *The Empty Space*, Penguin, Harmondsworth, 1972.

Cox, Harvey, *The Seduction of the Spirit, The Use and Misuse of
People's Religion*, A Touchstone Book, Simon & Schuster, New
York, 1973.

Eliade, Mircea, *Shamanism*, Routledge & Kegan Paul, London,
1964.

Halprin, Anna, 'Community Art as Life Process', *Drama Review*,
Volume 17, No. 3, (T-59), Oct. 1973.

Halprin, Anna, *Exit to Enter, Dance as a process for personal and
artistic growth*, Dancers' Workshop, San Francisco, 1973.

Halprin, Anna, *Collected Writings*, Dancers' Workshop, San
Francisco, 1973.

Halprin, Anna, *City Dance*, Dancers' Workshop, San Francisco,
1977.

Halprin, Anna, *Dance as a Self-healing Art* (written with James
Hurd Nixon), San Francisco, Dancers' Workshop, 1977.

Halprin, Anna, 'Moving towards Harmony', an interview with Anna
Halprin on New Horizons, *KPFA*, 4 July 1980.

Halprin, Anna, Cassette letter to James Roose-Evans, 3 Sept. 1980.

Halprin, Anna, Cassette letter to James Roose-Evans, 20 Sept. 1980.

Halprin, Anna, *Movement Ritual*, Dancers' Workshop, San
Francisco.

Halprin, Anna, 'The San Francisco Dancers' Workshop', (ed by Allen
Feinstein), *Theatre Papers*, First Series, No. 6, Dartington
College, Totnes.

Halprin, Lawrence, *The RSVP Cycles: Creative processes in the
human environment*, George Braziller, New York, 1969.

Halprin, Lawrence and Burns, Jim, with contributions from Anna
Halprin and others, *Collective Creativity*, M.I.T. Press,
Canterbury, Mass., Fall 1974.

Jean, Noram and Deak, Frantisek, 'Anna Halprin's Theatre and
Therapy Workshop', *Drama Review*, Volume 20, No. 1 (T-69),
March 1976.

Lommel, Andreas, *The World of the Early Hunters*, Evelyn Adams & Mackay, London, 1967.

'Mutual Creation', *Tulane Drama Review*, Fall 1968.

Rogers, Carl, *Encounter Groups*, Allen Lane Penguin Press, London, 1971 and Harper & Row, New York, 1970.

Toynbee, Philip, *Part of a Journey*, Collins, London, 1981.

Wain, John, *Sprightly Running*, Macmillan, London, 1962.

15 and 16 Grotowski and the Poor Theatre and Grotowski and the Journey to the East

Barba, Eugenio, 'Theatre Laboratory 13 Rzedow', *Tulane Drama Review*, Volume 9, No. 3, Spring 1965.

Barba, Eugenio, and Flaszen, Ludwik, 'A Theatre of Magic and Sacrilege', *Tulane Drama Review*, Volume 9, No. 3, Spring 1965.

Brecht, Stefan, Kott, Jan et al., 'On Grotowski', *Drama Review,* Volume 14, No. 2 (T-46), Winter 1970.

Craig, Mary, *Man from a Far Country*, Hodder & Stoughton, London, 1979.

Croyden, Margaret, an interview with Grotowski, *Drama Review*, Volume 9, No. 6 (T-45), Dec. 1965.

Croyden, Margaret, 'A Grotowski Seminar', *Drama Review*, Volume 14, No. 1 (T-45), Fall 1969.

Croyden, Margaret, 'New Theatre Rule: No Watching Allowed', *Vogue*, Dec. 1975.

Drozdowski, Bohdan (ed.) *Twentieth-Century Polish Theatre*, John Calder & Riverrun Press, Dallas, 1979.

De Chardin, Teilhard, *The Future of Man*, Collins, London, 1964.

Godard, Colette, 'Interview with Grotowski', *ITI Bulletin*, Winter/Spring.

Grimes, Ronald L., 'Route to the Mountain', *New Directions in Performing Arts*, London, Hamish Hamilton, 1976.

Grotowski, Jerzy, *Towards a Poor Theatre*, Odin Teatrets Forlag, Denmark, 1968; Methuen, London, 1975; Simon Schuster, New York, 1969.

Grotowski, Jerzy, 'External Order, Internal Intimacy', interview by Marc Fumaroli (translated by George Reavey), *Drama Review*, Volume 14, No. 1 (T-45), Fall 1969.

Grotowski, Jerzy, 'Holiday', *Drama Review*, Volume 17, No. 2 (T-58), June 1973.

Grotowski, Jerzy, 'Theatre of Nations Research University', Wrocaw, *ITI Bulletin*, Autumn 1975.

Grotowski, Jerzy, 'We look at those close to us', *ITI Bulletin*, Winter 1975.

Grotowski, Jerzy, 'The Healthy State of their Work', *ITI Bulletin*, Winter 1976.

Grotowski, Jerzy, 'The Art of the Beginner', *ITI Bulletin*, Spring/Summer 1978.

Grotowski, Jerzy, 'Theatre of Sources 1977-80', *ITI Bulletin*, Winter 1978.

'Grotowski at the Belgrade Colloquium', recorded by Jean-Jacques Daetwyler and translated by Alex Martin from the *CIRP Bulletin*, No. 1.

Hesse, Herman, *Journey to the East* (translated by Hilda Rosner), Holt, Rinehart & Winston, New York, 1956.

Hesse, Herman, *The Glass Bead Game* (translated by Richard and Clara Winston), Holt, Rinehart & Winston, New York, 1969.

Kantor, Tadeusz, 'Cricot Theatre, The Theatre of Death', *Theatre Papers*, Second Series, No. 2, Dartington College, Totnes, 1978.

Kumiega, Jennifer, 'Laboratory Theatre, Grotowski: The Mountain Project', *Theatre Papers*, Second Series, No. 9, Dartington College, Totnes, 1978.

Leabhart, Thomas (ed.) *Mime Mask and Marionette*, Volume 2, Summer 1978, published by Marcel Dekker, New York.

Magriel, Paul (ed.), *Chronicles of the American Dance*, Henry Holt, New York, 1948.

Mennen, Richard, 'Grotowski's Para Theatrical Project', *Drama Review*, Jan. 1976.

Puzaya, Konstanty, 'Grotowski's Apocalypse', *Drama Review*, Volume 15, No. 4 (T-52), Fall 1971.

Schechner, Richard and Hoffman, Theodore, 'Interview with Grotowski', *Drama Review*, Volume 13, No. 1 (T-41), Fall 1968.

Temkine, Raymonde, *Grotowski*, Avon, New York, 1972.

Trilling, Ossia, 'Nationum Theatrum Redivivum!', *Drama*, London, Autumn 1975.

Young, Marjorie S., *Journeys to Glory*, Harper & Row, New York, 1976.

17 Eugenio Barba and the Third Theatre

Barba, Eugenio, 'Barba's Kasperiana', *Drama Review*, Volume 13, No. 1 (T-41), Fall 1968.

Brook, Peter, *The Empty Space,* Penguin, Harmondsworth, 1972.

Barba, Eugenio, 'Letter from Southern Italy', *Drama Review*, Volume 19, No. 4 (T-68), 1975.

Barba, Eugenio, *Roots and Leaves*, Odin Teatret, 1975.

Barba, Eugenio, 'The Third Theatre', *ITI Bulletin*, Winter 1977.

Barba, Eugenio, 'An Offence against Nature', interview with Per Moth for the Danish magazine *Rampelyset*, Jan. 1977, and printed in English in the *University of Aarhus Theatre Newsletter* (ed. Karl-Heinz Westarp), No. 6, 1977.

Barba, Eugenio (ed. Ferdinando Taviani), *The Floating Islands Reflections with Odin Teatret*, Odin Teatret, 1979.

Barba, Eugenio et al., 'Theatre Presence, Sea Lanes, Sardinia, and Theatre Culture 1979', *Theatre Papers*, Third Series, No. 7, Dartington College, Totnes, 1980.

Daetwyler, Jacques, *Tiers Théâtre, L'Odin et la naissance*, Palindrome, Geneva, 1980.

D'Urso, Tony and Taviani, Ferdinando, *L'Etranger qui danse*, Maison de la Culture and Odin Teatret, Rennes, 1977.

Experiences, Odin Teatret, 1973

Fumeroli, Marc, 'Funeral Rites, Eugenio Barba's Ferai', interview with *Drama Review*, Volume 14, No. 1 (T-45), Fall 1969.

18 The Mountain with Many Caves: Peter Brook, Alfred Wolfsohn and Roy Hart

Attar, Farid ud-Din, *The Conference of the Birds* (translated by C. S. Nott), Routledge & Kegan Paul, London, 1961.

Brook, Peter, *The Empty Space*, Penguin, Harmondsworth, 1972.

Deschamps, Dominique, *The Roy Hart Theatre*,unpublished, 1971.

Maria Guther, letter to the author, 2 October 1973.

Hart, Roy, *The Objective Voice*, paper given at the Zagreb Congress of Psychotherapy through Music, 1970.

Heilpern, John, *Conference of the Birds*, Faber & Faber, London, 1977.

Heilpern, John, *Observer*, 11 May 1980.

Hughes, Ted, 'An interview with Tom Stoppard', *Times Literary Supplement*, 1 Oct. 1971.

Jung, Carl, *Sermones ad Mortuos* (translated by H. G. Baynes), Random House, New York, 1961; Stuart & Watkins, London, 1967.

Kretzmer, Herbert, *Daily Express*, 16 Sept. 1969.

Lorca, Federico García, *Lorca* (selected and translated by J. L. Gili), Penguin, Harmondsworth, 1971.

Nin, Anaïs, *Journals* (ed. Gunther Stuhlman), Volume 1, Peter Owen, London, 1966.

Shorter, Eric, 'Brook and others in Avignon', *Drama*, London, Autumn 1979.

Smith, A.C.H., *Orghast at Persepolis*, Eyre Methuen, London, 1972.

Waterhouse, J.F., *Birmingham Post*, 20 Oct. 1955.

Reynolds News, Nov. 22 1953, Wolfsohn.

The Illustrated, 3 April 1954, Wolfsohn.

Time Magazine, 19 March 1956, Wolfsohn.

The Work of Alfred Wolfsohn on the Human Voice, unpublished.

19 Towards AD 2,000

Brook, Peter, *Drama Review* (T-109), Spring 1986.

Brook, Peter, *The Shifting Point*, Methuen, London, and Harper & Row, New York, 1988.

Carrière, Jean-Claud, translated by Peter Brook, *The Mahabharata*, Harper & Row, New York, 1985.

Davies, Andrew, *Other Theatres*, Macmillan, London, 1987.

Drama Review, 'Is the Third Theatre Dead?' Volume 30, No. 1 (T-109), Spring 1986.

Halprin, Anna, in conversation with the author.

Harvey, Andrew, *A Journey to Ladakh*, Jonathan Cape, 1985.

Joffee, Linda, *The Christian Science Monitor*, 25-31 May 1987.

de Jongh, Nicholas, in conversation with the author.

Manning, Rosemary, *The Open Door*, Jonathan Cape, 1983.

Roose-Evans, James, *Inner Journey, Outer Journey*, Rider, 1987.

Schechner, Richard, *The Decline and Fall of the Avant Garde (The End of Humanism)*, PAJ Publications, New York, 1982.

Shared Experience, published by Shared Experience, London, 1985.

Siegel, Marcia B., *The Christian Science Monitor*, 16 Nov. 1987.

Williams, David, *Peter Brook – A Theatrical Casebook*, Methuen, 1987.

Williams, Tennessee, *Camino Real*, Secker & Warburg, 1956.

Epilogue

Anaïs Nin, *Journals* (ed. Gunther Stuhlman), Volume 1, Peter Owen, London, 1966.

RECOMMENDED FURTHER READING

Assembled with the assistance of Enid Foster, Librarian of the British Theatre Association, 9 Fitzroy Square, London W1.

I am indebted to Alexander Schouvaloff, Curator of the Theatre Museum in London, for introducing me to an essential source of information for all students of experimental theatre: the numerous volumes of *Les Voies de la création théâtrale*, published in France by CNRS. The volumes on the work of *Tadeus Kantor*, *Peter Brook* and *Le Théâtre du soleil* are especially valuable, while Volume 7 covers Pitöeff, Meyerhold, Evreinov, Piscator, etc. For the student who does not read French, the photographs alone are a valuable guide.

America

Shank, Theodore, *American Alternative Theatre*, Grove Press, New York, 1982.
Vinson, James, *Contemporary Dramatists* (2nd edn), St James Press, London, 1977.

Asia

Mackerras, Colin, *The Chinese Theatre in Modern Times, 1840 to the Present Day,* Thames & Hudson, 1975.
Scott, A. C., *The Theatre in Asia*, Weidenfeld & Nicholson, London, 1972.

Brecht

Bartram, Graham and Waine, Antony (eds), *Brecht in Perspective*, Longman, London, 1982.

Bentley, Eric, *The Brecht Commentaries 1943-80*, London, Eyre Methuen, 1981.

Demetz, Peter, *Brecht: A Collection of Critical Essays*, New Jersey, 1962.

Esslin, Martin, *Meditations: Essays on Brecht, Becket and the Media*, Methuen, London, 1981.

Ewen, Frederic, *Bertolt Brecht, his Life, his Art and his Times*, Citadel, New York, 1967.

Hiley, Jim, *The Theatre at Work: the story of the National Theatre's production of Brecht's Galileo*, Routledge & Kegan Paul, London, 1981.

Hill, Claude, *Bertolt Brecht*, Twayne, Boston, 1975.

Jacobs, Nicholas and Ohlson, Prudence (eds), *Bertolt Brecht in Britain*, T.Q. Publications, 1977.

Patterson, Michael, *The Revolution in German Theatre 1900-1933*, Routledge & Kegan Paul, London, 1981.

Völker, Klaus, *Brecht, a Biography* (translated by John Newell), Marion Boyars, London, 1979.

Weber, Betty N. and Heinen, Hubert (eds), *Bertolt Brecht: political theory and literary practice*, Manchester University Press, 1980.

White, Alfred D., *Bertolt Brecht's Great Plays*, Macmillan, London, 1978.

Witt, Hubert, *Brecht as they knew him* (translated by John Peet), Lawrence & Wishart, London, 1980.

Wulbern, Julian, *Brecht and Ionesco: commitment in context*, University of Illinois Press, Champaign, Ill., 1971.

British

Chambers, Colin, *Other Spaces: new theatre and the RSC*, Methuen, London, 1980.

Craig, Sandy (ed.) *Dreams and Deconstructions, alternative theatre in Britain*, Amber Lane Press, Ashover, 1980.

Itzin, Catherine, *Stages in the Revolution: Political theatre in Britain since 1968*, Eyre Methuen, London, 1980.

Goorney, Howard, *The Theatre Workshop Story*, Eyre Methuen, London, 1981.

Chaikin and the Open Theatre

Chaikin, Joseph, *The Presence of the Actor*, Atheneum, New York, 1972

Pasolli, Robert, *A Book on the Open Theatre*, Bobbs-Merrill, Indianapolis, 1970.

Information in Innes's *Holy Theatre* and Styan's *Modern Drama*, Volume 2 (see General section).

Craig

Marker, F.J. and Lowe, Lise, *Edward Gordon Craig and the Pretenders: a production revisited*, Carbondale, Ill., Southern Illinois Press, 1981.

Newman, L.M., *Gordon Craig Archives, International Survey*, Malkin Press, London, 1976.

Rood, Arnold (ed.), *Gordon Craig on movement and dance*, Dance Books, London, 1977.

General

The Mime Journal, edited by Thomas Leabhart, which started up in 1980, is an invaluable source, and is published yearly by the Pomona College, Theater Dept, Claremont, California 91711. See also the excellent series of *Theatre Papers*, edited by the Dept of Theatre, Dartington College of Arts, Totnes, Devon.

Allen, John, *Theatre in Europe*, City Arts, 1981.

Braun, Edward, *The Director and the Stage, from naturalism to Grotowski*, Methuen, London, 1982.

Innes, Christopher, *Holy Theatre: Ritual and the Avantgarde*, Cambridge University Press, 1981.

Pronko, Leonard, *The Experimental Theatre in France*, University of California, Berkeley, Calif., 1963.

Schevill, James, *Break Through in Search of New Theatrical Environments*, Swallow Press, Chicago, 1973.

Styan, J.L., *Modern Drama in Theory and Practice*, 3 volumes, Cambridge University Press, 1981.

Weightman, John, *The Concept of the Avantgarde: explorations in modernism*, Alcove Press, London, 1973.

Grotowski

Grotowski, *The Mountain Project*, pamphlet, Dartington, Totnes, 1978.

Kumiego, Jennifer, *Laboratory Theatre*.

Living Theatre

Biner, Pierre, *Le Living Theatre*, La Cité, Lausanne, n.d.

Information in Styan's *Modern Drama*, Volume 2, Schevill's *Break Through*, and Innes's *Holy Theatre* (see General section).

Meyerhold

Braun, Edward, *The Theatre of Meyerhold, revolution on the modern stage*, Eyre Methuen, London, 1979.

Hoover, Marjorie L., *Meyerhold: the art of conscious theater*, University of Massachusetts Press, Amherst, 1974.

Ariane Mnouchkine

Kirkland, Christopher, 'The Golden Age', *Drama Review*, June 1975, Volume 19, No. 2 (T-66).
Nes Kirby, Victoria, '1789', *Drama Review*, Volume 15, No. 4 (T-52), Fall 1971.

Piscator

Innes, C.D., *Erwin Piscator's Political Theatre: the development of modern German drama*, Cambridge University Press, 1972.
Piscator, Erwin, *The Political Theatre* (translated with introduction and notes by Hugh Rorrison), Eyre Methuen, London, 1980.
Piscator, Maria Ley, *The Piscator Experiment*, Carbondale, Ill., Southern Illinois University Press, 1967.
Willett, John, *Erwin Piscator: half a century of politics in the theatre*, Eyre Methuen, London, 1978.

Polish

Grodzicki, August, *Polish Theatre Directors*, Interpress, Warsaw, 1979.

Reinhardt

Styan, J.L., *Max Reinhardt*, Cambridge University Press, 1982.

Ronconi

Godard, Colette, 'Luca Ronconi's' *Drama Review*, Volume 15, No. 4 (T-52), Fall 1971.
Quadri, Franco, 'Luca Ronconi', *Drama Review*, Volume 21, No. 2 (T-74), June 1977.

Stanislavsky

Benedetti, Jean, *Stanislavski, An Introduction*, Methuen, London, 1982.
Centre Study Committee of International Theatre Institute International Seminar, *Stanislavski's Theatrical and Pedagogical Principles*, International Theatre Institute USSR, Moscow, 1981.
Toporkov, Vasily Osipovich, *Stanislavski in rehearsal: the final years* (translated by Christine Edwards), Theatre Art Books, New York, 1979.

Stein, Peter

Patterson, Michael, *Peter Stein: Germany's leading theatre director*, Cambridge University Press, 1981.

Robert Wilson and Richard Foreman

Aragon, Louis, 'Deafman Glance', open letter to Andre Breton in *Les Lettres françaises*, 2 June 1971.

Barnes, Clive, 'Deafman Glance', *New York Times*, March 1971.

Barnes, Clive, '12-hour Stalin', *New York Times*, 17 December 1973.

Brecht, Stefan, *Theatre of the City of New York from the mid 60's to the mid 70's*, Book 1 (T-90), MIT Press, Cambridge, Mass., 1981.

Dandrel, Louis, 'Prehistory in 24 hours', *Le Monde*, 16 November 1972.

Denby, Edwin, 'You never heard of a silent opera?', *New York Times*, 9 December 1973.

Foreman Richard, 'The Life and Times of Sigmund Freud', *Village Voice*, January 1970.

Gottfried, Martin, 'Listening to the sounds of silence . . . on stage', *Women's Wear Daily*, 13 December 1973.

Gottfried, Martin, 'The Life and Times of Joseph Stalin', *Women's Wear Daily*, 18 December 1973.

Gusson, Mel, '12-hour play', *New York Times*, 14 December 1973.

Jowitt, Deborah, 'Forgetting to remember the Walrus', *Village Voice*, 10 January 1974.

Kirkby, Michael, 'Richard Foreman's Ontological-Hysteric Theatre', *Drama Review*, Volume 17, No. 2 (T-58), June 1973.

Langton, Basil, 'Journey to Ka Mountain', *Drama Review*, Volume 17, No. 2 (T-58), June 1973.

Longchampt, Jacques, 'Eight days on the mountain of the soul', *Le Monde*, 14 September 1972.

Oliver, Edith, 'Deafman Glance', *New Yorker*, March 1971.

Oliver, Edith, 'The Life and Times of Joseph Stalin', *New Yorker*, 31 December 1973.

Rockwell, John, 'Brooklyn', *Opera News*, 2 February 1974.

Searle, Judith, 'Ka Mountain', *Sunday New York Times*, November 1972.

Trilling, Ossia, 'Robert Wilson's Ka Mountain', *Drama Review*, Volume 17, No. 2 (T-58), June 1973.

Index

Abbey Theatre, Dublin, 43
Adler, Stella, 37
Agate, James, 58
Alexander, F. Mathias, 12
Alexandrinsky Theatre, 25
Alfreds, Mike, 71, 192
American Group Theatre, 37
Ancient Theatre, St Petersburg, 26
Andreyev, Leonid, 19
Antoine, André, 15, 17, 53–4, 57, 73
Appia, Adolphe: 48–52; influence of, 90, 172; influence on Artaud, 74, 75–6, 77; influence on Reinhardt, 62–3; influence on Tairov, 31–2; writings, 48, 51, 78; Plate 4
Arp, 75
Arrabal, Fernando, 83–4
Artaud, Antonin: 74–8; Balinese theatre, on, 90; concept of non-verbal theatre, 3, 83, 188–9; influence of, 151; manifesto, 83, 90; plague enactment, 201–2; scenic reforms, 81; visionary, 90

Baigyoku, Nakamu, 55
Bakrushin, 30
Bamman, Gerry, 103
Barba, Eugenio: 163–73; group of actors, his, 12, 60–1; influence of, 139; poor theatre, 60–1; Théâtre des Nations, at, 155; training, on, 150; Plates 33 and 34
Barnett, Mike, 113
Barrault, Jean-Louis: Copeau's influence on, 56, 61; homage to Artaud, 74; Roy Hart theatre and, 181; staging of Gargantua, 78; use of film, 29

Barton, Craig, 95
Baty, Gaston, 60
Bauhaus, the, 41, 92, 145
Beaumont, Cyril, 93
Beck, Julian, 104–6, Plate 17
Behar, Serge, 183
Belasco, David, 17
Bel-Geddes, Norman, 44
Berliner Ensemble, 68–9, 73
Bernhardt, Sarah, 84
Bing, Suzanne, 60
Blin, Roger, 74
Blok, Alexander, 22, 25
Boleslavsky, Richard, 6
Bond, Edward, 70
Bornemann, Ernest, 69
Boulez, Pierre, 101
Bowra, Sir Maurice, 139, 160
Brahm, Otto, 62, 63
Brancusi, Constantin, 53
Bread and Puppet Theatre: 120–30; community of actors, 12; direction of, 114; influence of, 113; naming of, 86; ritual and, 143–4; Plates 21, 22, 23, 24
Brecht, Bertold: 66–70; Alienation Principle, 144; beliefs, 147, 167; fieldwork, 89; influence of, 90; lecture on experimental theatre, 73; people's theatre, 112; Plate 7
Brook, Peter: 174–80, 196, 199, 200; and ritual, 196–7; African tour, 76, 144, 184; company, his, 12, 166, 169, 171; Conference of Birds, The, 166–7; development of ideas, 26; Grotowski's influence on, 153, 155; importance of change in theatre, 188, 193–4; influence

of, 90, 139; John Heilpern on, 85, 144, 166–7, 170, 175, 177, 184–5; Martha Graham's influence on, 100; masks, use of, 56; *Midsummer Night's Dream*, 71, 85; *Orghast*, 102, 119; poor theatre, 60–1, 77; staging, his, 55, 78; Ted Hughes on, 174, 176–8; *The Ik*, 128; *The Mahabharata*, 194; Théâtre des Bouffes, at, 78; training actors, 150, 170, 184; writings, 103, 104, 107, 140, 145–7; Plates 32, 35 *see also* Heilpern
Byrd Hoffmann School of Byrds, 114
Bryden, Bill, 191

Cage, John, 75, 101, 181
Calderón de la Barca, 26
Capra, Fritjof, 87, 104
Chagall, Marc, 84–5, 111
Chaikin, Joseph, 106–9, 121, 128, 146, 155, Plate 19
Chardin, Teilhard de, 159
Chekhov, Anton, 8–9, 17–18, 33, 57, 62
Chekhov, Michael, 6, 36
Childs, Lucinda, 95, 119
Chinoy, Helen Krich, 63
Cieslak, Ryszard, 146; Plate 29
Circus Schumann, 63
Clurman, Harold, 37
Colette, 74
Comédie Française, 53, 76
Compagnie des Quinze, 12, 57–9
Copeau, Jacques: 53–61; improvisation, use of, 87–8; influence of, 90; stage space, use of, 77–8, 150; Vieux-Colombier, School of the, 12, 77; Plate 5
Coronet Theatre, 46
Cox, Harvey, 143, 197
Craig, Edward, 46
Craig, Gordon: 40–8; Appia and, 50–2; influence on Copeau, 56; influence on Kantor, 114; influence on Reinhardt, 62–3; influence on Taïrov, 31; vision of, 76, 90, 92
Crommelynck, Fernand, 28
Cunningham, Merce, 75, 95, 98, 100, 121

Dalcroze, Émile-Jacques, 32, 50, 56
Dancers' Workshop, 113, 131–44, Plate 27
Dappertutto, Dr, 25
Dasté, Jean, 60
Dean, Basil, 63, 65
Decroux, Étienne, 60
Deutsches Theater, 62
Diaghilev, Serge, 8
Dukes, Ashley, 59, 64
Dullin, Charles: Copeau and, 56, 60; group of actors, his, 12; homage to Artaud, 74; influence on Grotowski, 150–1; on Meyerhold, 29
Duncan, Isadora, 11, 19, 92
Duse, Eleanora, 44

Esslin, Martin, 64, 69
Evreinov, Nikolai, 22, 26, 27, 79
Experimental Theatre Studio, 22

Flazen, Ludwik, 146
Fokine, Michel, 91
Fontane, Theodor, 16
Fonteyn, Margot, 91
Foreman, Richard, 111, 114–18
Frost, Robert, 176
Fuller, Loie, 49–50, 66, 100

Garcia, Victor, 165
Garrick Theatre, 56
Genet, Jean, 97
Gide, André, 53
Gluszcak, Bohdan, 157
Gogol, 11, 29
Gorki, Maxim, 8, 71
Graham, Martha: 91–8; advice to students, 90; influence of, 3, 100; myths, use of, 149, 166; Noguchi's designs for, 101; *Notebooks,* 64, 166, 169, Plates 10, 11
Grand Magic Circus, 77, 83–7, Plate 9
Granville-Barker, H. G., 54
Gray, Spalding, 112
Gregory, André, 72, 102, 146, 155
Grein, J. T., 62
Grimes, Ronald, 157
Grosses Schauspielhaus, 63
Grotowski, Jerzy: 145–51, 152–62, 199; actors, on, 32, 59, 61, 150, 153, 176; and rituals, 187; Brook

and, 175–6, 181; encounter and performance, 163–4, 166; exercises for actors, 61, 108, 176; influence of, 90, 108, 139, 172; influence on Barba, 165–6; Okhlopkov, compared with, 81; people's theatre, on, 112, 113; Stanislavsky's influence on, 7; training actors, 32, 176; Plates 24, 32
Group Theatre, the, 6, 12, 37
Gurdjieff, G. I., 154, 169, 183
Guther, Maria, 182
Guthrie, Tyrone, 37, 79, 145
Gyesghem, André van, 18, 79, 80

Habima Theatre Studio, 36, 37
Hall, Peter, 189
Halle, Adam de la, 26
Halprin, Anna, 113, 131–44, 154, 156, 182, 199, Plate 26
Hampstead Theatre, 4–5
Hamsun, Knut, 8, 19
Hart, Roy, 77, 154, 169, 180–3, Plates 38, 39, *see also* Roy Hart Studio/Theatre
Harvey, Andrew, 194
Hauptmann, Gerhart, 9, 19
Heilpern, John: on Brook and actors, 170, 184–5; on Brook and *The Conference of Birds*, 166–7; on Brook and *Midsummer Night's Dream*, 85; on Brook and the Peulhs, 177; *The Conference of Birds* (book), 144, 175
Henze, Hans Werner, 180
Hepworth, Barbara, 87, 101
Herkomer, Hubert von, 45
Hesse, Hermann, 3–4, 158, 160
Hobson, Harold, 54
Hochhuth, Rolf, 67
Horan, Robert, 148
Houghton, Norris, 21
House of Interludes, 24, 25
Housman, Laurence, 46
Hovhaness, Alan, 95
Huelsenbeck, Richard, 75
Hughes, Ted, 174, 176–8
Hugo, Victor, 14
Humphrey, Doris, 33
Huxley, Aldous, 181
Huxley, Sir Julian, 181

Ibsen, Henrik, 8, 17, 44–5, 62, 71
International Theatre Research Centre, 174
Ionesco, Eugene, 74
Irving, Henry, 42, 48
Ivanov, Vyachleslav, 24

Janov, Arthur, 104
Jessner, Leopold, 41, 73
Johnson, Jennie, 181
Jones, Hywel, 179, 180, Plate 36
Jones, Robert Edmond, 44
Joseph, Stephen, 79
Jouvet, Louis, 56, 60
Jung, Carl, 87, 104, 166, 179, 194, 198

Kabuki Theatre, 55
Kamerny Theatre, 33–4
Kantor, Tadeusz, 114, 157
Kaprow, Allan, 121
Katchalov, Vassili, 18
Kathakali, dance tradition, 196
Kean, Charles, 15
Kerzhentzev, Platon Mikhailovich, 24, 27, 28
Kipphardt, Heinar, 67
Knapp, Bettina, 86
Komisarjevskaya, Vera, 12, 22–3, 26
Komisarjevsky, Theodore, 12
Koonen, Alisa, 32
Kostelanetz, Richard, 115
Kretzmer, Herbert, 183
Krishnamurti, 104
Kronek, Ludwig, 15, 17
Kumiega, Jennifer, 155

La Mama, 109
Laboratory Theatre, 146, 148, 156, 161, *see also* Polish Laboratory Theatre
Laing, R. D., 104
Langton, Basil, 120
Lauvik, Else Marie, 164
Lenin, Vladimir Ilyich, 26
Littlewood, Joan, 70, 104, 112, 120
Living Theatre, the, 12, 77, 88, 103–6, 114, Plate 18
Logan, Joshua, 18
Losey, Joseph, 78

Macready, William Charles, 15, 16
Maeterlinck, Maurice, 8, 9, 10, 22

Mahabharata, The, 192, 193, 194, 195, 197, Plates 41 and 42
Malina, Judith, 104
Maly Theatre, 6
Manhattan Theatre Project, 102, 155
Manning, Rosemary, 198
Marceau, Marcel, 60
Marshall, Norman, 42, 45, 54, 58
Martin, John, 91, 94, 95
Martinet, Marcel, 29
Maxwell Davies, Peter, 180
Meiningen, Duke of Saxe-, 15–17, 48
Meiningen Players, 11, 15–18
Mennen, Richard, 160
Mercier, Jean, 51
Mercury Theatre, 83
Meyerhold, Vsevolod: 21–30; Brecht and, 69, 73; Grotowski and, 150–1; influence of, 74; Lee Strasberg on, 38; Okhlopkov and, 78, 79; Reinhardt and, 63; Stanislavsky and, 8–9; Taïrov and, 33, 35; Plates 1, 2
Meyerhold Theatre, 31
Mnouchkine, Ariane, 71, 79, 87–90, 104
Molière, 55
Molina, Tirso de, 26
Monk, Meredith, 95, 100
Moorat, Joseph, 46
Moore, Sonia, 18, 36, 37
Morozov, 9
Moscow Art Theatre: 6–12, 17–20; Copeau's attitude to, 54, 57; Craig's *Hamlet* at, 43–4, 47; Meyerhold's development from, 22, 25; Taïrov's opinion of, 31; Vakhtangov at, 36

Nash, Xavier, 139
National Theatre, 62
Nemirovich-Danchenko, Vladimir, 7–9, 18, 21, 36, 39
Nijinsky, 93
Nikolais, Alwin, 28, 49, 92, 95, 98–100, Plates 13, 14, 15, 16
Nin, Anaïs, 187
Noguchi, Isamu, 4, 44, 101
Noverre, 120

Obey, André, 58, 59
Odin Teatret, 77, 144, 163–73, 185, 187, 191, Plates 33, 34

O'Horgan, Tom, 104, 109
Oida, Yoshi, 128
Okhlopkov, Nikolai, 71, 78–81, 109, Plate 8
Olson, Charles, 75
Ontological-Hysteric Theatre, 114
Open Theatre, 77, 106–9, 114, 121, 128–9, 170, 188, Plate 19
Opera Theatre, 30
Ostrovsky, Alexander, 8, 21

Partch, Harry, 102
Patterson, Michael, 72
Peaslee, Richard, 102
Penley's Theatre, 46
Performance Group, the, 77, 79, 102, 166, 171, 185
Phelps, Samuel, 15–16, 17
Picasso, Pablo, 102
Piscator, Erwin, 29, 65–8, 73, 145, 167
Pitoëff, Georges and Ludmilla, 60
Polish Laboratory Theatre: Anna Halprin on, 131; Chaikin on, 155; development of, 146, 148, 185; exercises at, 108; Grotowski's productions at, 81, 152; influence of, 144, 164, 171; role of, 144, 168, 171, 187, Plates 28, 29, 31
Porter, Andrew, 174
Purcell Operatic Society, 45–6

Quinze, Compagnie des, *see* Compagnie des Quinze

Raikh, Zinaida, 30
Rainier, Yvonne, 121
Rajneesh, Bhagwan, 104
Rauschenberg, Robert, 75, 101
Realistic Theatre, 78, 80
Reinhardt, Max, 22, 62–8, 71–4, 145, Plate 6
Rittner, Luke, 189, 190, 191
Robertson, Tom, 15
Rodin, Auguste, 49
Rogers, Carl, 104, 140
Rogoff, Gordon, 107
Rolland, Romain, 27, 112
Ronconi, Luca, 65, 79, 81–3, 104
Rosjak, Theodore, 104
Rothko, Mark, 170
Roy Hart Studio, 180

Roy Hart Theatre, 77, 171, 181, 183, Plate 39
Royal Court Theatre, 124
Royal Shakespeare Company, 71, 146, 174, 192
Rudkin, David, 97

Sadler's Wells Theatre, 15–16
Saint-Denis, Michel, 12, 55, 57–60, 78
St Denis, Ruth, 33
Sankovskaya, Yekaterina, 10
Satie, Eric, 53
Savary, Jerome, 83–7, 104 see also Grand Magic Circus
Saxe-Meiningen, Duke of, see Meiningen
Schaubühne Theatre, 71–3
Schechner, Richard, 79, 102, 104, 112, 123–4, 188
Schumann, Peter: 120–30; amateurs, use of, 111; group, his, 12; ideas on theatre, 86, 104, 143, 169; influence of, 113; role as director, 114; see also Bread and Puppet Theatre; Plate 21
Scriabin, Alexander, 24
Serlio, Sebastiano, 41
Shakespeare, William, 8, 166
Shared Experience Company, 71, 192
Shaw, George Bernard, 17, 47
Shaw, Martin, 40, 45, 46
Shawn, Ted, 33
Shchepkin, Mikhail, 10, 11
Simonson, Lee, 42, 48
Slonim, Marc, 22, 26, 32
Squat, 109–11, 114
Stalin, Josef, 30, 33, 34
Stanislavsky, Constantin; 6–13, 17–21; Brecht and, 68; Craig and, 43; influence of, 73, 90, 150, 151; Meyerhold and, 30; naturalism of, 62, 68; Paris visit, 57; staging, on, 145; training of actors, 69; Vakhtangov and, 36, 39
Stary Theatre, 146
Stein, Gertrude, 53
Stein, Peter, 65, 70–3, Plate 40
Steiner, George, 181
Stockhausen, Karlheinz, 180
Stoppard, Tom, 176
Strasberg, Lee, 6, 37, 78

Strindberg, August, 14, 17, 36, 62
Sukhovo-Kobylin, Alexander, 29
Sulerjitsky, Leopold, 12
Susuki, Tadashi, 171
Svoboda, Josef, 44
Swados, Liz, 177–8
Szajma, Josef, 157

Taïrov, Alexander, 21, 26, 31, 33–6, 79
Taylor, Paul, 98, 100
Terry, Ellen, 46
Terry, Megan, 109
Théâtre Alfred Jarry, 74
Theatre of the Bauhaus, 92
Théâtre des Bouffes, 78, 193
Théâtre des Champs Elysées, 57
Théâtre Français, 14
Théâtre Libre, 17, 53, 54
Théâtre des Nations, 146, 153, 154, 171, 181
Théâtre Panique, 83, Plate 9
Théâtre Sarah Bernhardt, 74
Theatre, School of, 44
Théâtre du Soleil, 87–8
Théâtre du Vieux-Colombier, 53–6, 58, 78
Theatre Workshop, 70, 120
Theatrical Studio, 9–10
Tolstoy, Leo, 8
Tomaszewski, Henryk, 157
Toynbee, Arnold, 140
Toynbee, Philip, 144
Tseretelli, 32
Tudor, Anthony, 95
Tudor, David, 75
Turnbull, Colin, 185
Tynan, Kenneth, 6, 68
Tzara, Tristan, 75

Vakhtangov, Evgeny, 26, 35–9, 73, 79, 150, Plate 3
Vega, Lope de, 26
Vestris, Madame, 15
Vieux-Colombier, School of the, 12, 59–60, 77, 145
Vieux-Colombier, Théâtre du, 53–6, 58, 78
Vilar, Jean, 60, 74
Vildrac, Charles, 54
Vincent, Vincent, 60
Vitrac, Roger, 74
Volksbühne, West Berlin, 66, 67

Wagner, Wieland, 44, 48
Wain, John, 144
Wardle, Irving, 149, 174
Weill, Kurt, 70
Waseda Little Theatre, 168, 171
Weiss, Peter, 67
Wethal, Torgeir, 164
Wigman, Mary, 92
Wilde, Oscar, 32
Wilson, Robert, 111–20, 128, 156, 165, 195
Wojtyla, Karol, 157

Wolfsohn, Alfred, 181–3, Plate 38
Woolf, Virginia, 3, 68, 94
Wyspianski, Stanislaw, 149

Yeats, W. B., 43, 45
Young, Marjorie B., 157
Young, Wayland, 181

Zhdanov, Andrei, 33
Zavadsky, Yuri, 146
Zola, Émile, 14, 17